Anonymous

A Collection of Testimonies

concerning several ministers of the gospel amongst the people called Quakers

Anonymous

A Collection of Testimonies
concerning several ministers of the gospel amongst the people called Quakers

ISBN/EAN: 9783337410988

Printed in Europe, USA, Canada, Australia, Japan

Cover: Foto ©Lupo / pixelio.de

More available books at **www.hansebooks.com**

A COLLECTION

OF

TESTIMONIES

CONCERNING

Several Ministers of the GOSPEL

Amongst the PEOPLE called

QUAKERS,
Deceased:

With some of their last Expressions and EXHORTATIONS.

LONDON:

Printed and Sold by LUKE HINDE, in *George-Yard, Lombard-Street.* 1760.

THE PREFACE.

THE YEARLY-MEETING obferving, that in many of the TESTIMONIES, received from the different Quarterly-meetings, much ufeful and profitable Matter was contained, tending to promote and encourage the Practice of Virtue, and of that Obedience and Self-denial, which the Gofpel of Chrift requires of his Servants; together with feveral fhort, but full Relations of the bright Examples, and folid and tender Expreffions of many who have had the Happinefs to finifh well, and leave behind them the beft Demonftration of their Belief of the TRUTH, and Excellency of the CHRISTIAN RELIGION, by giving a clear Evidence, of its genuine Fruits and Effects, in their Lives and Converfations; and, in the Conclufion, by being divinely favoured with an Affurance of that Life and Immortality, for which, above all, they had defired and laboured.

The PREFACE.

Under these Considerations, the YEARLY-MEETING directed the Collecting and Printing of such of these TESTIMONIES as were judged most likely to be of general Benefit; which COLLECTION is here presented to the *Reader*. But we must acknowledge we greatly regret, frequently to find the solid and weighty Expressions of our *dying Friends* omitted, under the Excuse of *Brevity*; when oftentimes they are the most important, and would be the most likely to be of Advantage to those to whom they are communicated; but, so it is in too many Instances: To avoid which, in future, Friends are desired not to be negligent at such Opportunities, but to make as full and authentick a Collection of the last Words, and Death-bed Expressions, of our worthy departing Friends, as they are capable; as these are generally the most lively and affecting, and have a stronger Tendency to stir up the pure Mind in the considerate Readers, and make them to desire and endeavour so to walk, in the Counsel of God, as to obtain the like precious Experience: In order to promote which, these TESTIMONIES are earnestly recommended to the Perusal and serious Attention of Friends in general, but especially to the Youth of both Sexes; for in them they may

The PREFACE.

may fee a Cloud of Witneſſes to the happy Fruits of an early Devotion, and the unſpeakable Advantages reſulting to thoſe who embrace the Viſitation of the Moſt High, and follow the Diſcoveries and Requirings of his holy Spirit, in the Way of Regeneration and the daily Croſs; Advantages which ſo far ſurpaſs every Thing, which hath been or can be exchanged for them, that, when put in the Scale, they all appear lighter than Vanity.

There are two Phraſes (in the following Collection) that frequently occur, which, to a Reader not of our Perſwaſion, may be miſunderſtood, and by being miſunderſtood, may give Offence; they are, *He, or ſhe, was deſcended from believing Parents*; or, *was convinced of the Truth*. To obviate which, it may be obſerved, that it is not thereby intended to circumſcribe the Belief of the Truth, in the general Acceptation of that Phraſe, to ourſelves; or to inſinuate, that other Societies do not believe the Truths of *Chriſtianity*: But, as the Words of Chriſt are, I AM THE TRUTH. This I AM, the eſſential, everlaſting, ſaving Truth, is that of which they were *convinced*, and in which they *believed*: *Convinced* of him by his own immediate, ſelf-evident Operation upon their Minds;

Minds; *convinced*, that this was the Spirit of Truth, of whom it was said, when he came, he should *convince the World of Sin, of Righteousness, and of Judgment.*

And being brought to this Rock and sure Foundation of living Faith, they became *convinced*, that as the Holy God is an omnipresent Spirit, so in Spirit and in Truth must he be acceptably worshiped; that as he is in himself infinite, and incomprehensible, *dwelling in the Light, which no Man can approach unto, whom no Man hath seen or can see*; so, through this *Spirit of Truth*, this Holy Mediator, Access only could be had, and true Worship performed, to the Father of Spirits. They were *convinced*, that as he is perfectly holy, so, except they were made in degree holy, their Prayers could never ascend with Acceptance, as the Incense of Saints, before the Throne of Glory. And altho' the Command and Declation to *Abram* is plainly exhibited in Scripture, *viz. I am the Almighty God, walk before me, and be thou perfect*; it seemed to them an impossible Attainment, till opened by him who hath the Key of *David :* They then saw, that *Perfection* arose from the Relation *Abram* stood in to an Almighty Creator; and were
convinced

The PREFACE.

convinced that this *Call* extended to the Seed of *Abram* through all Generations. And,

Being *convinced* of the Purity, so they were of the Peaceableness of this Gospel Dispensation. They not only read, but felt it breath, *Peace on Earth, and Goodwill to Men*; that there was to be *no hurting nor destroying in all God's holy Mountain.*

These are some of the important Truths, of which they were *convinced*; Truths which, we trust, will spread and prevail in the Nations of the World, till, in the Lord's Time, the Accomplishment of that memorable Prophecy, and Proclamation of the evangelical Prophet, be fully known, *viz. And it shall come to pass in the last Days, that the Mountain of the Lord's House shall be established in the Top of the Mountains, and shall be exalted above the Hills; and all Nations shall flow unto it: And many People shall go and say, Come ye, and let us go up to the Mountain of the Lord, to the House of the God of* Jacob, *and he will teach us of his Ways, and we will walk in his Paths; for out of* Zion *shall go forth the Law, and the Word of the Lord from* Jerusalem. *He shall judge among the Nations, and shall rebuke many People:*
And

The PREFACE.

And they shall beat their Swords into Plowshares, and their Spears into Pruning-hooks: Nation shall not lift up Sword against Nation, neither shall they learn War any more. O House of Jacob *! come ye, and let us walk in the Light of the Lord.* Isaiah ii. 2, 3, 4, 5.

AN
Alphabetical INDEX

OF THE

NAMES of those FRIENDS inserted in this Volume.

A	Pag.	B	Pag.
Henry Atkinson	31	William Beck	86
John Adam	42	John Batterſbie	102
Alex. Arſcott	101	Benjamin Bangs	140
Joseph Atkinson	113	Jane Briſcoe	159
Aaron Atkinson	130	Evan Bevan	197
John Aſhton	157	Robert Barclay	201
Eliz. Aſhbridge	295	Mongo Bewley	209
Peter Andrews	322	George Bewley	222
		Mabel Barker	253
B		Jonathan Barnes	268
		Elizabeth Bowing	279
Sarah Brown	21	George Brawn	292
Joseph Bunting	25	William Brown	294
William Beard	36	John Bevington	309
Joshua Barber	67	Daniel Bell	342
Mary Baker	80	Elizabeth Balfour	362

The INDEX.

C

	Pag.
Luke Cock	143
Joan Cale	167
Thomas Carr	243
John Corbyn	278
Rebecca Cowell	336

D

John Dodshon	15
Thomas Drewrey	17
Sarah Dixon	73
William Dixon	75
Francis Davis	85
James Dickinson	150
Elizabeth Dennis	214

E

John Everard	89
Mary Ellerton	95
John Ecroyd	288

F

Jonathan Freeth	111
Joseph Freeth	162
John Fothergill	180
Elizabeth Fletcher	259
Anna Flack	312
Abm. Farrington	338

G

	Pag.
Mary Godbold	12
Thomas Giddy	82
William Gray	96
Jane Gee	121
John Gurney	134
Joseph Gill	155
Mary Greer	169
Joseph Gurney	238
Archibald Gillespy	305
Thomas Gilkes	319

H

John Hands	117
Charles Howell	125
Benjamin Hornor	132
Jeremiah Hunter	146
Elizabeth Hands	175
Tabitha Hornor	191
John Horsfall	241
Alice Hall	303
David Hodgson	307
Ann Hart	317
David Hall	328
Charles Harrison	359
William Hartley	360

I

Elizabeth Jacob	123

K

Martha King	127
Benjamin Kidd	262

L

Mary Larcum	153

M

Samuel Maud	32
Susanna Martin	90
Joseph Moseley	99
Christopher Mason	194

N

Mary Neal	332

O

Samuel Overton	107
William Osborn	205
Jonathan Ostell	269
Joseph Ollive	348

P

Margery Peters	119
Kath. Peckover	148
Henry Payton	195

P

	Pag.
Rachel Proud	220
Isaac Pickerell	315

R

George Russell	34
George Rooke	170
Mary Ransom	206
Eliz. Rawlinson	246
Mary Richardson	286
Robert Richardson	321

S

Christopher Story	1
Thomas Scott	23
John Snashall	59
James Simpson	61
Bridget Story	78
Ann Scotten	115
Thomas Story	165
Mary Snowden	189
Thomas Smith	216
Joseph Storrs	256
William Sproule	265
John Scott	301

T

Sarah Tomlinson	29

The INDEX.

T	Pag.	W	Pag.
John Thompson	43	Thomas Wilkinson	46
William Taylor	224	Christopher Winn	49
Alice Thistlewait	250	Deborah Wardell	63
Michael Turpin	353	Wm. Williamson	177
		Thomas White	186
W		Abigail Watson	272
		Deborah Wilson	281
Thomas Wilde	7	Simeon Warner	283
Elizabeth Wheatly	27	Hannah Wilson	355
Elizabeth Wilson	37		

A COL-

A COLLECTION
OF
TESTIMONIES concerning
Publick Friends deceased.

A Testimony from the Monthly-meeting at Carlisle *in the County of* Cumberland; *containing a brief Account of the Life and Services of our dear and worthy Friend,* CHRISTOPHER STORY.

THIS our dear Friend, and worthy Elder, was born at *Rigghead* in the Parish of *Kirklinton*, and County of *Cumberland*, in the Year 1648; and was convinced of the blessed Truth, and received it in the Love of it, in the Year 1672, being about the Twenty fourth Year of his Age. And the Lord, who was graciously pleased to visit and gather him, as one of the first Fruits in this Part of the Borders of *England*, and called him to work in his Vinyard early, endowed him

him with a good Understanding of the Things pertaining to his Kingdom; and, in the Year 1677, bestowed on him a Gift of the Ministry, which he exercised freely; and we have good Cause to believe, he made good Improvement thereof, as appeared by his faithful and unwearied Labour in the Church of Christ in these Parts. His Service among us was great, and well accepted, he being one who ruled well in his own House, and also in the Church; for which he was counted worthy of double Honour.

He visited the Meetings in this Nation, and also in *Ireland* and *Scotland*, divers Times; and as his Service was great and well received amongst his Brethren, both at home and abroad, so likewise it was often his Concern, in our own County, to appoint Meetings amongst other People, which frequently proved to great Satisfaction, and caused many to confess to Truth; he being endued with a living, plain and powerful Testimony, to the reaching of the Hearts and Consciences of the Hearers.

His Care over the People of God was great, that all who professed the Truth might walk blameless, and come up in Faithfulness in every Branch of their Testimony. Zealous he was against undue Liberty, or going into Excess in eating or drinking, or into the foolish, vain and gaudy fashions of the World, in Superfluity of Apparel; and his circumspect Behaviour,

Behaviour, which was attended with much Meekness and Gravity, had often an awful Effect upon such.

He suffered Imprisonment and Spoiling of Goods with much Patience, which proved to be his Lot pretty early, by wicked Men who became Informers, seeking his Ruin, with many others; yet the Lord preserved him in Faithfulness, and brought him clean through all these Exercises. He stood firm in his Testimony against the *Anti-christian* Yoke of Tithes, that none might be unfaithful therein, either in paying or receiving them. And, having a Gift beyond many in the Government of Church Affairs, he exercised the same in much Wisdom and Prudence, and laboured diligently for the Peace of the Church, and to keep out every Thing that might appear to cause Strife and Debate. He had an excellent Gift of healing and making up of Breaches. And, although his Way was not to lay sudden Hands on any, yet he was indeed as a tender nursing Father, and watched with a careful Eye of Love over the Flock of Christ, that no hurtful Thing might get place amongst them. A great Lover and Promoter of good Order and Discipline, and very diligent to attend Meetings of that Nature, leaving his own Business to serve the Church. And when it was his Concern to deal with any by way of Rebuke, it was in much Tenderness and Solidity, and not in Harshness or Sourness.

He was a Pattern of Humility in his Conduct and Conversation, and bore a noble Testimony against Pride in every Branch of it, and also against Covetousness, and the eager Pursuit after the Things of this World, by launching into Trade and Business beyond Mens Abilities and Capacities, as being great Enemies to the Work of God, and the Prosperity of his Truth.

And as he was much loved and honoured amongst his Brethren, because of his Faithfulness, so he was greatly esteemed by his Neighbours, whom he was very ready to serve, in reconciling Differences, and preventing Lawsuits. And as he was not negligent in the Work of the Lord, to promote Truth and Righteousness, where ever his Lot was among any People, being of an universal Spirit, and concerned for the Good and Welfare of all ; so when at Home, about his lawful Affairs, he was not negligent in providing Things honest in the Sight of all ; and the Lord was pleased to bless his Endeavours, by affording him outward Mercies, and giving him Wisdom to use them in Moderation ; so that he was a good Example in his County, having his House and Heart open to receive and entertain the Lord's Servants and Messengers. He was a great Encourager of his Children and Servants to frequent Meetings ; but a great Discourager of their going to Markets and Fairs unnecessarily ; and often cautioned Friends, of

the

the great Danger that Youth were in, of being drawn into too much Liberty at such Times, and thereby bringing Reproach upon the Truth, and Disesteem upon themselves. And though he was much against Idleness, and such as spent their Time like the Sluggard, yet charitable and compassionate to the Poor, and such as were in Want, and would often provoke and stir up Friends to Liberality in Contributions, and was himself very exemplary therein.

And, as old Age came upon him, his Zeal and Fervency was not lessened; which was demonstrated by the living Freshness that attended his Ministry, and his continued Constancy in attending Meetings when under very great bodily Weakness; having been seized with a consumptive Distemper, which increased upon him about the Space of nine Months; in all which Time he bore his Affliction with abundance of Patience, though often in great Distress in his outward Man; yet his inward Man was strengthened and renewed, and his Memory and Understanding remained firm and perfect: Often commemorating the great and unspeakable Loving-kindness and Mercy of God, in visiting him in his young Years. And much was the good Counsel and seasonable Advice that dropt from him in Friends Meetings, even in the Time of his great Weakness; as also to many, of several Ranks and Degrees, who came to visit him; not forgetting to give tender and fatherly Advice frequently to his own Children.

And though it be our Loss, to be deprived of such a worthy and serviceable Instrument in the Lord's Hand, as he was, whose Memory will remain sweet among us; yet we firmly believe it is his great Gain, having faithfully finished his Day's Work, his Reward, we doubt not, is great with the Lord.

He departed this Life the 6th Day of the Eleventh Month 1720, and was buried the 8th Day of the same, being accompanied to the Burying Ground at *Hetherside*, by the greatest Number of Friends and others that has almost ever been seen in these Parts at any Burial. Aged Seventy two Years. A Minister Forty three Years.

A Testimony

A Testimony from the Monthly-meeting at Settle, *in the County of* York, *concerning* THOMAS WILDE.

OUR said Friend, by his own Account, was born in the Year 1649, and convinced of the Truth in the Twenty fourth Year of his Age; soon after which he became very zealous and circumspect in his Life and Conversation, and, for Truth's Sake, took up the Cross chearfully, and denied himself, not only of the former Pleasures and Delights he had accustomed himself to, but even also of the Trade and Imployment he was instructed in, and whereby he had his chief Supply, as to the Things of this World; for, being by his Trade a *Taylor*, he, under a religious Concern of Mind, soon after his Convincement, could not comply with the making such needless and superfluous Fashions in Apparel, as were then used by his Customers, and thereupon gave over the greatest Part of his Trade, and betook himself to other Business, in order to get a Livelihood; wherein Providence was favourably pleased to bless his Labours with Success: So that, although he never had a great deal as to the Things of this World, yet he had a Competency sufficient to support him in, and carry him through the same, with Satisfaction and Comfort. He was also made helpful to others in his Station, according to his Ability; for which he many Times publickly acknowledged his Thankfulness to the Lord, that he had been so merciful to him, in raising him from a low Degree to a State of Favour and Acceptance with him, as well as a Degree of Service and Unity among his People. It was not long after his Convincement, before his Mouth was opened in a publick Testimony amongst Friends, wherein, although for divers Years he had but a few Words in Meetings, yet his Appearance was both acceptable and useful to Friends. And as he approved himself faithful and diligent in the Gift bestowed upon him, the Lord was pleased to inlarge it, so that he became an able Minister of the Gospel, and therein his frequent Service amongst Friends was very edifying, and helpful to such as had the Opportunity of his Labours and Service amongst them.

He was not only instrumentally helpful in that respect, but the Lord having been graciously pleased to bestow upon him a good Degree of Understanding, he was thereby qualified to be very serviceable in the Discipline of the Church; so that such as knew him, and had the Benefit of his Labours and Services amongst them, had a valuable Esteem for him, both at home and abroad; for he often visited the Meetings of Friends in divers of the adjacent Counties; and, in the Year 1700, had a
Concern

Concern upon his Mind to visit Friends in *Wales*, together with the South and West Parts of this Nation; which Journey, in Company with another Friend, he accomplished to his Satisfaction; after his Return, saying, *The Lord had been near to and assisted him therein, in the greatest Exercises that he met with*; and also, *That he found a favourable and kind Reception among Friends where he travelled; which bowed him down in Spirit before the Lord, in Thankfulness to acknowledge his great Goodness to him in many Respects.* He was often made to rejoice both in publick and private, that the Lord should be so graciously pleased to visit him, and in any degree to make him serviceable in the Church and among his People.

At a certain Time, when visited with Sickness, whereof many thought he would not have recovered, he expressed himself on this wise to Friends then present; — *I have been often brought very low in my Mind, when I considered the exceeding Goodness of the Lord to me, in visiting my Soul with the Inshining of Truth, whereby I was made to see the miserable and wretched State I was then in, having spent so much of my precious Time in Vanity, and in following of my own foolish Imaginations; but the Lord, through his infinite Mercy, in his own due Time, was pleased to correct and chastise me for the same, and, in measure, I came to be redeemed therefrom; although, I may say, I was neither a Prophet nor a Prophet's Son, but a poor*

poor forlorn Creature, which causeth me the more to admire his Loving-kindness to me ; for I can say, when at any Time I have gone astray, his Rod and his Staff have upheld me, and therefore I have come to witness Deliverance. I speak not these Things to gain your Applause ; no ! I am far from that ; there is no Desert in me ; my own Unworthiness, as a Man, I have reason to bear in Mind ; but it is the Lord's Goodness to me that occasions me thus to express myself.

He was often concerned for Friends Growth and Prosperity in the Truth ; and especially, that the Youth might be preserved from the many hurtful and entangling Snares of this World ; endeavouring to excite in Friends a diligent Care after their own Growth therein, and that they might not too much depend upon instrumental Means, which frequently leads to a Neglect of attending upon the Gift in themselves. Thus he was often engaged in Spirit for the Good of those he laboured amongst. He also was a very diligent Attender of Meetings, until old Age and Infirmity of Body rendered him uncapable, and therein was very exemplary to others. His Life and Conversation corresponded with his Doctrine. He was not apt to appear in Meetings, after a publick Manner, unless he had a Necessity upon him so to do; and then his Exercise tended to the Edification and Comfort of those who sat under his Ministry, which was living and powerful.

In

In his last Illness, which continued many Months upon him, he manifested a great deal of Patience and Resignation of Mind to the Will of the Lord, saying to some Friends who visited him, — *I have had many comfortable Times amongst Friends, the Lord having been good to me in many Respects, and under various Exercises and Temptations that I have met with; and I hope, as I continue faithful to the End, he will be near me still, and at that Time give me an Inheritance among the Righteous, which I have no Cause to doubt of; for although this Affliction he has now laid, or permitted to be brought upon me, be exercising, yet if it should continue and increase, I know that I ought to bear with Patience; for the Lord has been good to me many Ways, as I have reason to acknowledge, and hope he will continue so to be to the End.*

We doubt not but the Desire of his Soul was answered in that Respect, and that he now enjoys the Fruit of his Labours, *Peace with the Lord*, and *Assurance for ever*. And although, by reason of his old Age, and the Infirmity of Body that had long attended him, he at Times was not so strong in his Intellects, as in the Time of his Health he used to be, yet he was in a good degree preserved in a sweet and inoffensive Disposition of Mind, and was sometimes very lively and clear in his Understanding, and manifested the same in his last Moments.

He

He departed this Life, in great Patience and Stilnefs, the 10th of the Ninth Month 1728, and was buried in Friends Burying Ground in lower *Bentham* in *Yorkſhire*, on the 12th of the fame, being in the Eightieth Year of his Age.

A Teſtimony from the Monthly-meeting at Woodbridge, *in the County of* Suffolk, *concerning our well-beloved Friend* MARY GODBOLD.

MARY GODBOLD, late Wife of *Robert Godbold*, of *Bredfield* in the County of *Suffolk*, was born in the Pariſh of *Dallingo*, in the County aforefaid, about the Year 1665. She was well inclined from her Youth, and, for the Sake of the bleſſed Truth, did deny herſelf of thoſe Things which ſhe ſaw would prevent her from doing her Duty to God and Man. About the Year 1706, it pleaſed the Lord to call her into the Work of the Miniſtry. She was very zealous and faithful in the Diſcharge of her Duty therein, to the Honour of God, and the Comfort of his People.

She was a tender nurſing Mother, both in her Family and in the Church of Chriſt, and had a fervent Zeal for God and his bleſſed Truth; and ſhe was very loving and ſerviceable in entertaining Friends; alſo zealous in exhorting and building up both Old and Young

in

in the most holy Faith: And the very Stream of her Testimony tended wonderfully to perſwade the young Generation to Faithfulneſs to God, and Love one towards another. She was alſo concerned to bear her Teſtimony againſt that *ſeparate Spirit* that hath appeared amongſt us of late. And though ſhe was often very weak in Body, yet very careful and diligent in viſiting Meetings, in and about the Counties of *Norfolk*, *Eſſex* and *Cambridgſhire*, as well as thoſe in the County wherein ſhe dwelt; and whilſt ſhe had Strength of Body to attend publick Meetings, ſhe had often therein a Word to ſpeak in Seaſon, ſuitable to the Conditions of many; and was inſtrumental, in the Hand of the Lord, to keep Things in good Order, relating to Church Affairs. But about the 12th of the Seventh Month 1728, ſhe was taken very ill, and much afflicted in Body; yet through fervent Travail of Soul to the Lord, in the living Faith which ſhe received of Chriſt the Author of it, ſhe was kept ſtedfaſt, in the true Patience, to the End of her Days, and obtained Victory, which God in his own good Time did manifeſt to her; and which moſt excellent Enjoyment ſhe often declared of unto others, to their Joy and Refreſhment alſo. She would frequently ſay, in the Time of her Ilneſs, *That the Work of Regeneration was bravely compleated in Chriſt, and all Doubts and Fears were removed; and now ſhe waited to be with him her Redeemer.*
She

She likewise often spoke *of the sweet Enjoyment of God's living Presence, which she was favoured with*; for which she was thankful, and praised the Lord for his great Goodness towards her Soul. At other Times she wept and prayed on behalf of others, and begged *that the Lord, in his great Goodness and Mercy, would be pleased to visit the Souls of all, as he had visited her.* And in this sweet, quiet and heavenly Frame of Spirit, she continued to the End of her Illness; and on the 4th Day of the Eleventh Month 1728, being then very still and quiet, and in a Lamb-like State, she gave up the Ghost; and we have good reason to believe she died in true Peace with the Lord, and in right Good-will towards all Mankind, and is gone to receive a Crown of Righteousness, and a joyful Reward with the Lord, the God of her Salvation, for ever. And certainly the Loss of her is very great to the Church, but undoubtedly our Loss is her Gain and Comfort in Christ, World without End.

On the 7th of the Eleventh Month 1728, she was decently buried in Friends Burying Ground in *Bredfield* aforesaid.

A Testimony

A Testimony from the Monthly-meeting at Asquith *in* Yorkshire, *concerning* JOHN DODSHON.

THIS our dear deceased Friend was descended of believing Parents, and by them carefully educated in the Way of Truth and Plainness. In his young Years he became concerned in Spirit to fear and seek the Lord, that he might feel and witness in himself the sanctifying Work of his Spirit; and by attending thereto, he grew up a good Example to the Youth of his Time. Thus persevering to love Truth and religious Meetings, and waiting therein upon the Lord for his quickning Power, he had a Gift of the Ministry committed to him. His Labour and Exercise therein tended to Friends Comfort and Satisfaction, the same being adorned with an innocent Life, and a grave and peaceable Conversation; and through the Openings of the divine Power, his Understanding came to be enlarged in the Mysteries of the Kingdom. He was truly beloved and esteemed amongst us in his Services for the Truth. He visited many of the Meetings of Friends in this County, and in some other Counties, North and South, to the Satisfaction and Comfort of Friends; having also often had good Service in divers publick Meetings, on sundry Occasions, where

where many People of different Professions were gathered. He was a very diligent Attender of our Monthly-meetings, and very serviceable therein in many Respects, promoting Peace and Righteousness; also a frequent Attender of our Quarterly-meeting, and often at the Yearly-meeting, and other Meetings for Truth's Service.

He was a loving and kind Husband, a gentle and prudent Master, and a good Neighbour; whose Readiness to be assisting in many Cases, gained him a general Respect amongst them; a Lover of Peace, and very instrumental in composing of Differences; so that his Removal from us seems not only to be a Loss to the Church, but others also; yet his great and everlasting Gain.

Some Months before his Departure, he told some Friends, *he did not expect to continue long amongst us*; and, in the particular Meeting whereunto he belonged, he seemed in his Exercise like a Person hasting to be discharged of his Day's Work; which was particularly remarked by some.

On the 8th of the First Month 1728, he was suddenly seized with a *Fever*, and though the Distemper was very violent upon him, he bore it with *Christian* Patience and Resignation. He gave good Advice to young People, and others who visited him, and often spoke thankfully *of the Goodness of God to him, and of the Sweetness of true Love, right Unity, and Brotherhood,*

Brotherhood, which he had laboured to promote, and then recommended. He appeared without any Surprife at the Approach of fo fudden a Change; often praying for *divine Help to bear and go through*; and nigh his laſt Moment defired, *that he might have to draw his Breath in the Senſe of Life*; which fome there prefent fully believed was mercifully granted him; and that he is now entered into the Kingdom of Glory and Peace that never ſhall have an End.

He departed this Life the 14th, and was buried in Friends Burying Ground at *Hardcaſtle Garth* the 16th of the Firſt Month 1728, being attended to his Grave by many Friends and others. Aged about Fifty three Years. A Miniſter nigh Thirty Years.

A Teſtimony from the Quarterly-meeting, held at Pardſhaw-hall, *for the County of* Cumberland, *concerning* THOMAS DREWREY *Senior.*

THOMAS DREWREY *Senior*, of *Bolton* in the County of *Cumberland*, was convinced of the Truth about the Fourteenth Year of his Age: There being but very few in thoſe Days who made Profeſſion thereof, he was much vilified, derided and reproached, by his Parents, Relations and others, who ufed what Means they could to perfwade him not to

leave

leave the Way of his Anceſtors; during which Time, he underwent great Afflictions upon ſeveral Accounts; yet, being ſupported by the Power and Virtue of that which he profeſſed, he was enabled to ſtand through all. As he grew in Years, he grew in Strength and ſaving Knowledge, and by degrees came to witneſs an Improvement in that Gift the Lord had beſtowed upon him, ſo that in due Time he was engaged to open his Mouth in publick Teſtimony, and to declare unto others, what the Lord had made him an Experiencer of. His diligent and fervent Labour was, that all might be made Sharers thereof. He was not eloquent of Speech, nor accompliſhed with Literature, but was attended with the Life and Power of Truth, which is the Subſtance of the true Miniſtry: This made his Offerings beneficial and edifying to the Church. He did not travel much abroad, except ſometimes into the South and Weſtern Parts of *England* and *Wales*, but very diligently attended the Meetings he belonged to; and alſo often viſited Meetings in his native County. He was a good Example in a blameleſs Life and Converſation, and a faithful Sufferer for the Teſtimony of Truth, in the Time of Perſecution. He had a Fine of Twenty Pounds impoſed upon him for keeping a Meeting at his Houſe, and the ſame being levied, made great Havock of his ſmall Stock; yet, as he often ſaid, *he never ſuffered Want.* His Heart was

was open to entertain Friends, and often to contribute to the Neceſſity of the Poor, which he frequently adviſed Friends unto, ſaying, *the Lord loves a cheerful Giver.* So being an Encourager of Good, in all reſpects, he found the Bleſſing and Comfort thereof in his declining Days, inſomuch, that when he advanced in Age, and Infirmity of Body grew upon him to that degree, that he was unable to attend Meetings, he was preſerved in a tender and ſweet Frame of Spirit; during which Time, the Viſits of Friends were very acceptable to him, having great Love to them for Truth's Sake, and ſaying, *He greatly loved the Company of Friends, and hoped he ſhould die in Unity with them* ; and that, *as Truth had been his Choice in his Youth, it was his Support and Comfort in his old Age, or elſe his Infirmity of Body would be heavier to bear.* Yet he often expreſſed his Deſire to be diſſolved and to be at Reſt, feeling nothing but Peace with God and Goodwill towards all Men. And being ſenſible the Time of his Departure drew near, he was very deſirous of his eldeſt Son *Thomas*'s Company, who had many ſolid Times of Conference with him, about Truth and the Affairs thereof; but the moſt memorable and weighty Expreſſions which he uttered, near the Time of his Concluſion, were to this Effect. — *I have lived to a good old Age, and gone through divers Exerciſes and Trials; and, through all, the Lord hath been my Help and Support;*

Support ; and now I have so much Peace and Satisfaction in my inner Man, that it seems to me, if I had my Days to spend over again, I could not spend them better.

After this, his Time was but short; his Body weakned, and his Speech failed, so was not well to be understood ; and as Peace had been his Delight in his Life-time, he was favoured with a peaceable and quiet End, without either Struggle, Sigh or Groan.

He departed this Life the 29th Day of the Third Month 1729, in the Ninety first Year of his Age. A Minister Fifty Years, or upwards.

Some Account of SARAH BROWN, *of* Pickering, *with some of her dying Sayings, as near as can be remembered : From the Monthly-meeting of* Malton *in* Yorkshire.

SHE was carefully educated, by her Parents, in the Principles of Truth ; and, when very young, she fell under a Concern of Heart, that she might come to be acquainted with the Lord for herself ; and, in order thereto, as she in the Time of her last Illness declared, *She was made willing to seek out private Places, to pour forth her Supplications to the Lord* ; beseeching him, *to make the Way of Truth more fully known to her* ; and also, *to enable her to walk therein.* Which Concern he was pleased to regard, in his own Time, to his Praise, and to her Growth and Incouragement in the Truth ; for about the Twenty second Year of her Age, a Part in the Ministry was committed to her, which became a very close Concern upon her, being such a Cross, that she said, *She had rather have parted with her natural Life* ; but could find no Peace without answering the Lord's Requirings; and therefore she resolved, through his divine Assistance, *to be obedient unto him, though all Sorts of People might hiss at her.*

She travelled in the Service of the Miniftry, in this and feveral neighbouring Counties, and was well received, fhe being of a grave, modeft and exemplary Behaviour, as became her Vocation, and our holy Profeffion; and the Lord was pleafed to favour her with *Chriftian* Courage to the laft: For in the Time of her late Ilnefs (it being a pining Diftemper) fhe fignified, *that fhe had freely given up herfelf, and all that was near to her, to the Lord;* and, in great Sweetnefs of Spirit, very frequently expreffed her earneft Defire for the Prefervation of *her Hufband and Children in the Truth.* She often bewail'd the loofe Profeffors of our own Society, and alfo the Blindnefs and Prophanity of many in other Profeffions, expreffing her Defire for the Good of all People; and faid, *that fhe had no Caufe to diftruft the Lord, for he had been wonderfully kind.* And near her End fhe had many fick Fits, yet often broke forth in great Sweetnefs, faying,— *Glory be to the eternal God, whom,* fhe faid, *fhe felt to be near her in that the Time of her great Affliction of Body.*

About half an Hour before her Departure, fhe feemed to have an hard Struggle with Death, and fpake not much more to us; but a few Minutes before fhe drew her laft Breath, fhe appeared eafy, and very fweetly cried out, —*Glory be to the eternal God!* And fo long as fhe could fpeak, in Sweetnefs of Spirit gave Glory to God. And although fhe hath finifhed her

her Courſe in this World, her Memory is ſweet to us that are left behind.

She died the 18th of the Fourth Month 1729, in the Thirty third Year of her Age, and was buried at *Pickering* aforeſaid.

A Teſtimony from the Quarterly-meeting at Pardſhaw-hall *in* Cumberland, *concerning* THOMAS SCOTT *of* Newbiggin.

HE was born at *Hetherſide*, in the Year 1678, in the ſaid County. His Parents were of the Church of *England*, in which Way he was educated; but being at a Meeting of Friends, the Lord was pleaſed, through the Miniſtry of his Servants, to reach his Underſtanding, ſo that he was fully convinced of the Truth, and joined with Friends, took up the daily Croſs, and denied himſelf of his former Pleaſures and Paſtimes.

He was of an innocent Behaviour, and grew in the Truth; and after ſome Time, the Lord endued him with a Gift of the Miniſtry. His Appearance was in a lowly, humble, Frame of Mind, in the Demonſtration of the Spirit and Power, and attended with a ſweet and heavenly Authority, to the edifying and refreſhing of the Church. He was juſt upon the Workers of Iniquity, though conſolating to the True-hearted. His Care of the Church was great, and the Profperity of Truth much in his View. He was well efteemed by Friends. He vifited the Churches in divers Parts of this Nation, and alfo in *North Britain*, where he had good Service.

He was a good Example to the Youth; a loving Hufband, and a tender affectionate Father to his Children, and often fupplicated the Lord for them.

Being at a Meeting one Firft-day, he livingly preached the Gofpel; and in his Return was taken with an Ilnefs, which increafed and remained upon him near three Weeks; during which Time, he was patient and refigned to the Will of the Lord, faying, *that Death was no Terror to him*.

He departed this Life the 8th Day of the Sixth Month 1729, in great Unity with us, and was interred in Friends Burying Ground at *Hetherfide*. Many Friends attended his Burial, and the Truth was powerfully declared, to general Satisfaction. Aged Fifty Years. A Minifter Twenty Years.

A Teftimony

A Testimony from the Monthly-meeting of Pard-shaw-hall, *in the County of* Cumberland, *concerning* JOSEPH BUNTING.

HE was born in *Ireland,* and descended of honest Parents, whose Names were *Joseph* and *Jane Bunting.* They brought him over with them when young, and settled upon a Farm, within the Compass of *Allenby* Meeting in this County, for several Years.

He was educated in the Way of Truth, and, in his young Years, much inclined to read the holy Scriptures, and the Writings of Friends, being endued with a large natural Capacity.

About the Twelfth Year of his Age, the Lord was pleased to visit him; so that he hath since been heard to say, *He should then have opened his Mouth in publick Testimony in Meetings; but not giving up in Obedience, was, through the subtil Workings of the Enemy, for a Time led away after youthful Vanities.* Afterwards, about the Twenty second Year of his Age, it pleased the Lord to give him a second Visitation, by the powerful Ministry of our worthy Friend *Mary Ellerton* of *York,* then in this County. Soon after, he gave up in Obedience to what he believed was required of him, and came forth in a publick Testimony, in a few Words, which was attended with the Power and Authority of the Truth, and, being preserved in an humble, lowly Mind, he grew in his Gift, and became an able Minister of the Gospel.

He visited Friends in most Parts of this Nation and *Ireland*, having good Service for the Truth, whereof many are Witnesses. His Ministry was found, living, clear, powerful and prevalent ; just upon the Workers of Iniquity, yet very tender and consolating to the least Child in the Truth.

He was married to an honest young Woman of *Allenby* Meeting about two Years ago, and removed to *Whitehaven*, where he had good Service amongst Friends and others, who much lamented his Death. His Testimony was very affecting to People in many Places. He was willing to spend and be spent for Truth's Sake. His Conversation was solid, savoury and exemplary. We cannot but lament the Loss of so serviceable an Instrument in the Hand of the Lord. Several were convinced by him and joined with Friends. He was diligent in attending Meetings when at home.

In his Sickness he was patient, and said, *It was a brave Thing to have a clear Conscience at such a Time.* And calling his dear Wife to him, said, *He must leave her, and commit her into the Hands of a good Keeper* ; adding, *What Cause have I to be thankful, that I have had Time to remember, and call on him who will take*

take me to himself. He declared often, that *he was very easy*; and in his Sickness he was at Times wonderfully drawn forth in Prayer.

He departed this Life, in great Unity with Friends, the 29th Day of the Ninth Month 1729, and we believe is at Rest. He was buried, the 1st Day of the Tenth Month, in Friends Burying Ground in *Whitehaven*, where a great many Friends and others attended, and divers living Testimonies were born to the Truth. Aged about Thirty four. A Minister Twelve Years.

A Testimony from the Quarterly-meeting of Durham, *concerning* ELIZABETH WHEATLY.

SHE received the Truth in her young and tender Age, in the early Breakings forth thereof, about the Year 1656. At her first Convincement she met with Hardships from her Mother, who was a Widow, and so severe against her, that she turned her out of her House to shift for herself; but this Suffering was made easy in a little Space: Some Relations being convinced, one of them entertained her, at whose House she remained some Years; and in this Time she not only became well settled and grounded in the Truth, but was raised up to give a fresh and lively Testimony to others of its Goodness, to the Comfort of the Meeting

ing to which she belonged, and to the edifying of many. And being made willing to give up to what was manifested and called for at her hand to bear Testimony unto, she became a very serviceable Instrument in the Hand of the Lord, to the comforting and strengthning of many, by her continued Labour of Love; which was not only acceptable to the neighbouring Parts where she first had her Service, but she was frequent in Travels, visiting most Counties in *England*, and several Parts of *Scotland*, being zealously concerned for the Growth of Truth amongst the Professors of it, that they might arrive at the true Knowledge thereof. She was of a good Savour amongst her Neighbours and Acquaintance, and of good Service even to very old Age; and finished her Course in this Life in the Ninety second Year of her Age; having been a Preacher of Righteousness, not only in Word and Doctrine, but also in Life and Conversation, for about Seventy Years. And having laid down her Head in Peace, she rests from her Labours, and her Works follow her.

She departed this Life at *Iveston*, being the Place of her Abode, the 20th of the Twelfth Month 1729.

The Testimony from the Quarterly-meeting of Lancaster, concerning SARAH TOMLINSON.

OUR Friend *Sarah Tomlinson* was born in *Cheshire*. She was educated by her Parents in the Principles of the Church of England, her Father being a Priest. The manner of her Convincement we cannot rightly shew, there being no Footsteps to be found amongst her Papers that give any Information thereof: But this we know, that upon her embracing our Principles, and joining in Society with us, she was turned out of her Father's House; whereupon our Friend *Tabitha Ardern*, of *Stockport* in *Cheshire*, charitably took her under her Care, where she became confirmed in the Principles of Truth she had before embraced; and in due Time it pleased the Lord to commit to her a Gift in the Ministry, in which she laboured, both in the Meeting to which she belonged, and in many Parts of *England* and *Wales*. Her Ministry was attended with Life and Power, as many have experienced to their Comfort and Refreshment. She was very serviceable in Meetings established for Church Discipline, being peculiarly qualified for it; charitable to the Poor, particularly when under Infirmity of Body, she having great Judgment in applying

proper

proper Remedies for their Relief, and her Death is therefore by them much lamented. In all thefe and many other Services, fhe laboured to the Time of her laft Ilnefs, which was a *Fever*. Many Friends and Neighbours who then vifited her, found her in a patient Refignation to the Lord's Will. She often expreffed her earneft Defire, *that Friends might profper in the Truth, and live in Unity one with another*; and but a few Hours before her Departure, recommended her dear Love to all Friends, fignifying her Satisfaction in her approaching Diffolution; which was comfortable to thofe attending her; and we have reafon to believe fhe is gone to Reft.

She died at her own Houfe in *Warrington* the 24th, and was buried the 27th of the Twelfth Month 1729, at Friends Burying Ground there, her Body being accompanied to the Grave by many Friends and Neighbours.

A Teftimony

A Testimony from the Quarterly-meeting in Cumberland, *concerning* HENRY ATKINSON.

HE was descended of believing Parents, at *Mosthorn* in the said County, who died when he and their other Children were young. Hereupon this our Friend was received by a Relation, a Member of the Church of *England*, who educated him in that Way. He was then a sober Youth, and was bound Apprentice to a *Taylor* in *Newcastle* upon *Tyne*. After some Time he removed to *London* and settled there, and was convinced of the Truth, and joined with Friends at *London*, and mostly continued there for Fourteen Years. He then returned into his native Country and settled there, and was well esteemed by Friends; being often melted and broken by the Power of Truth in Meetings. He came forth in a publick Testimony, and was serviceable therein. He was of a clean sweet Conduct, redeemed from the World, and the Spirit of it; and often bore his Testimony, in the Authority of Truth, against the same. He was of a cheerful Temper. He visited the Churches divers Times in *North-Britain* and *Ireland*, and we believe had good Service.

Near the latter Part of his Time, he was concern'd to visit the South Parts of this Nation.

Nation. He had a Certificate from the Monthly-meeting he belonged to, and, as we underſtand, was enabled to accompliſh his Service; but in his Return was taken with a *Fever* and *Ague* at a Friend's Houſe near *Banbury* in *Oxfordſhire*, where he departed this Life, about the Sixtieth Year of his Age. A Miniſter Thirty Years.

The Teſtimony from the Monthly-meeting of Newcaſtle, concerning SAMUEL MAUD, *late of* Sunderland.

WE think it our Duty, and hope it may be of Service, to recommend to Poſterity the good Example of this our dear deceaſed Friend. He was born at *Leeds* in *Yorkſhire*; his Parents being *Preſbyterians*, he was educated in that Way till about the Eighteenth Year of his Age; at which Time he came to live with *William Maud*, his Uncle, at *Sunderland*, who was a Profeſſor of Truth in its early Breakings forth; with whom he continued not long, before he was convinced of the ſame, and made open Profeſſion thereof; demonſtrating to the World the bleſſed Effects of the Power of Truth, by a ſober and religious Converſation, in which he ſeemed daily to improve, until he was raiſed up to bear a publick Teſtimony to the Light of Jeſus, which

which had wrought his Reformation. His Labour of Love was well accepted of by his Brethren, he appearing well qualified for the Work of the Miniſtry, being lively and edifying in his Teſtimony, found in Doƈtrine, and exemplary in a ſteady pious Conduƈt. A Lover of Peace and Unity, which he not only frequently recommended to others, but ſo fully demonſtrated his own Regard to it, that in ſome Conteſts he meekly reſigned his Right for the Sake thereof. He kept a more than ordinary Government over his own Spirit, which made the Work of the Spirit of Truth ſhine forth very eminently both in his Life and Doƈtrine. This rendered him dear to us, and well eſteemed by others. And ſo ſenſible are we of his eminent Services, both in the Miniſtry and Diſcipline of the Church, that the Spirits of many are bowed down in a deep Senſe of the Loſs we ſuſtain by his Death.

 He departed this Life the 4th Day of the Second Month 1730. Aged Sixty three.

A Testimony from Carloe *Monthly-meeting in* Ireland, *concerning* GEORGE RUSSEL.

THIS our dear deceased Friend hath been known by some of us about Fifty five Years. He was a Man of an innocent Life and blameless Conversation, zealous for the Promotion of Truth, and the Discipline of the Church; constant in attending Half-year's, Quarterly and Province-meetings, as well as the particular Meeting to which he belonged; and often had a Concern upon him to advise Friends to make right Use of Time, that their Day's Work might be done in the Day: For that *an exercising Time and Day of great Mortality was coming on, which would be a dreadful Day to the Unfaithful and Disobedient amongst us; and that there would be no Safety in that Day, but in the Lord's Arm of Power*; saying, *we should be safe under it, and not otherwise.*

The Substance of this he was frequently concerned, under great Dread and Weight, to declare amongst us; and, to some who visited him in his Ilness, said, that *What he had so often been concerned to declare amongst us, would come to pass.* His Appearance in Meetings was always under a reverent Awfulness. And as he was diligent in attending Meetings, so was he frequently concerned to press Friends to visit

visit Families within the Compass of our Monthly-meeting; saying, *The Lord often owned them in that Concern, as there was a waiting upon him in the Service.* In such Visits, he at times had a clear Sight respecting the State of Families, and would drop very suitable Advice upon those Occasions. His Love was such to Friends and Truth, that he suffered not his outward Affairs to hinder his attending the Service of the Church, but was always ready, when of Ability, to join Friends therein, and mindful to encourage others. He was one who took the Over-sight of the Flock, not by Constraint, but willingly; and we have, with his Wife and Children, to whom he was a loving Husband and tender Father, a sensible Loss of so worthy a Friend and Elder, who was taken from us, lively in old Age.

He endured the Pain of his last Illness with great Patience, and in Spirit was attended with divine Sweetness, which supported him through. He had his Request granted, of *an easy Passage out of this Life*; and we have no Cause to doubt he enjoys the Fruit of his Labours, and is entered into the Rest prepared for the Righteous.

He departed this Life the 18th of the Sixth Month 1730. Aged about Eighty, a Minister about Forty Years.

A Testimony from the Quarterly - meeting at Hurstperpoint, *in the County of* Sussex, *concerning* WILLIAM BEARD.

HE was a meek, humble, innocent and inoffensive Man, a sincere Lover of the Truth, and of the Friends of it. He diligently frequented Meetings so long as Ability of Body would permit. And as it pleased the Lord to commit to him a Part in the Ministry, we believe he faithfully discharged his Duty therein. His Delivery was in Plainness of Speech, frequently in great Tenderness and Brokenness of Spirit. He seldom appeared in many Words at a time; yet what he delivered, seemed always to spring from the divine Fountain, it being attended with Life and Power, and was greatly to the comforting and Refreshment of many. He used with much Earnestness to exhort and press all to Diligence in Meetings, and that none would sit down easy under a bare Profession of Religion, but labour and strive after the inward Work, that they might know Sanctification and Holiness perfected in themselves. He was oftentimes very fervent and powerful in Prayer. He was a good Example to others, and well esteemed by Friends and Neighbours. His Removal from us is a Loss to our County, and especially to the Meeting at *Brighthelmston*, to which he belonged.

In the time of his Ilness, and but a little before his Death, he did several times express, that *he enjoyed inward Peace*, and that *he was well satisfied in the Will of the Lord, whether it were to live or die*.

He departed this Life the 27th Day of the Seventh Month 1730, and was buried the 30th of the same in Friends Burying Ground at *Rottingdeane*. Aged about Seventy three Years.

The Testimony of Friends from the Moate *Monthly-meeting in* Ireland, *concerning* ELIZABETH WILSON.

THIS our dear Friend was born at *Waterstown*, in the County of *West Meath*, in the Year 1694; the Names of her Parents were *Jacob* and *Jane Fuller*, who, being honest and religious Persons, carefully educated their Children in the Way of Truth; and she was dutiful to them to the End of their Days.

And as she grew in Years, she had religious Inclinations, and thereby came sensibly to know the Want of an inward Acquaintance with the Lord in Spirit, which, Education of itself could not give her. Thus the Lord began to prepare her, by his Word and Power in her Heart, for future Service. And her Love increasing in the pure holy Fear, she was preserved out of the Vanity and Folly, which too much abound in some of the Youth of our Day.

She loved Retirement, and often, with a tender, humble and broken Spirit, waited for a further Manifestation of the pure holy Principle of Light and Grace; and, in those inward Exercises, she frequently witnessed the Comfort of divine Love.

When she grew to mature Age, by the Consent of her Parents, she joined in Marriage with *William Watson*, a religious young Man, who lived but a short time with her. She remained a Widow several Years, in which State she behaved well, and received a Gift in the Ministry. She was of an innocent and sober Conversation, well beloved, both by Friends and Neighbours.

In the Year 1721 she married our Friend *Thomas Wilson*, who frequently gave her up to answer such Services as were required of her; and as she, by Faithfulness, had obtained to a good degree of Advancement in the Truth, she was not hasty nor forward to offer her Gift, but waited in the pure Silence, to be endued with Power from on high, which is the true Qualification of all who are called into that weighty Work of the Ministry; whereby she became skilful in dividing the Word suitably to the States of the People.

And

And although she seldom appeared large in Testimony at home, the tender Frame of Spirit she frequently sat under, in our silent Meetings, was very observable; yet when she did appear, what she delivered was sound and weighty, often being as glad Tidings of Life and Salvation, by Jesus Christ, to the true Mourners in *Sion*, and Consolation to the needy Soul: This seemed to be her particular Gift; yet, at times, the Power and Dread that she appeared in, did strike at the very Root and Mystery of Iniquity, that works, and too much prevails in the Children of Disobedience; hating the Appearance of Evil in any, but greatly concerned that Peace and Unity might be maintained amongst Friends, and that the ancient Testimony and Discipline, settled amongst us, might be kept up; and was serviceable therein, through her Zeal for the Prosperity of Truth.

She was a diligent Attender of Meetings, when at home; also our Quarterly and National Meetings. She sometimes visited Friends, both in the North and South of this Nation; and also, in Company with our dear Friend *Elizabeth Pease*, visited Friends in *Scotland*, and some Parts of the North of *England*. And in the Seventh Month 1729, she, with her dear Companion *Jane Gee*, having had a Concern upon their Minds for some time to visit Friends in *Wales*, and some Parts of *England*, in full Unity they left us: And for a further

further Account of her Labour and Service in that Nation, we refer to the following *Postscript*, wrote by her Companion; and have ground for Hope, that she is entered into that Rest prepared for the Righteous. She was a Minister about Eleven Years.

A Postscript by JANE GEE.

"MY dear Friend and Cousin *Elizabeth Wilson*, having for some considerable Time had a Concern upon her Mind to visit Friends Meetings in *Wales*, and some Parts of *England*, opened her Mind to me; and, having the like Concern, I found much Freedom to join with her in that Service. Taking our solemn Leave of our Husbands and Friends the 20th of the Seventh Month 1729, we landed near *Chester* the 23d of the same; so visited Friends Meetings in *Wales*, and divers Parts of *England*, spending about a Year in that Service. She grew in her Gift, and was well accepted where she came. Her exemplary Deportment and innocent Behaviour, with a solid and religious Conversation out of Meetings, which tended to Edification, was an Ornament to her. She was favoured with a Sight of her Death some Months before her Sickness, which made her very desirous to get her Day's Work done. She was taken ill at
"*Rushworth*

" *Rushworth* near *Halifax* in *Yorkshire*; but
" having a Defire to be with her Friends at
" *Manchester*, got there; and her Diftemper
" prevailing upon her, fhe took to her Bed
" and lay about two Weeks, moftly in a
" retired fenfible Condition, patiently bearing
" her Affliction; and a few Hours before her
" Departure, having lain fome time in Stil-
" nefs, fhe faid, that *fhe had enjoyed the fweeteft
" Spring of divine Love that ever fhe felt in all
" her Days*; and took Leave of me with a
" moft fweet, compofed and pleafant Counte-
" nance. And as fhe lived in the Fear of the
" Lord, I do firmly believe fhe died in his
" Favour.

" She departed this Life the 16th of the
" Eighth Month 1730, about the feventh
" Hour in the Evening, and was buried in
" Friends Burying Ground at *Manchefter* the
" 18th of the fame."

A brief

A brief Testimony from the Monthly-meeting of Owstwick *in* Yorkshire, *concerning* JOHN ADAM.

HE was descended of believing Parents, and educated in the Way of Truth, and was religiously inclined from his Childhood. He became a Minister about the Twenty fifth Year of his Age, and travelled frequently, in the Service of the Ministry, into *Scotland, Holland* and *Germany*; thrice into *Ireland*; also divers times in *Wales*, and the South and West Parts of this Nation.

He was remarkably innocent, peaceable, meek and humble; which, with sundry other Virtues and Qualifications, gained him the Esteem both of Friends and Neighbours. In short we may say, he was a Preacher of Righteousness, in Life and Conversation, as well as Doctrine; and we doubt not but our Loss is his exceeding great Gain.

He departed this Life at his own Habitation in *Welwick*, the 21st of the Sixth Month 1731. Aged about Fifty seven, a Minister about Thirty two Years.

A Testimony

A Testimony from the Quarterly-meeting in Westmorland, *concerning* JOHN THOMPSON.

OUR ancient and worthy Friend *John Thompson*, Son of *John Thompson* of *Crook* near *Kendal* in *Westmorland*, was born in the Fifth Month 1667. His honest Parents zealously educated him in the Way of Truth. Notwithstanding which, for some Years he was very inclinable to many of the Pastimes and Diversions of Youth, to the great Grief and Affliction of his religious Parents; but nothing proved sufficient to restrain him, until it pleased God, by the merciful Visitation of his Light and Grace, to shew him the Folly of his Ways, and the evil Consequence that would ensue a Continuance therein; which, as he gave way to, wrought so powerfully in him, as to reclaim him from his former Courses.

He received a Gift of the Ministry about the Eighteenth Year of his Age, and in a short time visited Friends Meetings in some adjacent Counties; after which, being seized with Sickness, he underwent great Afflictions, both of Body and Mind, for several Months: And thus being baptized in the Deeps, he was led to behold the Wonders of the Lord; and having the Mysteries of the Gospel opened to him,

him, he became an able Minister thereof. He travelled much abroad in his young Years, not only in this Nation, but also in *Scotland* and *Ireland*, and had good Service both among Friends and others; though at times, from the violent Insults of some unreasonable Men, he was exposed to imminent Danger, but through the Protection of Providence was preserved from bodily Harm.

When at home, he was diligent and exemplary in attending Meetings both for Worship and Discipline. The Simplicity of the Gospel very much appeared in his Ministry, to the Edification of the Church, and the reaching and convincing of several. He was also zealously engaged in Meetings of Discipline, at home and abroad, for the Preservation of Unity and good Order in the Church. Whilst Ability of Body would permit, he very much devoted himself to the Service of Truth; but being apprehensive, of late Years, that his Stay here would not be long, he several times very fervently cautioned and warned Friends, in their Meetings, against *Formality*, and *a dead empty Profession*; and that in a particular manner about two Weeks before his last Ilness.

Upon a young Man's coming to visit him, when under considerable Weakness of Body, he expressed himself to this Effect; *My Day is now almost over, and this is thine: Give thyself up freely to the Service of Truth, and spare*

spare no Pains to publish the Gospel ; we have but once a Time : '*Tis my Comfort that I have freely devoted myself to the divine Requirings, and I have great Peace now in my declining Years.* From hence 'tis evident, that the divine Power which called, brought forth and supported him under various Exercises in the Series of his Life, continued to uphold him near his dying Moments.

About the 25th of the First Month 1731, he was seized with a violent *Fever*, and a Complication of other Distempers, which were very strong upon him ; yet he bore his Pain with great Patience, intimating his Resignation to, and Contentment in the Will of God.

He quietly departed this Life at his own House in *Crook,* on the 2d Day of the Second Month 1731, and was buried in Friends Burying Ground near his own House the 5th of the same, being accompanied by a considerable Number of Friends and others. In the Sixty fourth Year of his Age, having been a Minister upwards of Forty five Years.

The Testimony of the Quarterly-meeting of Cumberland, *concerning* THOMAS WILKINSON *of* Beckfoot.

THIS our ancient Friend descended of honest Parents, though not of our Profession, and was born in the Year 1653. They died when he was young. He was educated, by a Relation, in the Way of the Church of *England*, and was by Nature wild, though not guilty of gross Evils. About the Fourteenth Year of his Age it pleased the Lord to visit him, and bring him under Conviction for his youthful Vanities; which he divers times expressed his Thankfulness for in his last Ilness; commemorating also, the Lord's Working upon him, and how he came to know a passing through the Ministration of Condemnation, which he patiently abode under, till he came to witness Justification and Peace. And being fully convinced of the Way of Truth, he joined himself with Friends; and after some Time, waiting in Silence with them, he received a Gift of the Ministry, and travelled, when but young, through most Parts of this Nation and *Wales*; and several times visited Friends in *Scotland* and *Ireland*; approving himself a faithful Labourer according to his Measure, and was instrumental in turning several to Righteousness.

His

His Miniftry was not with enticing Words of Man's Wifdom, but in the Demonftration of the Spirit and Power: And he was endued with an excellent Gift of Prayer. And as he bore a faithful Teftimony in Word and Doctrine, his Converfation was agreeable thereto. He alfo bore a zealous Teftimony againft Tithes; and for Non-payment of a fmall *Modus* out of his Eftate of Land, he was profecuted, in the Court of *Exchequer*, by the Farmers of Tithes; upon which Account he fuffered Imprifonment at *Carlifle*, and in the *Fleet* at *London*, fixteen Years before he was difcharged: All which Suffering he patiently bore without murmuring; and often faid, *he never enjoyed more of the Lord's Favour than in his Confinement.*

He paffed through many Hardfhips, and great Exercifes, by the * *Pearfons*, and bore a faithful Teftimony againft them, and the Spirit they appeared in, at the Meeting to which he belonged: As his Dwelling was near the Meeting-houfe, he fuffered many Abufes by them in their Malice and Rage; but that which was moft afflicting, was the Danger the Meeting was in, of being laid wafte by them:

Under

---

* *Thofe* Pearfons *were Ranters; bitter Enemies to the Society; frequently difturbed their Meetings for Worfhip in an unprecedented manner, and treated Individuals with great Outrages and Infults.*

Under which Affliction this our Friend stood firm, himself and Family being instrumental to uphold the Meeting, and were a great Strength to Friends. In his last Ilness, some Friends sitting by him, he said, *He had no Trouble in his Mind for any Thing he had done concerning them, they being rebellious against God and his People.*

He was visited with an intermitting *Fever* about three Weeks; during which Time, he was patient and sensible, and freely resigned himself up to the Lord's Will; often signifying, *that nothing stood in his Way,* and *that he had the full Evidence of Joy and Peace.* He gave good Advice to Friends, and to his Children and Family, desiring, *the Lord might bless them with the Dew of Heaven.*

He was of good Service in the Church. His Heart and House were open to serve and entertain Strangers. He departed this Life the 20th of the Eighth Month 1731, in full Unity with Friends, and was decently interred the 22d of the same, in their Burying Place at *Beckfoot*; his Corps being accompanied by many Friends and sober Neighbours, where divers living Testimonies were born for the Truth. Aged upwards of Seventy eight, a Minister about Fifty Years.

A Testimony

A Testimony from the Quarterly-meeting of Kendal *in the County of* Westmorland, *concerning* CHRISTOPHER WINN.

OUR dear and worthy Friend *Christopher Winn* was born near *Sedbergh* in *Yorkshire*, in the Year 1655, and educated in the Way of the Church of *England*. He was convinced of the blessed Truth, about the Year 1680, by that eminent and worthy Minister of Christ *Roger Haydock*: For a farther Account of which, we refer to a following short Narrative, left by him in *Manuscript*.

He was called to the Work of the Ministry about the Year 1683, in which he laboured fervently and faithfully, being suitably qualified for the same; and in Testimony would frequently speak of the Lord's gracious Dealings with his People; exhorting Friends to a Resignedness of Mind to serve him faithfully; and even travailed in Pain, that Christ might be formed in all. He was powerful in Prayer, and in Supplication oftentimes favoured with a near Access to divine Goodness.

His great Care and Concern for the Welfare of *Sion*, fully manifested his sincere Love to Truth and the Brethren. He was diligent in attending Meetings; a strict Observer of the Hour appointed: And the Care of the Church grew

grew daily upon him ; being concerned in a particular manner, that a godly and zealous Difcipline fhould be maintained, fo that Judgment might be placed upon every Tranfgreffor, and the Church be made clean : And although he ufed to deal plainly with Backfliders, yet, in a truly *Chriſtian* Spirit, entreated with fuch Meeknefs, and moving Tendernefs, as generally had a good Effect, being duly cautious of hardening or hurting any. He was full of Love, and meek in Expreflion to the Babes in Chrift.

He was a Man of an innocent, inoffenfive Conduct, and cheerful in Converfation ; and what rendered the fame more agreeable, profitable and edifying, was his being attended with a reverential Awe in what Company foever he came, left he fhould fpeak or act any thing prejudicial to Truth : Thus perfevering in true Watchfulnefs, Humility and Circumfpection, he adorned his holy Profeffion, and gained general Favour and Acceptance, both amongft Friends and others.

About the Beginning of the Sixth Month 1731, he was vifited with a *Fever*, of which he partly recovered ; but the Relicts thereof threw him into a gradual Decay, which in time occafioned his Death.

During his laft Sicknefs, which continued feveral Months, he was frequently vifited by feveral Friends, who had great Satisfaction therein, wholfome Advice and fweet Expreffions

often

often dropping from him : Some few of which are as follow. Being one time left in the Room, a Friend going in, told him *He was alone.* He answered, *No, he had the Company of the Father.* Another time being asked, *If he would have a little Wine?* He answered, *He was favoured with the Wine of the Kingdom.* At another time his Wife, who was tender over him, told him, *He was poor;* meaning in Body. He cheerfully answered, *He should in a little time be rich enough.* Another time, holding up his Hand, said, *It looks poor and withered, and almost fit for the Grave;* adding, *it was no Terror to him; because the Soul would be accepted in the Day of Account.* And after a little Pause, said, *It's a noble Thing to endure to the End; such obtain the promised Salvation.* Another time, when very weak of Body, a Friend being about to take Leave of him, he expressed himself thus; *Dear Friend, shall we not have Times of Pain and Distress? Nevertheless, let us not faint: It is my Faith, I am near upon entering into eternal Rest.* The Friend answered, *She was fully of the same Mind.* He said, *That's well:* And added, *Be of good Cheer; do thy best to please God, and be not afraid of what may befal thee; but be obedient to thy known Duty: Fear the Lord, and he will preserve thee.* At another time, a Friend visiting him, asked, *How he fared?* He answered, *He was favoured with the Presence of the Lord, and thereby*

thereby refreshed both in Soul and Body. Another time being asked, *How he was?* He spake pretty largely of the *Goodness and Mercy of God extended to him, and the Seal and Evidence he had of eternal Salvation.* And at the same time return'd upon himself, and said, *Though it be thus with me, the Words of the Apostle are fit to be remembered,*—Let him that thinketh he standeth, take heed left he fall: And added, *Such a Pitch of Strength and Safety should not be presumed upon; we should watch always.* In short, he was a Pattern of Holiness; and we think it may with as much Justice be said of him as of most Men, that *he was an Israelite indeed, in whom there was no Guile.* Thus this virtuous and honourable Man, having lived to a good old Age, and kept the Faith, hath therein finished his Course, and, we doubt not, obtained that glorious Immortality and Rest which is prepared for the Righteous.

He departed this Life, at his House near *Sedbergh,* on the 22d of the Second Month 1732. Aged Seventy seven, a Minister Fifty Years.

A short

A short Narrative, left in Manuscript, *by* CHRISTOPHER WINN, *relating to his Convincement,* &c.

"DURING the Time of my late Indis-
"position of Body, the gracious Deal-
"ings of the Almighty with my Soul have
"often been revived in my Mind; as also,
"how I have answered the End of my
"Creation: And in the Course of my Expe-
"rience, I concur with the great Apostle of
"the *Gentiles,* that *The Flesh lusteth against
"the Spirit, and the Spirit against the Flesh*;
"but Thanks be to God for his Mercy, who
"in a good degree hath given me, through
"the Help of his divine Spirit and Power,
"Victory over the Lusts and Inclinations of
"the Flesh: Therefore I cannot but earnestly
"recommend all, carefully to observe what
"brings Pain and Uneasiness to the Mind,
"and look upon it as Correction and Instruc-
"tion from above; which, if duly regarded,
"will bring all into a degree of the same
"comfortable Experience.

"I was born in the Year 1655, and edu-
"cated in the Way of the Church of *England,*
"so called, and was, according to my Power
"and Capacity, a diligent Observer of its
"Doctrine and Worship, till such time as I
"found

"found a Longing of Soul for other Food,
"though I knew not where to find it. I do
"remember, in my young Days, something
"at work in me, reproving for Sin and
"Transgressions, teaching and leading in the
"just Man's Path. The Lord was near at
"hand, but I knew him not; so that I often
"transgressed afresh, and Fear seized me;
"insomuch that I petitioned the Lord, *he
"would in Mercy deliver me from the gnawing
"Worm, and Fire unquenchable.* It was usual
"with me to repeat the Lord's Prayer, when
"I laid down in my Bed, and often reproved
"myself, if I suffered any other Thoughts to
"intervene in the time of repeating it; de-
"signing to do my best to please God.

"After a time, by the Direction of divine
"Providence, at a Meeting of the People
"called *Quakers*, held at *Briggflats*, it was
"put into the Heart of that worthy Messenger
"and Man of God, *Roger Haydock*, to define
"*who had Right to call God* Father, *and who
"had not :* By which Doctrine my Under-
"standing was opened, and my Heart en-
"larged, to consider Friends Principles; which
"I perceived gradually fitted me for receiving
"the Grace and Spirit of God, and the Reve-
"lation of his Son in me. Then I became
"more sensible of a Cross that was to be
"born; which when I went from under, I
"was smitten with great Fear and Horror;
"so that I evidently saw the bearing thereof,
"was

"was the Way to the Kingdom of God.
"And I remember, that to use the *plain*
"*Language* was none of the least; for I
"sheltered and covered with this Expression,
"when I spoke to any,—*How doth' Body?*
"But this would not do: Peace was not to
"be obtained without Obedience. This kept
"me weak for a time; but when I gave
"up, Strength returned, and I had the Answer
"of *Well done, thou hast not denied my Name.*
"Here was matter of rejoicing, which I write
"for the Encouragement of such as may be
"weak in the like case; and let it be observ-
"ed,—Disobedience always brings Feebleness,
"whether in this or other of the Lord's
"Requirings.

"Being convinced, and in measure con-
"verted, I had Desires to become more and
"more the Lord's holy Temple, which called
"for Simplicity, and, in measure, Purity, as
"the Truth is in Jesus. I was willing, in
"degree, to imitate *Zaccheus*, by restoring
"what I had wronged any of, whether by
"gaming or otherwise; the first of which I
"was addicted to in my Youth. The Sentence
"passed in me; I obeyed and Peace followed.

"About the Year 1683, being watchful
"over my own Spirit, and faithful to the
"Lord's Requirings, I grew in Favour with
"him; and waiting diligently in Meetings
"for his divine Power, I had given me to
"believe, I should 'ere long have a publick
"Testimony

" Teſtimony to bear for him; and when the
" Day came, a terrible one it was; the Word
" of the Lord burned in me like a Fire,
" ſaying, *This is the Day, neglect it not*; ſo
" that I was willing to ſpeak a few Words.
" And it has been my chief Care ever ſince,
" to miniſter in the Ability that God gives:
" Beginning with the Oil, and ending when
" it ſtayed; which I know by manifold
" Experience, is the only Way to pleaſe God
" and profit the People.

" About the Year 1686, having ſome Incli-
" nation to marry, I had one in view; but
" conſulting him who anſwers from between
" the Cherubims, from the Mercy Seat, as I
" always did in Matters of moment, he was
" pleaſed to give me a View of one, at that
" time many Miles diſtant, which he after-
" wards gave me; a ſuitable Help-meet and
" dear Companion to this Day.

" Soon after I was married, the Enemy
" aſſaulted me afreſh, reſpecting the Cares of
" this Life, with which I much feared I
" ſhould be ſwallowed up; but my God and
" Saviour helped me to pray, and, in the time
" of Expreſſion, gave me Faith in his Power,
" that he who ruleth in Heaven and Earth
" would give me Strength to Victory. At the
" ſame time he gave me to know, I was too
" remiſs in frequenting Week-day Meetings;
" and upon my giving up to the Witneſs of
" God in me, he gave me a bleſſed Promiſe,
" *That*

"That the little Meal in the Barrel should not
" fail, and, that my End should be happy, as
" I continued faithful to him; whose Promises
" I have witnessed to be *Yea and Amen.*
" Blessed be his Name for ever.

" About the Year 1694, I joined dear
" *Gilbert Thompson*, my Wife's Brother, in
" the Management of his School, with whom
" I had true Fellowship; being sensible, in
" our Communication, that Jesus drew near.

" While I lived there, the Lord put it into
" my Heart to visit Friends in *Wales*, such a
" Day in such a Month; which if I had not
" answered, I had missed a Meeting, held
" only once a Month, at which was convinced
" a Woman of considerable Family; for
" which I humbly and thankfully bless God
" through Jesus Christ. I may also say, in
" several of my Visits to Friends in *Cheshire*,
" *Yorkshire* and *Cumberland*, some were con-
" vinced; which I mention only to encourage
" Gospel Ministers to Obedience.

" It likewise remains with me to signify,
" what the Lord put into my Heart by way
" of Prophecy, at a General-meeting at *Gray-
" rigg*, viz. I WILL BEND THE CEDARS, I
" WILL HUMBLE THE HEATHEN, AND
" ENLARGE ISRAEL'S BORDERS. And fervent
" Prayer continues upon my Mind for the
" young Generation amongst Friends, that
" the Lord would be pleased to prepare them
" against that Day. I also earnestly entreat
" that

"that our Elders, in their particular and
"Monthly-meetings, would watch in a godly
"Care and zealous Difcipline over them,
"that they may live and act agreeable to a
"*Chriftian* Converfation; for unlefs *the hidden*
"*Things of* Efau *and* Achan *be deftroyed,* as
"well as difcovered, the *Ifrael* of God can
"neither journey forwards, nor ftand before
"their Enemies. I am fully of the Mind,
"that when ever it may pleafe God to redeem
"and recover his Church out of her prefent
"languifhing Condition, the Line of *Difci-*
"*pline* muft be vigoroufly ftretched over all
"Tranfgreffors; Judgment laid to the Rule,
"and Righteoufnefs to the Balance; fo fhall
"every one receive what is right, according
"to the Ufe or Abufe of their Talents.

"Now to God the Father, for all his
"unnutterable Mercies, through Jefus Chrift
"his Son, who by the gracious Aid and divine
"Influences of the holy Spirit, hath hitherto
"helped and preferved me, and given me
"Faith and Hope of a Manfion amongft the
"Sanctified, be rendered and afcribed all
"Honour and Praife, Dominion and Glory,
"henceforth and for ever. *Amen.*

Milnthrop *near* Sedbergh, "CHRISTOPHER WINN."
the Eleventh Month 1731.

A Teftimony

A Testimony from the Quarterly-meeting at Brighthelmstone *in the County of* Sussex, *concerning* JOHN SNASHALL.

TO us it appears a laudable Practice to preserve the Memory of the Righteous, in order to excite the Living to follow the Footsteps of the Flock of Christ Jesus, our good and holy Shepherd. Such is the Motive in making mention of our worthy Friend and Elder *John Snashall*, deceased, who was an exemplary Pattern of Piety; descended of honest and religious Parents.

He was born at *Keymer*, near *Hurstperpoint*, the 9th Day of the Second Month 1656. His Father was of the national Church, his Mother a *Baptist*. Being but a Child when his Father died, he fell chiefly under the Care of his elder Brother, a *Presbyterian*. When he grew up to Years of Understanding, he sought after Religion, and inclined to go with his Mother among the *Baptists*; till having Notice of a Meeting of Friends at *Blatchington*, near *Brighthelmstone*, he went, and he heard the Truth so powerfully preached there by *Thomas Turner*, that he most readily received the Word and kept it; and his Heart being prepared as the good Ground, the heavenly Seed increased and brought forth in him the Fruits of the Spirit.

About

About the Year 1700, it pleased the Lord to favour him with a Gift of the Ministry, in which he experienced Improvement. He was found in Word and Doctrine, and oftentimes confolating to the Churches of Christ; fo that we have good reafon to believe he was inftrumental in convincing fome, who continued faithful.

And altho' he did not fee his Way clear to vifit many Meetings out of his native County, yet he was diligent, many times through great Difficulties, to attend the Monthly, Weekly, and Quarterly-meetings.

He was zealous againft that antichriftian Yoke of *Tithes*; for which, we believe, he was a faithful Sufferer, being an open and couragious Oppofer of the hireling Priefts, and the corrupt Part of their Doctrine in general; as well as of *George Keith* in particular, while *Keith* lived in *Suffex*, and fought to maintain his Apoftacy.

In his natural Temper he was very loving and courteous to all; in Charity univerfal; a good and kind Neighbour, hardly withholding from any that wanted to borrow. A tender Father; frequent in Exhortation to his Children and Grand-children, to fear the Lord; very often expreffing, *It would be his greateft Joy, could he behold the bleffed Truth profper in his Day.*

He bore his Sicknefs, which was but fhort, in great Meeknefs and Patience, and in a fweet
composed

compofed Frame of Mind, was often heard to
fay,— *My Lord, my Light and my Salvation.*
And we firmly believe he had a full Affurance
the Lord was fuch to him before his Departure,
which was on the 11th of the Seventh Month
1732, in the Seventy fixth Year of his Age.

A Teſtimony from the Monthly - meeting of
New - Malton *in* Yorkſhire, *concerning*
JAMES SIMPSON.

HE was educated after the manner of the
Church of *England*, and, in his young
Years, came to live within the compafs of our
Meeting. Being zealoufly concerned for the
Good of his Soul, his Cries were to the Lord,
who in his own time opened his inward Eye,
letting him fee the Emptinefs of the National
Worſhip in which he had been educated; and
by the Illumination of divine Light, convinced
him of the Truth as profeffed by us. So, in
great Humility and Refignation of Mind, he
came to fit down amongſt us, where he found
a Remnant feeking after the faving Knowledge
of God, with whom he came into a religious
Fellowſhip; and in true Stilnefs of Mind
waited upon the Lord for the further Dif-
coveries of his Will. Thus continuing in a
State of humble Dependance, the divine Being,
of his infinite Mercy, brought him to witnefs

a better

a better State; and in procefs of time opened his Mouth to fet forth his Praife, and to preach the Gofpel, which he did with Power, as one having Authority, to the refrefhing of many Souls; wherein he approved himfelf a faithful Minifter, and laboured in divers Parts of this Nation, where he was well received amongft Friends. And after his Return, his Travails were to promote the Truth and good Order amongft Friends, labouring in the Difcipline of the Church; the Care whereof feemed to be very much upon him the remaining Part of his time, that it might be kept up in good Order, and in the Power of God, and that we thereby might become a Praife to his Name in the Earth.

He was not forward to open his Mouth in the Church, but waited to feel the Lord's Power to fill his Heart; and in the flowing of his Love he difpenfed with Faithfulnefs, to the Refrefhment of many thirfty Souls, who were waiting for Confolation.

His Care was great for the Children of Friends, that they might walk in the Footfteps of the Flock of Chrift, which will bring to the Place where he feeds his People. At the laft publick Meeting he attended, which was about a Month before his Departure, he very earneftly befought the Almighty to reach to our young People, and incline their Hearts to keep his Laws. He was then in an ill State of Health, which increafing upon him, he

continued

continued in great Refignation of Mind to the Will of God, whether to live or to die; fignifying to fome of us, *That the Sight of Death was not a Terror to him.* Thus continuing in great Stilnefs, he waited for the Diffolution of his earthly Tabernacle, till the 23d of the Eighth Month 1732, when he died; and was buried the 25th of the fame in Friends Burying Ground at *Barton*, accompanied by his Friends and many Neighbours; where the Lord was pleafed to appear both immediately and inftrumentally, to the tendering of many Hearts.

A publick Preacher about Thirty Years.

A Teftimony from the Monthly - meeting of Newcaftle *upon* Tyne, *concerning* DEBORAH WARDELL.

THERE remains in our Hearts a fhort Teftimony to give for our dear Friend and Sifter *Deborah Wardell*, who died in the Seventieth Year of her Age. She was even like a Shock of full ripe Corn, gathered in its due Seafon; and we doubt not but the Lord has received her Soul into the Manfions of Glory, where the Wicked ceafe from troubling, and the Faithful are at Reft.

Her Miniftry was very lively; fhe was found in Word and Doctrine, and very edifying;

preaching

preaching the Coming of our Lord Jesus Christ in his spiritual Appearance; frequently opening the Scriptures, and the Mysteries of Life and Salvation; with fervent Exhortations to serve the Lord in Righteousness and true Holiness.

Her *Christianity* did shew itself greatly by her meek and peaceable Spirit. She was many times fervent in Prayer to the Lord, for the rising Generation, that *they might come up in the Places of the Faithful who are gone before.*

In the Time of her last Ilness, which continued above three Months, she oftentimes was in a very sweet Frame of Mind, and frequently used to say, *The Thoughts of Death were no Terror to her;* but was entirely resigned to the Will of the Lord; and often expressed the Hope she had in her latter End.

Two Days before she died, having a very sick Fit, upon her being a little recovered of it, she desired to see her Children, and expressed herself to them after this manner: —*I did not think I should have been alive till now. I hope it will be an happy Hour for me. I pray God bless you in all your Undertakings, and that he may be with you, as he has been with me, to the End of your Days.*

LANCELOT

Lancelot Wardell's *Testimony concerning his dear deceased Wife,* Deborah Wardell, *who died the 7th of the Tenth Month* 1732.

"SHE was descended from honourable
" Parents, namely, *John* and *Margaret*
" *Walton* of *Bishop-Aukland,* who were early
" convinced, in the Morning of the Day,
" wherein Truth was published by *George Fox*
" and others. They kept an open Door for
" Travellers who were sent abroad in the
" Service of Truth, to promote the Gospel of
" our Lord and Saviour Jesus Christ; as, since
" their Death, did most of their Children;
" who are all gone to their Rest, as Shocks of
" Corn gathered in due Season, of which she
" was the last.

" She was a true Yokefellow, an affectionate
" Wife, a tender Mother, and faithful La-
" bourer in the Vineyard of the Lord; and,
" where her Lot was cast, of good Service
" both as to her Ministry and in Meetings of
" Business; having been an approved Mother
" in our spiritual *Israel,* for her Care, Conduct
" and Advice.

" Some Years since, being visited with
" Sickness, she ordered her Children to be
" brought into her Chamber; at which time,
" it was her Concern to admonish them to be

" faithful

"faithful to the Lord's Requirings, that they
"might obtain a Crown of Life: In order
"thereto, she said her Desire was, *That they*
"*might live in the Fear of the Lord, and keep*
"*near to his preserving Power, that they might*
"*witness his Peace, when the Time of Dissolu-*
"*tion came;* which would be of more Value to
"them than all the World: For what would
"all the World signify to her now, if she
"wanted that? If this be the Time of my Dis-
"solution, said she, *I am not afraid to pass*
"*through the Vale of Death, being fully per-*
"*swaded it will be a Passage into everlasting*
"*Light, where Sorrow and Sighing, Pains and*
"*Afflictions, shall be at an End;* and instead
"thereof will be *Joy and Rejoicing*, in an un-
"disturbed Rest and Felicity, without End.
"Adding, *if the Lord lengthen my Days, I*
"*desire they may be devoted to his Service.*

"In the latter Part of her Life she was
"attended with an *Asthma*; yet, whilst she
"was able to attend Meetings, she was very
"diligent and serviceable therein. And tho'
"my Loss be very great by her Removal, yet
"being satisfied it is her eternal Gain, I
"earnestly desire I may be fully resigned to
"the Will of the Lord therein."

A Testimony

A Testimony from the Monthly-meeting of Brighouse *in the County of* York, *concerning* JOSHUA BARBER.

OUR dear and worthy Friend *Joshua Barber*, Son of *Samuel* and *Elizabeth Barber*, was born at *Esholt* in the Parish of *Guisely*, in the Year 1660. His Father died a Prisoner for attending the Meetings of the People called *Quakers*, before this his Son was two Years old; so that his Mother, who was a religious Woman of the Church of *England*, educated him in that Way; and he being brought up in the Trade of a *Smith*, about the Seventeenth Year of his Age went to *Doncaster* to work, where, having an Inclination to go to a Meeting of Friends, he made Enquiry, if there was any in that Part of the Country? Hearing of one kept at the House of *Thomas Kellam*, of *Balby*, he went twice to it, and was there reached by the Testimony of our Friend *Thomas Aldam*.

After that, he returned to his Mother's House, not far from *Rawden*, and being informed of a great Convincement thereaway, and that *Jeremiah Grimshaw*, his former Acquaintance, was joined with Friends, and become a publick Preacher among them, he had a Desire to go to their Meeting, which he did the next First-day after his Return from *Doncaster*, and was there effectually reached; divers living Testimonies being born by *Jeremiah Grimshaw* and others; so that he went but once after that Meeting to the publick Worship he had been educated in, but joined with Friends of *Rawden* Meeting, amongst whom he lived, and married a Friend's Daughter within the Compass thereof.

He was a Prisoner in *York* Castle, for Tithe, some time; and about three Years after he was set at Liberty, he removed with his Family to live at *Burley*, in the Parish of *Leeds*; where he became zealously engaged in the Cause of Truth amongst Friends of *Leeds*, who were under a fresh Visitation; although no publick Friend then belonged to the Meeting, yet many were convinced, and came to join with Friends in that Time of Silence, to the Enlargement of the Meeting considerably: In which Time, this our Friend's Mouth was opened in publick Testimony among Friends, under which Concern he had been many Years; and as he grew in the Gift, he faithfully and zealously laboured among Friends, both at home and abroad, travelling in the Service of Truth through *Wales* to *Bristol*, and several long Journeys in this Nation, *Ireland*, and part of *Scotland*.

Toward the latter Part of his Time, great bodily Infirmity coming upon him, he often expressed his Thankfulness, *That he had endeavoured to discharge his Trust amongst the Churches,*

Churches, whilst Health and Strength lasted: having been many times, and in divers Places, engaged to bear a faithful Testimony against false Liberty, and plainly and particularly to deal with Offenders: And also some, whose Ministry he believed proceeded not from the Renewing of Life, but were got into a Form of Preaching without the Power; unto such he was a good Example in Meetings, steadily waiting, in deep Silence, upon the Movings of the holy Spirit, both to enable him to worship God, and to open Counsel, before he durst appear by way of Ministry, how great soever the Peoples Expectation might be from him; being very careful to minister in the Ability that God gives; so that his Ministry was living, truly edifying, and generally well esteemed.

He was a diligent Attender of Meetings, on First-days and other Days, both for Worship and Discipline, wherein he was very serviceable, having a Spirit of Discerning beyond many; and was, as the Apostle says, *swift to hear, but slow to speak*, in such Meetings.

He was greatly beloved by the generality of the Meeting he belonged to, for his good Example, steady Walking, and impartial Judgment, even among his nearest Friends, as well as others. When he thought there was Occasion for Advice, he dealt in great plainness with all, where he was concerned, as he found his way open in the Truth, so that he became a

Terror to Evil-doers, though a Comfort to them who did well.

Notwithstanding his bodily Infirmity, he diligently laboured in his Vocation so long as he was able, being not slothful in Business, but fervent in Spirit, serving the Lord; rejoicing in Hope, patient in Tribulation, continuing instant in Prayer, and much delighted in the Enjoyment of divine Goodness, which failed him not when he was confined to his own House, the last four Months of his Time, by an *Asthma* and *Dropsy*; but he would often say to Friends who visited him, — *Although he had been sometimes counted over zealous, like the good Man of old, who said,* The Zeal of thy House hath eaten me up; *yet he now reaped the precious Fruits of his Faithfulness unto his great Lord and Master, who spake Peace to his Soul, and gave him the Earnest of everlasting Rest, by overshadowing him many times with his heavenly Love, and lifting up his Mind above his great Afflictions of Body, to rejoice in his holy Name and Power.* And near his Conclusion he said to a Friend present, — *It was his Faith, the Lord would overturn that dark Power which so often prevailed in the Churches, and would raise up many that should stand for his Name.* We well know that his Travail of Spirit, in this respect, had been often very deep before the Lord, and his Mourning great for the true Seed's sake.

Upon

Upon taking leave of his Friends, a few Hours before his Departure, he said, *It has been my Judgment a long time, and I am still of the same Mind, that there is none can worship, praise and glorify God, but in a measure of his own divine Spirit.*

He departed in great Peace, Comfort and Hope in Christ, the 2d Day of the Eleventh Month 1732. Aged Seventy two.

An additional Testimony from the Quarterly-meeting of York, *concerning* JOSHUA BARBER.

WE esteem ourselves under an Obligation, in gratitude to the Memory of so useful and serviceable an Instrument, to give this further Account of him, who, whilst amongst us, was well known and truly esteemed, for his Service sake, by Friends in this Quarterly-meeting, which he often attended, to our true Help and Comfort in the Work of the Lord.

Our sincere Value for this our Friend and Brother, engages us to declare, His exemplary Life and Conversation, as well as truly zealous and faithful Labour among us, was very acceptable, as its Tendency was to the discouraging of all Appearance of Evil, the promoting of the Life of Righteousness, and the building up of the Church in the most holy Faith,

Faith, that she might bring forth the Fruits of the Spirit. And although he was not forward in his publick Appearance amongst Friends, yet the weighty Travail of Spirit before the Lord, which was much upon him, was truly helpful to us, and comfortable to remember; so that though he be removed from us, his Life and Labour yet speak, and the Remembrance thereof is precious.

He was found in Judgment; steady in a true and fervent Zeal against corrupt Liberty in Conversation; as also for promoting a steady Faithfulness amongst all Friends in the several Branches of our Testimony, and particularly that against Tithes; being well assured, that so doing is one way whereby we are called to confess Jesus Christ before Men. He was also frequently under a weighty Care and Concern of Mind, for the Preservation of a truly living Ministry in the Church; and that the Spirit, Will and Wisdom of Man, might be always in due Subjection unto the Power of God, so that God in all Things might be glorified. And as thus he lived and laboured, to the Comfort and Edification of the Upright-hearted among us; so he died in Faith and full Assurance of Peace, the Reward of the Faithful: An Evidence whereof he has in a lively manner left behind him, which induces us to give this brief Account, in order that it may excite others to labour to succeed him in so religious and good a Conduct amongst
Mankind

Mankind in general; and to recommend such his religious Life and Labour for the Good and Welfare of the Church of Christ, and the Exaltation of the Glory and Renown of the Lord, our most gracious God, who alone is worthy for ever.

A Testimony from the Quarterly-meeting held at Wigton, *for the County of* Cumberland, *concerning* SARAH DIXON.

SHE was the eldest Daughter of our Friends *John* and *Anne Wilson* of *Graythwait*, and educated in the Way of Truth; sober from a Child; dutiful to her Parents, and a good Example in the Family.

It pleased the Lord to visit her often, in her young and tender Years, with his Heart-melting Love; and though some Hinderances prevailed for a while, yet, about the Twentieth Year of her Age, she joined with the Visitation, and became truly religious, heartily seeking after Peace with God. A few Years after, she came forth in publick Testimony, to the Satisfaction of Friends; and divers times visited the Churches in this County, and other adjacent Counties; and, we believe, had good Service, according to that Gift bestowed upon her. And though she was not large in Testimony, yet her Doctrine was watering,
sweet

sweet and sound, to the tendering the Hearts of those who sat under her Ministry, which evidently sprung from the right Fountain.

About the Thirtieth Year of her Age, she was married to our worthy Friend *William Dixon*, of *Lowsewater* in the said County; and after that, she visited Friends in some neighbouring Counties. When at home, she was diligent in attending Meetings; earnest and careful for the Maintenance of Discipline and good Order in the Church; and that Elders, and those engaged therein, might stand fast in, and keep close to, the Testimony of Truth. She was a dutiful, affectionate Wife; grave and sober in her Conversation; a loving, kind Neighbour to Poor and Rich; and the Loss of her is lamented by many, she being universally beloved by Friends and others. Her House and Heart were open to entertain Friends.

She was taken with a lingering Ilness, like a *Consumption*, which continued upon her above half a Year; and though she was afflicted with sharp Pains at times, she bore them with great Patience; often saying, *I am fully resigned to the Will of the Lord, and dare not desire to know, whether Life or Death; however, I am perfectly easy.* And a few Days before her Death, being sensible her Time was far spent, she desired some Friends, who came to visit her, *To stand fast by the Testimony of Truth;* with divers other weighty Expressions, which

which we omit for Brevity's fake. At another time she said, *Though I have had some poor low Times in my Ilness, now I have sweet Times.* And her Husband sitting by her, she was drawn forth in a living Frame of Spirit, and gave good Advice to him; also saying, *I never had so much of divine Comfort in all my Life as I now enjoy.* She lay still and quiet, and departed this Life like a Lamb, without either Sigh or Groan, on the 11th Day of the Seventh Month 1733, and was decently buried the 13th of the same, in Friends Burying Ground in *Eaglesfield,* her Corps being accompanied by a great many Friends and others, and divers living Testimonies born to the Truth.

Aged near Thirty three, a Minister about Ten Years.

A Testimony from the Quarterly-meeting of Wigton, *concerning* WILLIAM DIXON.

HE was descended from believing Parents, and educated in the Way of Truth; a Member of *Pardshaw* Meeting in the County of *Cumberland,* and his Residence was at *Waterend* in *Lowseswater.*

It pleased the Lord to visit him early in his tender Age, whereby he became acquainted with his Teaching, and freely gave up to follow the Leadings thereof, which was apparent by the visible Progress he made.

About

About the Twenty firſt or Twenty ſecond Year of his Age, he came forth in publick Teſtimony; and, as he was faithful to that Gift beſtowed upon him, he grew and became very ſerviceable amongſt us. He travelled pretty much, in his early coming forth, into moſt of our adjacent Counties; as alſo into *Cornwall* and other Weſtern Counties; and we are ſatisfied had good Service.

He was of a weak Conſtitution of Body. His Doctrine was ſound and watering, which did often drop as the Dew, and diſtil as the ſmall Rain, upon the tender Plants. Rather backward in Appearance; but in his Miniſtry attended with a Spring of Life and Sweetneſs: Not with the enticing Words of Man's Wiſdom, but in the Demonſtration of the Spirit; often ſpeaking of the Joys of Heaven. He was very fervent in his Approaches in Prayer, and teſtified his full Aſſurance and ſtedfaſt Faith, *of the Lord's Arm being ſtretched forth to gather the Nations*; ſupplicating the Lord, *That he might die in the Faith thereof, if he never lived to ſee it*; craving of him, in that Earneſt of Faith, *That he might ſpread his Goſpel from Nation to Nation, and from Iſland to Iſland.*

About the Thirtieth Year of his Age, he was married to the eldeſt Daughter of our Friend *John Wilſon*, of *Graythwait*. He was a kind and loving Huſband; free and open hearted to entertain Friends: And, being often
weak

weak in Body, he did not travel much abroad afterwards; yet was diligent in attending Meetings at home, as alfo neighbouring Meetings, when Ability of Body permitted; and amongft other People he had good Service, and grew brighter, fo long as he was able to appear abroad.

About the Thirty fixth Year of his Age he fell into a Decline, which continued upon him near three Quarters of a Year, and at length proved mortal; during which time, his dear Wife lay on her Death-bed, and was taken away about half a Year before him. He fome time afterwards came to Meetings, and did appear in Teftimony; though his Voice was much weakened, yet he was as ftrong as ever in the Power of Truth.

In the time of his Ilnefs feveral fweet Expreffions dropt from him: He faid to a Friend who fat by him, *I am entirely eafy; and though I have had the Lofs of a good Wife, I do not fret myfelf;—am fatisfied when this poor Body goes to Duft, there is a Place of Reft prepared for my Soul; and I am thankful I have nothing to do but die; though fome Places have been before me to have vifited, if I had Strength of Body, but I believe the Will fhall be taken for the Deed; for I never delayed Time when I had Ability. Oh! it is good to make Ufe of Time. I rejoice that I die in Unity with my Friends, and that the Lord is now near me.* He fpoke this with a weak Voice, but very affectingly,

being

being much broken. Another time he said to a Friend who bore him Company, *That the glorious Light of the Lord shined over him, and his Goodness was to him ; and he had nothing in his Heart but Goodwill to all.*

He departed this Life, in good Unity with Friends, the 24th Day of the First Month 1734, and was decently interred the 27th of the same, in Friends Burying Ground at *Eaglesfield.* Aged near Thirty seven, a Minister about Fifteen Years.

A Testimony from the Quarterly - meeting of Wigton, *concerning* BRIDGET STORY.

BRIDGET STORY, Wife of *Christopher Story,* of *Rigghead* in the County of *Cumberland,* was convinced of the blessed Truth about the Twentieth Year of her Age, and, according to the Manifestation given her, became a faithful Follower thereof. She was of a good Conversation among her Neighbours; a Pattern of Humility, Self-denial, Plainness and Circumspection, in her own Family; and often concerned in that universal Love, which did abound in her Soul, to advise her Children, as they grew up to Maturity, and others under her Care, to keep in God's holy Fear, and walk in the Footsteps of the Faithful who were gone before.

She

She was called into the Work of the Ministry some Years after her Convincement, and, according to her Capacity, laboured faithfully in the Discharge of her Duty therein; frequently appearing in publick Testimony in the Meeting she belonged to; not with inticing Words of Mens Wisdom, but in the Zeal and Simplicity of the Gospel; and was very fervent in Supplication to the Almighty; both which, did often tend to the Edification and Refreshment of the Living. She was of an undaunted Spirit, and noble Disposition of Mind, not regarding the Frowns of Men, in any Case wherein she believed the Testimony of Truth was concerned. Diligent and very exemplary in attending Meetings of Worship and Discipline; zealous for promoting and maintaining good Order in the Church; and, in particular, concerned for the inward Growth and Preservation of the rising Generation, that all Superfluity of Naughtiness might be avoided, and Decency and Plainness kept to, which becomes the Followers of Jesus; so that it may be truly said, *She was a nursing Mother in* Israel *indeed.*

She was also concerned, in the Love of Truth, at divers times to visit the Meetings of Friends in this and other Counties adjacent; also the Churches in *Scotland* and *Ireland*; and we have ground to believe she had good Reception among the Faithful, wheresoever her Lot was cast.

And

And though she was confined at home, in her declining Age, through the Decay of Nature, yet she retained her Integrity, and continued in great Innocency and Simplicity, to the Comfort of those who came to visit her, and finished her Course in this World, in a living Frame of Spirit, and in great Tranquility, the 21st of the Second Month 1733, in the Eighty second Year of her Age. A Minister Thirty Years.

A Testimony from the Monthly-meeting of Aylesbury *in the County of* Bucks, *concerning* MARY BAKER.

WE do not find any particular Account to communicate, of her first Convincement; those ancient Friends, who were her Contemporaries, being long since removed; but we have sufficient Cause to believe, she received the Truth while young, in the Love of it, and in an honest Heart; the Seed which was sown bringing forth Fruit to the Lord, who was graciously pleased to endow her with divers excellent Qualifications.

For many Years last past, some of us were well acquainted with her, and from a sense of her honest and innocent Life, we find ourselves engaged to give this brief Testimony concerning her.

That

That she was an inward and heavenly-minded Woman, and from her own Experience of the Virtue of Truth, she was often drawn forth in a living Testimony thereto; exhorting to a diligent Exercise and Travail of Spirit after the true Enjoyment of Life; in which Services she was many times made an Instrument of Edification and Comfort to the Faithful, as well as of Admonition and Reproof to the Negligent and Disobedient.

She was zealously concerned for good Order and Discipline in the Church in general, and particularly in our Womens-meeting, bearing the chief Weight of the Affairs thereof for many Years; which she diligently attended so long as she was of Ability. Her Labour and Service in the Church, both personally and by her outward Substance, and her exemplary Conversation, in Humility, Temperance and Self-denial, has left a sweet Memorial of her. She was courteous, kind, and religious in her Deportment to her Neighbours, frequently administring to the Help of the Necessitous. She was honourable in her Profession, and obtained a good Report in general.

The sweet Frame of Spirit and Peace of Mind, which, with great Comfort, several of us beheld her in, upon a Visit a few Days before her Departure, gives us good Cause to believe she died in the Lord, and is entered into everlasting Rest.

She departed this Life the 12th Day of the Ninth Month 1734, and was decently interred in Friends Burying Ground at *Jordans* the 16th following. In the Eighty sixth Year of her Age.

A Testimony from the Monthly-meeting of Falmouth, concerning THOMAS GIDDY.

IT pleased the Lord to open his Understanding, and favour him with the Knowledge of his blessed Truth, in his early Years, bestowing on him a Gift of the Ministry, and enduing him with the Spirit of true Government in the Church of Christ, for divers Years before many of us can remember; and we have been so sensibly reached by that Power which attended his Ministry, and Concern for maintaining the Discipline of Truth, since we knew him, that we cannot wholly pass it over in silence.

His Habitation being within the Compass of this Meeting, we were frequently favoured with acceptable Visits from him, as well as at Meetings of Business, of which he was a due Attender, when at home and able; and the Lord was pleased to make him a serviceable Instrument amongst us, and a Strengthener of those who were right minded, who had the Honour of God at Heart; he being, though zealous for the Maintenance of every Branch

of

of Truth's Teſtimony, ready to ſympathize with the Weak, and cheriſh the leaſt Appearance of Tenderneſs. His Houſe, as well as his Heart, was open to receive the Servants of the Lord; his exemplary Care and Induſtry in temporal Affairs being bleſſed with Succeſs.

He preached the Goſpel freely, and was frequently concerned, in the Diſcharge of his Duty, to ſpeak in plainneſs to Particulars, where Occaſion required; and we have reaſon to believe his Advice ſo given, oftentimes reached the living Witneſs, and proved of good Service.

Some conſiderable time before his Deceaſe, he laboured under many and great bodily Infirmities, by which his Memory and Underſtanding, in outward Things, were much impaired; yet, as one who had made Heaven his Choice, he was concerned and enabled, in ſundry Meetings, to bear his Teſtimony for God.

Towards the Concluſion of the laſt Quarterly-meeting, ſave one, he was at in this County, after having undergone pretty much Exerciſe, he exhorted Friends *to maintain their antient Teſtimony againſt all Wars and Fightings;* being apprehenſive we might be affected by an ACT then on foot for regulating the *Militia*.

Some time after this he went to the Yearly-meeting at *London*, and was comforted in his Journey; and notwithſtanding his great

Weakness of Body, returned in Safety to his Habitation.

The next Quarterly-meeting, after his Return, was at *Penzance*, where he went, and gave an agreeable Account of his Journey to *London*, and the Meeting there; and was zealously concerned to advise Friends *to a faithful Discharge of their Testimony against Tithes*.

The Farewel-meeting next Day at *Marazion*, was the last that any of us were at with him; in which, the good Presence of God eminently overshadowed our Assembly, to the tendering many Hearts, and his Life, like Oil, flowed over all. At the Conclusion of which we parted in much Love, he returning to *Penzance*, to be clear of that Meeting; and at the finishing of his Testimony in a Weekday-meeting there, was seized with violent Convulsions, which it was feared would have carried him off immediately; however it proved otherwise: But he lay under great Weakness and Affliction of Body about three Weeks, and then finished his Course the 6th Day of the Ninth Month 1734.

He was very sensible during his last Ilness, and appeared perfectly resigned to the Will of God; expressing very emphatically his Satisfaction, *that there was a Reward in Store for the Righteous*. Aged about Seventy three, Convinced Fifty two, a Minister about Forty Years.

A Testimony

A Testimony from the Monthly-meeting of Horslydown *in* Southwark, *concerning* FRANCIS DAVIS.

HE was born the 29th of the Fourth Month 1684, descended from religious Parents, and early discovered an Inclination to Virtue. He was exemplary in his Conversation; a diligent Searcher of the holy Scriptures, by means of which, being improved by the lively Influences of the Spirit of God, he became well qualified to defend the Doctrines of the Gospel.

About the Year 1701, he was called to the Ministry, and visited the Meetings of Friends in divers Parts of this Kingdom, several times in *Holland*, and Part of *Germany*; in which Station he was serviceable to the Church of Christ. He acquitted himself as one well instructed to the Kingdom, and was esteemed and accepted as an able and faithful Labourer in the *Christian* Vineyard.

He was taken ill the latter end of the Seventh Month 1734, and though in great Weakness and Affliction, yet that Meekness which attended him, bespake the Resignation of his Mind to the Will of God. His last Expressions were, *Thou Preserver of all those that put their Trust in thee: Saviour! Saviour! O, blessed be thy Name.*

He departed this Life the 25th of the Eighth Month 1734, and was buried the 30th of the fame, in Friends Burying Ground in *Long-lane.* In the Fifty firſt Year of his Age. A Miniſter about Thirty three Years.

A Teſtimony from the Quarterly-meeting of Kendal, *in the County of* Weſtmorland, *concerning* WILLIAM BECK.

OUR antient and well beloved Friend *William Beck,* was born in the Year 1641, near *Hawkſhead* in *Lancaſhire;* deſcended of honeſt and religious Parents, who were convinced of the bleſſed Truth, in or about the Year 1652, by the Miniſtry of that faithful Servant of Chriſt *Edward Burrough.*

His Father died when he was about Fourteen Years of Age; after which, he lived with his Mother, and learned his Father's Trade, which was that of a *Skinner* and *Glover;* and though their Circumſtances in the World were but ſmall, yet, being careful and induſtrious, they lived comfortably, till he entered into Trade for himſelf, which was when he was about Twenty Years of Age. He was religiouſly inclined, and it pleaſed the Lord to proſper him in his Buſineſs, and to give him Credit with thoſe he dealt with, being conſcientiouſly concerned to perform his Words and Contracts punctually.

After

After some time, it pleased the Lord to bestow upon him a Gift of the Ministry, in which he faithfully laboured, according to the Ability received; he was a diligent Attender of Meetings, rightly concerned for the Promotion of Truth and Righteousness in the Earth, and for the Preservation of Love and Unity amongst Friends. He was faithful and stedfast in his Testimony against Tithes, suffering joyfully the Spoiling of his Goods; and an Encourager of all, who made Profession of the Truth, to Faithfulness therein, and to Diligence in attending their Meetings, even in the hottest Times of Persecution; and he suffered deeply on that Account, his Circumstance considered. His Conversation being peaceable and inoffensive, he was well beloved. His Testimony was not with Eloquence of Speech, yet living and edifying to the Hearers. He was ready to do Good to all, and more especially to the Houshold of Faith; and as he loved Peace, so he laboured fervently to prevent Strife and Contention. Sound in Judgment; and his Conversation adorned his Doctrine. He lived to old Age, and retained his Integrity, Memory, Understanding, Love and Zeal for Truth and Righteousness, to the last; and would often, after he had lost his Sight, commemorate and speak of the many Favours, Preservations, Blessings and kind Dealings of the Lord to him, through the whole Course of his Life. He bore a living and faithful

Testimony in Meetings to the Goodness of God, and the Encouragement of Friends to trust in him, wait upon him, and to be faithful in their Testimony, careful in their Conversation, and true and sincere in their Love to him; and that then he would abundantly bless them every way, and prosper his Work in the Earth.

He was a good Example in his Family, a loving Husband, a tender Father, a kind Neighbour, and one who sought the Good of all Men. And though his Strength gradually declined through old Age, of which he was sensible, yet he continued in a sweet Frame of Mind, often signifying *his Resignation to the Will of the Lord*; and that it was a great Satisfaction to him, *that he had answered the Lord's Requirings, and done his Day's Work faithfully*, and had therein *great Peace and Assurance of his future Well-being*; and was like a Shock of Corn fully ripe, when he departed this Life the 19th of the Third Month 1734, and was buried on the 22d of the same, in Friends Burying Ground at *Colthouse*. Aged near Ninety three Years.

A Testimony

A Testimony from the Quarterly-meeting of Norfolk, *concerning* JOHN EVERARD.

OUR worthy Friend and Elder *John Everard*, was born at *Putham-Mary-Magdalen* in this County, in the Time of the Civil War, but we cannot be certain in what Year, there being at that time a Defect in the Parish Register. His Parents were poor, but of a sober religious Character, his Mother being by Profession a *Puritan*.

He was convinced by the Testimony of our Friend *Richard Hubberthorn*, and became a publick Preacher among us before he was Twenty Years of Age; in which Capacity he frequently visited divers Parts of this Kingdom, and once the Nation of *Ireland*, as Companion to our worthy and much esteemed Friend *William Penn*. A Blessing attended his Labours, for great Numbers were convinced by him; some of them are still living, to whom his Memory is very precious. He was not without great and trying Exercises, and from some who were nearly related to him: But in these times he was mercifully preserved, to the great Comfort of himself, and Satisfaction of his Brethren.

We think we may safely say of him, that he was a sound, edifying Minister, an exemplary Elder,

Elder, a faithful and affectionate Friend, and one who through a constant and careful Walking before God, witnessed a Victory over his last Enemy, which was Death; for he beheld its Approaches with that Comfort and Satisfaction, which can only possess the Minds of good Men.

He died at *Wandsworth* in the County of *Surry*. Aged near Ninety, a Minister above Sixty Years.

A Testimony from the Quarterly-meeting of Sussex, *concerning* Susanna Martin, *Wife of* Benedict Martin, *of* Hunt's Green.

WE have this to say concerning her; she was born in our County, descended of honest religious Parents, who strictly educated her in the Profession of Truth, and their Care of her was crowned with Success, for she was religiously inclined from her Youth; and it pleased the Lord to commit to her Trust a Gift of the Ministry, about the Twenty third Year of her Age.

She was a faithful Labourer, being a serious, weighty concerned Woman in her Spirit, and underwent deep Exercises. A true Mourner in *Sion*; had the Gift of Discerning; so that she often spoke suitable to the States of those to whom she ministered. She travelled to visit Friends

Friends through the greatest Part of this Nation, and *North Britain*, divers times, to the Edification of the Churches, being well received by Friends in general.

She was zealously concerned, that the Discipline of the Church might be maintained, in its several Branches; often, in the Spirit of Love and Tenderness, admonished and reproved the Unfaithful; desirous that the Poor might be relieved, according to their Necessities, especially such as were worthy; and generally kind and assisting, out of her own Bounty, to the Poor of all sorts. She was much concerned for the Unity of the Church, that her Members might be preserved in the Bond of Peace; and also for the spreading of the Gospel of Peace. She had a solid, savoury Testimony for the Truth, and was faithful and diligent in it; yet not forward in ministring, but waited upon the Lord until she did believe a Necessity was upon her.

She gave much good and seasonable Advice to her Children, in the time of her Health, with many Tears and Prayers to the Almighty for them, *that they might grow up in his Fear, and follow the Footsteps of the Faithful, and do their Day's Work in the Day time, that the Blessing of God might be their Portion here and eternally.*

She was an affectionate Wife, a real Sympathizer with her Husband in Affliction, a tender Mother, and a good Neighbour; so that the

Loss

Loſs of her is generally lamented by thoſe who knew her: Yet we do not ſorrow as thoſe who have no Hope, being ſenſible ſhe continued faithful to the laſt; and though ſuddenly ſurprized with Death, yet ſhe was prepared for it.

She died in the Lord, and laid down her Head in Peace, the 29th Day of the Twelfth Month 1735. Aged Sixty three.

The following Account, wrote by Suſanna Martin, *after her laſt Journey on a Viſit to Friends, is thought proper to be ſubjoined to the foregoing Teſtimony,* viz.

"— From *Windſor* I came to *Stains*,
" *Samuel Hopwood* being there. We had a
" Meeting, which was the laſt I had before I
" came home, and a very good time we had.
" The ſeaſoning Word of Life was witneſſed,
" and the Hearts of many were melted before
" the Lord; and that Peace, which paſſeth
" the Underſtanding of the natural Man, was
" known as a ſweet Return into my Boſom;
" for ever magnified be the Name of the
" Moſt High!

" Thence I came to *Rygate*, lodged at
" Brother *Thompſon*'s; and thence home in
" great Peace. Oh! the matchleſs Love of
" our God! who can declare it? He did not
" only draw me by the Cords of his Love, to
" viſit his Seed in the Hearts of the Children
" of

" of Men, but he was also Mouth and Wis-
" dom, as well as Riches in Poverty, Strength
" in the greatest Weakness, and a Brook by
" the Way, of which my weary Soul often
" partook; and I praise his most worthy
" Name, in that he had counted me worthy
" to be separated, from what was near and
" dear to me, for the Gospel sake, and to serve,
" follow and obey him in his Requirings.
" And though he led me sometimes through
" many Tribulations, and my Soul down into
" the Deeps; yet he did not leave me there,
" but his own Arm wrought Salvation and
" Deliverance to me; so that I was still en-
" couraged to follow him who is the Captain
" of our Salvation, who puts forth his Sheep,
" goes before them, and they hear his Voice
" and follow him. May his Love encourage
" many Thousands more to follow him faith-
" fully, that they may come to know him,
" who is the Lord of Life and Glory, to be
" their Shepherd and the Bishop of their Souls,
" is my hearty Desire and Prayer to God for
" them; that in Blessing he might bless them,
" and in multiplying he might multiply his
" Mercies upon them: For I can say, it is
" good to serve the Lord, and to give up the
" Strength of our Days to honour him with
" it, who hath given it unto us. And, having
" tasted and felt how good the Lord is to
" them who are given up to follow him,
" I have wrote these few Lines for the
                            " Encouragement

"Encouragement of those whom I may leave behind, when I may be in the silent Grave, that they may be given up to serve the Lord in their Day, and may be willing to go through Tribulations for the Gospel sake; knowing this, That great will be their Reward in Heaven, if faithful to the End; for it is the Willing and Obedient, who eat the Good of the Land that flows with Wine, Milk and Honey; the Sweetness of which, my Soul hath been a living Partaker of since my Return. Magnified be the right Arm of his Power, by which he hath upheld my Spirit to this Day, and hath been as a strong Tower, in which there has been Safety for all the tribulated Followers of him. Thanksgiving and Glory shall be ascribed to him for ever."

A Testimony

A Testimony from the Quarterly-meeting of York, concerning MARY ELLERTON.

OUR dear Friend, *Mary Ellerton*, came forth in a publick Testimony when young in Years, and travelled much in the Service of Truth. She was an able Minister of the Gospel of our Lord and Saviour Jesus Christ, by whom she was endowed with Power from on high, which made her Ministry powerful and edifying, and very comfortable to us here, and also to the Churches abroad, wherein she laboured faithfully; having many times travelled in Truth's Service through her native Country of *England*, visiting the Churches there; also *Scotland* and *Ireland*; divers Parts of the Plantations in *America*; and *Holland*.

She departed this Life, in the City of *York*, in a good old Age, well esteemed; but having many Afflictions of Body to struggle with, made her desire, if it pleased the Lord, *she might be freed from them and be dissolved*; which he was graciously pleased to answer in his own due time; and we believe she died in the Life and Power of divine Faith, and is now gone to that Rest which is glorious.

A Testimony

A Testimony from Friends of the Province of Ulster *in* Ireland, *concerning* WILLIAM GRAY.

AS there are some still living amongst us, who remember this our dear Friend from his Youth, and knew him then to have been of a sober Life and Conversation, and one who had a Regard to the Fear and Grace of God in his Heart; so there are many more of a younger Generation, who do know and very well remember his Services in the Church, for upwards of Thirty Years past.

And therefore, in Testimony to the good Spirit and Grace of God, which qualified him for those Services, wherein he afterwards became eminently serviceable ; as well as for the stirring up and encouraging others to come up in Faithfulness, we find a Concern in our Minds to say something concerning him, both as to those Qualifications with which he was endued, and also as to his Service in the Church.

He was plain and exemplary, of a grave and solid Deportment, had a ready Utterance, and of a sound discerning Judgment, and had a clear and ready Understanding in difficult Cases ; by which Qualifications he was enabled, not only to be very helpful in composing Differences, and speaking to Things he

observed

observed amiss; but also having acquainted himself with the Rules and Order of Friends, could speak pertinently and clearly in our Meetings of Business; and being invited by Friends of the *Select Meeting*, to join with them in that Service, he was cautious in accepting thereof, doubting his own Qualifications; but being afraid to reject the Love and Good-will of Friends to him, for his Growth and Perseverance in the blessed Truth, he accepted of Friends Invitation, and became a Member of that Meeting; in which he behaved himself with much Submission, Care and Preference to elder Friends. And as it pleased the Lord to call his fellow Elders to Rest and Peace with him, the Concern came more weighty upon this our Friend, which he faithfully discharged to the last; seldom omitting, in Meetings for Business, to advise Friends to Faithfulness, Care and Circumspection, in an orderly Conversation; and that all might come up in their respective Services, and in duly attending Meetings for Worship, both First-days and other Days; in which he was a good Example; and that they might be truly concerned therein to wait upon the Lord, to know their Strength renewed in him, that so they might come to lay down their Heads in Peace, whenever it should please the Lord to call them hence.

Towards the latter Part of his Time, he was concerned to bear a publick Testimony in Meetings,

Meetings, though in a Cross to his own Will, tenderly exhorting Friends to give all Diligence to make their Calling and Election sure; to witness which, would out-ballance all that this World can afford; and not barely to satisfy themselves with coming to Meetings, but to wait for that Bread which nourisheth the Soul up unto eternal Life.

His House was always open for Friends, who were received with much Freedom, Love and Care, and he loved the Company of honest, faithful Friends, both Ministers and others.

More might be said concerning him, but we are not willing to enlarge; yet we may say, he was an honest Man, a good Friend and Neighbour, a loving Husband, a kind Father, and one who was very helpful, both to poor Friends and others who were in want.

He took his last Illness coming from the Third Month's Half-year's Meeting in *Dublin*, and was only in one Meeting afterwards. And though his Pain at times was violent, he endured it with much Patience and Resignation of Mind, and quietly departed this Life the 20th Day of the Fourth Month 1736.

Aged about Seventy four. A Minister about Six Years.

A Testimony

A Testimony from the Monthly-meeting of Nottingham, *concerning* JOSEPH MOSELEY.

HE was born at *Appleby*, in the County of *Derby*, in the Year 1677, and was educated in the Way of the Church of *England*. About the Twenty third Year of his Age, it pleased the Lord so to influence his Understanding, as to shew him his undone State by Nature; and he was so wrought upon, that from that Time he was desirous of serving the Lord in Newness of Life. A little after, he joined himself to those People called *Presbyterians*; but not finding that Pearl of great Price, which his Soul longed for, he retired from them, not joining with any Profession until about the Year 1707, and the Thirtieth Year of his Age, when he was convinced of the blessed Truth, at a Meeting at *Hart's-hill* in *Warwickshire*.

About two Years after his Convincement, it pleased the Lord to call him to the Work of the Ministry; in which he was a faithful and serviceable Labourer, to the comforting and refreshing of the Honest-hearted. He was not only of singular Service in publick Ministry, but likewise in private Conversation, generally giving good and wholsome Advice to those who stood in need of it. He was naturally of a sweet a sweet and chearful Disposition, yet innocent; which made him acceptable to most Sorts of People. He lived at *Appleby*, the Place of his Nativity, until the Year 1736, and then found Freedom to come to live at *Nottingham*: And as he was of great Benefit to the Meetings to which he belonged, when he lived at *Appleby*, so was he of like Service whilst he lived amongst us, which though but a short time, yet we can truly say, we have a great Loss of him.

His last Ilness, which was a *Fever*, he bore with much Patience, being totally resigned to the Will of the Almighty. On the Day of his Death, being the First-day of the Week, several Friends being present, he appeared in Testimony, which tendered them very much. About half an Hour before his Departure, he prayed earnestly to the Lord, which he continued to do until near his Dissolution, and went away like a Lamb, being the 18th of the Eighth Month 1736. In the Fifty ninth Year of his Age. A Minister of the Gospel about Twenty seven Years.

A Testimony

A Testimony from the Mens-meeting of Bristol, *concerning* ALEXANDER ARSCOTT.

IT having pleased Divine Providence to remove from us our worthy and valuable Friend *Alexander Arscott*, we have the following Testimony to give concerning him.

His Life and Conversation was agreeable to the holy Principle he made Profession of; his Ministry gave Evidence of its Purity, being accompanied with divine Wisdom, Power and Life: And we hope those Writings he has left, will prove serviceable to many, both in the present and succeeding Generations.

His Delight was in doing Good to all Men, and in a particular and especial manner, he was careful to promote Love and Unity amongst those in Profession with us. Much of his Time was spent in serving his Friends and Neighbours, of which the Widow and the Fatherless, and such as laboured under Difficulties in Body or Mind, had a large Share; and to those who wanted Food or Raiment, he not only generously contributed himself, but encouraged others to do the same.

His Labour was accompanied with tender Love and close Sympathy, with the Sick and Disconsolate, which frequently had the desired Effect, in relieving the Afflicted. He was often

often applied to by many labouring under Difficulties, to whom he had been a true Friend in time of Need.

He departed this Life the 30th of the First Month 1737, in the Sixty first Year of his Age; whose Memory remains with a good Savour to those who were acquainted with him.

A Testimony from the Monthly-meeting of Settle, *in the County of* York, *concerning* JOHN BATTERSBIE.

OUR dear and antient Friend, *John Battersbie*, of *Lower Aegden*, in the Parish of *Gisburne* and County of *York*, was born, so far as can be gathered from the best Account, in the Year 1652, and was by his Parents educated in the Way of the Church of *England*, they being of that Profession; and very zealous in that Way, for a time, until some Doubts arose in his Mind, *whether it was agreeable to the Doctrines and Precepts laid down in the holy Scriptures:* And being more and more led to consider thereof, grew uneasy with the Profession he was in. He read much, and was very desirous to find out what he chiefly wanted, *viz.* inward Peace; which he continuing to seek after, went to a Meeting of the People called *Quakers*; although he had entertained

tained a very mean Opinion of that People, and taken them for an ignorant, new Sect; and like the Sect of the *Nazareens,* spoken against every where, *Acts* xxviii. 22. *Alexander Parker* was at that Meeting, and his Testimony was very much to his Condition; which made him wonder how it could be so, seeing he had no outward Knowledge of the State that he was in: By which said Testimony he was so reached and broken, as he never had been by the Ministry of any Man.

Soon after, he came to be throughly convinced, which was in the Years 1682 or 1683, being near the Thirty first Year of his Age; and in about a Year after, his Mouth was opened in a publick Testimony, in which he grew; so that in a short time he became a very able Minister of the Gospel of Christ.

At a certain Time, he had a Necessity upon him to go into the Steeple-house which he had before frequented; and going quietly towards the Place where he used to sit, having his Hat on, the Priest of the Place, whose Name was *John Miers,* being preaching when he went in, left off, and, with a loud Voice, bid *Take that Fellow away;* but none being forward to do it, he called a second and a third time, *Take that Fellow away.* In the Interim our Friend spake as followeth: John, *if thou hast a divine Commission to preach, go on, I do not interrupt thee.* At length some who were there did take him away. And although he neither
molested

molested the Priest, nor the Congregation, more than is aforesaid, yet notwithstanding, the Priest prosecuted him, and used Means to get him imprisoned; and accordingly he was had to *York* Castle, where he continued upwards of two Years, save that he had Liberty to go home at times. The said Priest was so malicious and inveterate, that he appeared at the Assize, and endeavoured to incense the Judge against him; which the Judge observing, rebuked the Priest, asking him, *If he would have the Man's Life?*

After he was released from his Imprisonment, he laboured much in the Work of the Ministry, in the Meeting to which he belonged, and Parts adjacent; his Testimony being large, plain and convincing, he often had good Service on publick Occasions, *viz.* Marriages, Burials, and also at such Meetings as were appointed for the sake of other People, where Meetings were not commonly held: His Ministry being acceptable to them, some were thereby convinced of the Truth he bore Testimony to, and came to make publick Profession thereof.

He was very industrious in his outward Calling and Business, being *Husbandry*; so that, although he had a Wife and eleven Children, who all lived till they came to Men and Women's Estate, besides some who died in their Infancy, and had no great Substance to begin the World with, yet notwithstanding, he he lived very reputably, being always careful to make due and punctual Payments of what Money he owed on any Account.

He had a watchful Eye over his Children for their Good, and spared not to rebuke and correct them, when he saw a Necessity for it; and we believe his Care on that Account was not in vain; they, most of them, having been orderly in their Conduct hitherto. He was likewise a sharp Reprover of such, as by their loose Conduct gave Occasion for the Truth to be evil spoken of; being moved thereto by a godly and *Christian* Zeal for the Honour of it, and the Welfare of their Souls: But was always very tender towards, and ready to encourage, the Well-minded.

He was a very constant Attender of Meetings on First-day and other Days; not omitting any, except Indisposition or extraordinary Affairs hindered. Some Years before he died, his Bodily Strength was much decayed, so that he was incapable of going to any neighbouring Meetings; but he constantly attended their own; and, as it had always been his Practice, was careful to observe the Hour appointed; in which, when he appeared, it was in great Zeal and Fervency of Spirit, earnestly pressing Friends *to a diligent Waiting upon the Lord, as a Means whereby they might come to know their Strength renewed, that they might be enabled to live to his Honour:* The Honour of God, and his own Peace, having been

been that which above all Things was most dear to him, as appears by the following Expreſſions of his to a Friend, at a certain Time; *It,* ſaid he, *hath always been my Care, to keep my Peace with the Lord.* And the ſame Friend being with him a few Weeks before he died, he ſpoke to him as followeth: *I deſire to be diſſolved; I have no Guilt upon my Mind; I ſee nothing in my Way; I am not afraid to die.*

When he grew ſo weak of Body, that he was obliged to keep his Room, he deſired, *that the Meeting might be kept there, that he might have the Benefit of Friends Company:* By which it appears, that his Love to Truth and Friends was fervent to the laſt; and wherein we ſtedfaſtly believe he finiſhed his Days, and is entered into that Reſt prepared for the Righteous.

We conclude our Teſtimony, concerning this our deceaſed Friend, with the following ſummary Account: He was a loving Huſband, a tender Father, a peaceable Neighbour, and a good *Chriſtian.*

He died the 1ſt of the Tenth Month 1737, Aged Eighty four Years and two Months. A Miniſter upwards of Fifty two Years.

A Teſtimony

A Testimony from the Quarterly - meeting of Birmingham *in the County of* Warwick, *concerning* SAMUEL OVERTON.

SAMUEL OVERTON, late of *Grovefield*, in the Parish of *Hampton Lucy*, in the County of *Warwick*, was born in the Parish of *Tachbrook* in the said County, the 14th of the Seventh Month 1668, and was educated in the Way of Truth as professed by us.

In his Youth, for some Years, he was much inured to Labour, and very helpful in the Management of his Father's Affairs, being his eldest Son.

About the Year 1695 he entered into a married State, and engaged in Business for himself; yet still continued a filial Affection and dutiful Care towards his Parents, and was a great Assistant to them and their Family: Being endued with a comprehensive natural Capacity, he exerted himself in an industrious and prudent Management of his temporal Affairs; in which, through the divine Blessing attending his honest and skilful Endeavours, he was favoured with a comfortable Subsistance on a Farm, where his honest Parents had laboured under very great Difficulties; for the Lord was pleased to bless him in the Basket and in the Store. He had several Children who

who died in their Minority, besides seven who survived, whom he gave considerably to, and saw them well settled; yet notwithstanding that, and his many Labours and Travels in the Work of the Ministry, in which he spent much Time, he died in plentiful Circumstances.

In his Youth he received a Visitation from on high; to which being faithful, about the Year 1694 the Lord was pleased to commit unto him a Dispensation of the Gospel to preach, wherein he faithfully laboured until Weakness of Body prevented him, which was but a very short time before his Death.

In the Course of his Ministry he several times visited the Meetings of Friends in many Counties in *England*, particularly in the Western Parts thereof, and sometimes in *Wales*; and for many Years attended the Yearly-meeting at *London*. And his Mind being freely devoted to discharge his Duty, he often appointed Meetings for the Information and Benefit of those of other Persuasions.

He was very serviceable in attending Marriages and Burials amongst Friends, both in the County wherein he resided, and those adjacent. He had an excellent Gift in the Ministry, and his Labours therein were generally very acceptable, he being found in Doctrine, and mighty in the Scriptures.

He was likewise very serviceable in Meetings of Discipline, being one of the first who was
concerned

concerned in settling of them in those Parts, which he also diligently attended, and was of a sound Jugdment and steady Deportment, often advising Friends *to keep cool in their Minds, and to speak from a Sense of Truth.* He was also a Pattern of Meekness and Brotherly Condescention.

He was a loving and affectionate Husband, a tender Father, a kind and liberal Master, a true and faithful Friend, a generous and good Neighbour, particularly to the Poor and Afflicted. His House and Heart were always open to entertain his Friends, especially those who were Strangers. He was often made use of as an Arbitrator, to compose Differences amongst our own Society and others, in which Office he was very successful.

He did not only, in Doctrine, zealously and repeatedly recommend a holy and circumspect Life and Deportment, but was a lively Pattern and Example thereof, in his own Conversation and Conduct.

He had a lingring Ilness for several Months, which he bore with *Christian* Patience; and, as often as the Intermission of his Distemper would admit, he was very diligent in attending Meetings, wherein he very devoutly exercised his Gift, and was supported and carried through, in the Discharge thereof, beyond what could in the Eye of Reason be expected, being freely given up to spend and be spent for the Service of Truth; and even at the last Meeting

Meeting he had amongst Friends at *Warwick*, which was the same Week he died, notwithstanding the Infirmities of his Body, he was deeply and excellently concerned in Testimony; and, as if sensible of his approaching Death, and the Loss which the Church was likely to sustain by his Removal, (which indeed is very great) he very fervently in Prayer *besought the Lord of the Harvest, that out of his abundant Goodness, he would be pleased to raise up and send more faithful Labourers thereinto*; which was very affecting and Heart-tendering to several then present: And we earnestly desire, that his ardent Prayer may be answered, and that it may please the Divine Being, to pour forth, upon the rising Generation, a double Portion of that Spirit which so eminently attended many of our worthy Friends, who are gone to Rest and Peace; of which Number we doubt not but this our worthy Friend was one, for we believe he lived and died a faithful Servant of Christ and his Church.

He departed this Life the 23d of the Seventh Month 1737, and was honourably buried in Friends Burying Ground in *Warwick* the 27th of the same, being attended by a great Number of Friends and Neighbours, and generally lamented by all Sorts of People.

Aged Sixty nine, a Minister about Forty eight Years.

A Testimony

A Testimony from the Quarterly-meeting of Birmingham, *concerning* JONATHAN FREETH.

HE was born at *Smithwick*, in the Parish of *Harboone*, in the County of *Stafford*, upon the 20th of the Tenth Month 1661, descended of honest Parents. And as he grew in Years, was religiously inclined, and diligently attended the Meeting he belonged to, to wit, *Birmingham*, two Miles from his Habitation, even in the Times of Persecution, when the Door of Friends Meeting-house was sometimes shut up, and they obliged to meet in the Highways.

He entered into a married State in the Year 1686, and about four Years after, removed with his Family to *Birmingham*; and, in the Year 1695, was concerned to bear a publick Testimony to the Truth.

He was found in his Doctrine, and often advised Friends *to love and fear the Lord*; and was a Man very thankful to God for his Goodness and Mercy, which was to him extended divers ways. And though he did not travel much, especially of late Years, yet he was very serviceable in his own Meeting, his Testimony being generally well accepted amongst Friends; and he was very diligent in attending Week-day Meetings. In his Life and

and Converfation he was an Ornament to his Profeffion, being an Example of Piety and Virtue, worthy of Imitation; plain and felf-denying; temperate, if not abftemious; prudent and wife in his Conduct, juft in his Dealings, of good Report amongft Men, and beloved by Friends and others. His Difpofition was quiet, peaceable and eafy; in Evennefs of Temper beyond many; not exalted in Profperity, nor dejected in Adverfity. He was a Lover of Peace and Unity in the Church, and was often qualified to advife in the Affairs of Truth, and was ready to entertain Strangers.

He was a faithful Friend, a tender Hufband, a loving Father, concerned for the good Education of his Children in the Way of Truth and Sobriety; and we have reafon to believe that his Endeavours, through the divine Bleffing, had a good Effect, fome of his Sons having received a Gift in the Miniftry.

He died in a good old Age, like a Shock of Corn gathered in due Seafon, after a fhort Ilnefs of about thirty feven Hours, on the 25th of the Eleventh Month 1738, and we doubt not hath finifhed his Courfe with Joy, and is entered into everlafting Reft.

Aged Seventy feven, a Minifter about Forty three Years.

A Teftimony

A Testimony from the Quarterly - meeting of Wigton in the County of Cumberland, concerning JOSEPH ATKINSON.

OUR dear and worthy Friend was born at *Masthorn*, in the Parish of *Stapleton*, and County of *Cumberland*. His Parents were esteemed very honest Friends; but they both dying, left several of their Children very young; and this our worthy Friend, being the youngest, was taken into the Family of an Unkle, who was a Member of the Church of *England*, and there remained a pretty many Years, till he was nearly arrived to mature Age; and, being religiously inclined, had it in his Mind to come to the Meeting of Friends, with whom his Parents had been in Communion. He was fully convinced and satisfied, and never again went to the national Worship, but continued to frequent the Meetings of Friends very diligently; and as he gave Attention to that holy Principle to which he was directed, and in which he lived, he, after some Years, received a Gift in the Ministry, and knew a gradual Growth therein; often appearing in the Power and Demonstration of the Spirit, his Testimony being attended with a holy Warmth and living Zeal, full of Innocence, Love and Sweetness, which tended to the Comfort and Edification of the Church.

And although he travelled not very much, yet he visited pretty many Meetings at sundry times, within this Nation and *North Britain*; and we doubt not but his zealous and faithful Testimony had a good Service abroad, as well as at home.

His Life and Conversation was very regular, coupled with the Fear of God; and in all his Dealings he had a tender Regard to the Testimony; and, being pretty much concerned in Trading and Merchandize, was very careful to ask the Counsel of his Friends, and to embrace it.

He was of a chearful Countenance, a free and unaffected Behaviour, and a courteous Disposition, which made his Company desirable, being tempered with a religious Gravity. In short, he was a loving Husband, an affectionate Father, a real Friend, and peaceable Neighbour. And notwithstanding he met with many heavy Exercises, and deep Afflictions in the Course of his Pilgrimage through the World, yet he bore all with a remarkable Courage, Meekness and *Christian* Patience; being supported, no doubt, by an invisible Hand, upon which he secretly leaned, and to whose divine Protection he was entirely resigned.

About the Sixty fifth Year of his Age, having been a Minister Thirty eight Years, after a short Ilness, having fought the good Fight of Faith, he finished his Course, at his House belonging to *Righead* in *Kirklinton*, in
a sweet

a sweet Frame of Mind, as appeared by the tender, fervent and warm Expreſſions that dropped from him in the time of his Sickneſs: And being paſſed from Works to Rewards, we firmly believe, through the Mercy of God in Jeſus Chriſt, he is entered into Reſt.

He was buried at Friends Burial Place at *Hetherſide*, the 12th of the Fifth Month 1738, his Corps being accompanied by many Friends and others; and living and powerful Teſtimonies were born, to the Honour of that holy Arm and Power which had raiſed and ſupported him in all his Services, and carried him through his Afflictions and Troubles; and to the Satisfaction and Comfort of all, or moſt, who were preſent.

A Teſtimony from the Quarterly - meeting of Birmingham, *concerning* ANN SCOTTEN.

OUR dear Friend, *Ann Scotten*, was Daughter of that worthy and eminent Servant of the Lord in his Day, *John Banks* of *Cumberland*. And having the Advantage of ſo pious an Example, as well as Education, ſhe became a ſober virtuous young Woman.

She was married to *Stephen Scotten*, of *Coventry*, in the Year 1700, and was a loving and faithful Wife, a tender and affectionate Mother, a ſincere Friend. She had a great Love for Friends who travelled in the Miniſtry, and her Heart and House were always open to receive them.

She came forth in the Ministry in the Year 1711, we believe, according to the Will of God. She was a Woman of a good natural Understanding, sound in Ministry, weighty and fervent in Prayer, stedfast in the Faith and Doctrines of our Lord and Saviour Jesus Christ, as she had experienced the Virtue and Efficacy of his Power to be her Comfort in Affliction, and Support in the Ministry.

She was often zealously concerned to recommend *a steady Dependance upon him, in whom is Salvation and Strength*; and though she was not large in her Testimony, yet in her Ministry she was frequently divinely favoured, to the Edification and Comfort of the Church.

She travelled in divers Counties in this Nation, in the Work of the Ministry, and her Labour therein was acceptable. She was very serviceable in our Womens Meeting of Business, was much concerned for the Honour of God, and the Peace and Concord of the Church. She was an Example of Piety to her Neighbours; and it may be truly said, she adorned the Doctrine of God our Saviour, by a sober and godly Conversation amongst them, by whom she was well respected, and her Death much lamented.

In her last Illness she seemed fully resigned to the Will of God. She often spoke of the Peace of Soul she enjoyed, and said, *that nothing*

nothing stood in her Way. We have no Reason to doubt but she finished her Course with Joy, and is at Rest with the Faithful.

She quietly departed this Life the 21st of the Tenth Month 1739, in the Sixty eighth Year of her Age; a Minister about Twenty eight Years.

A Testimony from the Quarterly-meeting of Birmingham, *concerning* JOHN HANDS.

OUR dear deceased Friend, *John Hands,* was born at *Warwick,* the 15th of the Twelfth Month, in the Year 1656. His Parents, who were of the Church of *England,* were honest and zealous People, and had this their Son, as well as the rest of their Children, educated after the most strict Manner thereof; but by a Paper of his own Hand-writing it appears, that even whilst he was very young, he was dissatisfied with that Way of Worship, not finding thereby the Wants of his Soul satisfied, which thirsted after something more substantial than Externals could administer to it; and that nothing short of the Bread of Life would relieve and satisfie him: Yet, though he was secretly convinced, and had this Satisfaction given him, *That such of the People called* Quakers, *who were faithful to the Manifestation of the Spirit of God in their own Hearts,*

Hearts, were the People of the Lord, he did not for many Years after join in Society with them.

But about the Beginning of the Year 1677, he being at the Congregation he assembled with, in their publick Place of Worship, and attempting to join them in singing Psalms, the Lord smote him for the same; and then and there, under great Sorrow for his former Unfaithfulness, he came to a Resolution, through the Lord's Assistance, never more to join with them in their Worship. *So the Lord*, says he in the Paper above mentioned, *brought me out from amongst them by his divine Power.* From which time he became a zealous and constant Frequenter of Friends Meetings, was a good Example in strictly keeping to the Time appointed, and watching diligently against Dulness and an unconcerned Spirit therein; and so continued until old Age and Infirmities rendered him uncapable to attend them.

In the same Year that he joined in Society with Friends, he received a Gift in the Ministry, in which he faithfully laboured. He visited Meetings in this, and several adjacent Counties, in which his Service was very acceptable, his Ministry being not in the enticing Words of Man's Wisdom, but in Demonstration of the Spirit, and also holding fast the Form of sound Words. He was not often very large in Testimony, but powerful and affecting; and his Conversation adorned the

the Doctrine of God our Saviour; for which he was generally esteemed amongst Friends, and of a good Report amongst all Sorts of People.

A Year or more before his Death, he was, through Weakness of Body, frequently confined at home; yet seemed much pleased with the Visits of Friends. When very weak in Body, he signified, *he was not afraid to die, the Sting of Death being taken away*. Weakness and the Decays of Nature, through Age, gradually increased upon him till the 28th of the Tenth Month 1739, when he departed this Life in great Peace with God, we doubt not, and in the Love and Unity of Friends.

Aged near Eighty three, a Minister about Sixty two Years.

A Testimony from the Quarterly-meeting at Collumpton *in* Devonshire, *concerning* MARGERY PETERS.

OUR antient and worthy Friend, *Margery Peters*, departed this Life the 18th of the Second Month 1739, about the Ninety second Year of her Age. She was the Widow of *John Peters* in *Cornwall*; they were both, a few Years after their Marriage, convinced of Truth in one Day, and likewise, a short time after, received the Gift of the Ministry; in which she was frequently exercised, to the

Edification of many. She was remarkably modest in her Deportment, of a courteous and obliging Behaviour, and of exemplary Piety, sweet and chearful in her Conversation, very instructive, and on that Account, equally entertaining and profitable; which added a Lustre to her Ministry, and made it more extensively serviceable.

She was tender and compassionate to all, doing good and communicating, according to the Ability which God had given her; a Pattern of Meekness and Humility, and so far from Self-exaltation, that she was much in the Practice of preferring others to herself; of so grateful a Disposition, as if she thought, when the least Kindness was shewn her, she could not discharge the Obligation.

During her Life, she was generally beloved by such as were acquainted with her; and notwithstanding her great Age, she retained her Memory and Understanding to the last, often expressing her great Love to Truth and the Friends of it; and, but a few Days before her Dissolution, she expressed herself to a Friend who visited her, to this Effect: *That she would have him remember her Love to all Friends, and tell them, that she had but a few Days to live; but that she should die in Peace with God, and with all Men.*

A Testimony

A Testimony from the National Half-year's Meeting in Dublin, *concerning* JANE GEE.

SHE was descended from honest Parents, and religiously inclined in her young Years; of a free and affable Disposition, courteous and solid Deportment, and often expressed the Satisfaction she had in the Company and Conversation of honest Friends.

In the Year 1714, she joined in Marriage with our Friend *John Gee*; was a tender and affectionate Wife, charitable to the Poor, and by her prudent and religious Conduct gained a good Report.

In or about the Year 1721, she received a Gift of the Ministry, which, through the Cross, she gave up to; having first known, in a good measure, the Work and Power of Truth in her own Heart to sanctify, fit and prepare her for that Service; and having the Prosperity of Truth in view, she joined with Friends in several Services of the Church, being gifted also for the Discipline thereof, particularly for that of *visiting Families*; wherein she was well accepted. She frequently recommended inward Retirement, to wait upon the Lord.

She was diligent in attending Meetings for Worship, and, when of Ability, travelled through divers Parts of this Nation in the
Service

Service of Truth. In the Year 1729, having a Concern to visit the Meetings of Friends in *Wales*, and some Parts of *England*, she went, with the Concurrence of her Friends here, in Company with her dear Friend and Companion *Elizabeth Wilson*. They travelled through *Wales*, and divers Parts of *England*; and on her Return at *Manckester*, her dear Companion was removed from her by Death, which sorrowfully affected her; yet she patiently submitted to the Lord's Will; and soon after returned home, to the Comfort and Satisfaction of her Husband and Friends.

She afterwards visited most or all the Meetings of Friends in this Nation.

Her mild and innocent Conversation and Deportment corresponded with the Doctrine she preached, and engaged Friends Love greatly, Self being of no Reputation with her.

The Indisposition of Body, which occasioned her Death, was of long Continuance, and attended with great Pains at times, which she bore patiently, and seemed resigned to the Will of God, whether to live or die. And, as she drew near her Conclusion, was frequent and fervent in Prayer and Praises to the Lord, under a Sense of his gracious and merciful Dealings with her.

A little before her Departure, several Friends coming to visit her, she sat up in Bed, though very weak, and in a fresh and lively Sense of divine Favour, expressed her Satisfaction in
their

their Visit; and desired, *That the Lord might be with them, in their Mens and Womens Meetings; and that Friends might be careful in the Education of their Youth.*

Her Supplication was earnest with the Lord, *that he would be with her in her last Moments*; which was graciously answered, she having a Taste of the living Springs of divine Goodness; and being filled with heavenly Joy, she could sing Praises to God, magnifying him for his Mercies, having a full Assurance of her Salvation, saying, *Lord, now come, thy Servant is ready*: And so concluded with heavenly Expressions, to the Admiration of those about her, being sensible to the last; and we doubt not is entered into that eternal Rest which is prepared for the Righteous.

She departed this Life the 28th of the Tenth Month 1739.

A Testimony from the National Half-year's Meeting of Ministers and Elders in Dublin, *concerning* ELIZABETH JACOB.

OUR dear Friend and Sister *Elizabeth Jacob*, deceased, was born at *Ardee* in *Ireland*, of believing Parents, (*Thomas* and *Agnes Head*) and went over into *England*, where she lived some Years. From whence she returned to this City, where she went through many and deep Baptisms, before Self came

came to be sufficiently abased, and she made willing to bear a publick Testimony for her Lord and Master, which she did in this City, as some of us well remember.

She continued about seven Years amongst us, and then joining in Marriage with our Friend *Richard Jacob* of *Limerick*, removed thither, and was of great Service in that City and Province, being an able Minister of the Gospel, and well qualified for Discipline in the Church.

She travelled in the Service of Truth, not only in this Nation, but several times, in *England, Scotland, Wales*, and also in *Holland*; and many were the Seals of that living powerful Ministry with which she was endowed, both in this Nation and elsewhere.

She had a very clear and distinct Utterance in her Ministry, which was attended with great Reverence and Tenderness, to the reaching and tendering the Hearts of Friends and others; she was fervent and weighty in Prayer, and had deep Concern for the Youth amongst us, many of whom were often much affected by her Ministry; so that we may say, she was made, in the Lord's Hand, an Instrument of much Good. And in her late Years, although often attended with Infirmities of Body, it was her Delight to see and visit Friends. So long as she was of Ability, she duly attended the Meeting she belonged to, appearing lively in her Gift to the last.

An

An Abstract of the Testimony from Munster *Province-meeting in* Ireland, *concerning* CHARLES HOWELL.

HE was born at *Gorey* in the County of *Wexford,* in the Year 1671, and educated according to the Manner of the Church of *England*; and, when grown up, was put Apprentice to our Friend *Nicholas Lock,* by Trade a *Sadler*; in which Time it pleased the Lord to visit him with the Knowledge of the Truth, which brought him to see the exceeding Sinfulness of Sin; to deny himself of that vain Conversation to which he was naturally inclined, and to live a righteous, sober and godly Life.

He bore a faithful Testimony against the Payment of Tithes, and on that Account suffered a long and close Imprisonment, which he bore with Patience and Chearfulness. Soon after his Release, about the Year 1695, it pleased God to bestow on him a Gift of the Ministry, wherein he approved himself a faithful Labourer. He travelled abroad, not only in this Nation, but also in some Parts of *England* and *Wales*. His Ministry was plain, sound and suitable. He was a diligent Attender of Meetings, both for Worship and Discipline, and of an exemplary Life and Conversation.

He

He was taken ill the 19th of the Eighth Month 1740, being seized in a sudden and violent Manner, which he bore with Patience and Resignation to the Will of God; and though his Pains were very great, he said, *It was the Lord's Goodness in supporting him under the same.* And when he was asked, *If he would have a Doctor?* he said, *He believed his Time was come, and that his Dependance was not on Doctors, but on the great Physician of Souls; and that what he had laboured for in his Lifetime, he was now going to enjoy.* And seeing his Wife and Children in Trouble about him, said, *Why do ye afflict yourselves so? Sorrow not for me as without Hope. I have not my Day's Work to do now; for though my Body is full of Pain, my Mind is easy.* And further said, *The Lord who promised to be an Husband to the Widow, and a Father to the Fatherless, I make no doubt will be so to you, if you keep near to him.*

He departed this Life the 23d of the Eighth Month 1740, we are satisfied, in Peace with the Lord.

Aged about Sixty nine, a Minister about Forty four Years.

A Testimony

A Testimony from the Monthly-meeting at Woodbridge, *in the County of* Suffolk, *concerning* MARTHA KING.

A Concern is on our Spirits, to give the following Testimony concerning this our antient and worthy Friend. She was born in the Parish of *Chaffield*, in the County of *Suffolk*, 1645. She was soberly inclined in her Youth, and when arrived to Woman's Estate, she was favoured with the Visitation of God's Love unto her Soul; and by Virtue thereof, she became zealously concerned to get to Meetings, both on First and other Days of the Week, though situated many Miles from her Habitation.

About the Thirtieth Year of her Age, the Lord was pleased to call her into the Work of the Ministry, wherein she had good Service amongst Friends, in the time of Persecution, by Exhortation and Example, in going constantly to Meetings, though she often met with Mockings, Scoffings, and Abuse, from the rude People; and sometimes was haled out of Meetings and carried to Goal; which she suffered with Patience and *Christian* Courage. She would frequently say, with great Thankfulness to the Almighty, *That, in the Midst of all her Exercises and Trials, the Lord was her Comfort*

Comfort and Support ; in which Enjoyment she would often, even in the Prison-house, praise the Lord, with rejoicing of Soul, amongst her Friends in Confinement. She hath also been of good Service amongst us, in her old Age, both in Conversation, and in the Work of the Ministry ; the Stream of her Testimony being attended with lively and powerful Exhortations unto all, but in particular to the Youth amongst us.

She travelled in the Work of the Ministry through several Counties in *England*, with a very solid and becoming Conduct, suitable to such a great and weighty Work ; and with like Service and Conduct she continued amongst us, even to a good old Age. Though she lived some Miles from Meetings, yet she would, if possible, constantly attend both First and Week-day Meetings, till about the Eighty sixth Year of her Age ; and several of those Years she travelled to Meetings on foot, with her Husband *Thomas King*, a very antient and steady Friend. But Friends considering the Difficulties she laboured under, thought proper to remove her into the Dwelling belonging to the Meeting-house at *Woodbridge*, for her better Conveniency in attending Meetings. She had not lived there long, before she buried her aged Husband, who had been her comfortable Companion for many Years.

As to her inward Condition, we have good reason to believe, in Concurrence with her own

own Testimony, that *She dwelt so near to the Lord in Spirit, that she often was favoured with inward Peace of Soul.* She sometimes said, to such as visited her, *That the Lord, in the Riches of his Love and Mercy, was still pleased to favour and bless her with the Enjoyment of his living and comfortable Presence, now in her old Age*; for which, she would express so much Joy and Thankfulness to him, for his continued Love to her poor Soul, as shewed her Heart to be filled with Praises to him, in the sensible Enjoyment thereof. And for several of the last Years of her Life, when lame and feeble as a Child, yet she would desire to be led into Meetings; and was frequently enabled to drop many innocent and comfortable Exhortations, to the Admiration of many. She earnestly desired, *That the Lord would be pleased to enable her to hold out unto the good End that crowns all.* And it may be said of her, that she lived and died a Servant of the Lord and his People, and hath left a good Savour behind her.

She departed this Life the 16th of the Third Month 1740, in the Ninety fifth Year of her Age.

K   *A Testimony*

A Testimony from the Monthly-meeting of Brighouse in Yorkshire, *concerning* AARON ATKINSON.

HE was born at *Masthorn* in the Parish of *Stapleton*, and County of *Cumberland*, about the Year 1665. His Parents dying when he was young, the Care of his Education was committed to some Relations who were of the *Presbyterian* Profession, among which People he walked till about the Twenty second Year of his Age; when being at a Meeting at *Christopher Taylor's*, at *Hetherside* in the Parish of *Kirklinton*, and County aforesaid, he was there convinced of the Truth, by the powerful Preaching of our late esteemed Friend *Christopher Story*, and became an eminent Example of Plainness and Sobriety.

He was anointed for, and called to, the Work of the Ministry in his young Years, in a very extraordinary manner; and preached the Truth, not in the Wisdom of Man, but in the Power of God. He had a lively and affecting Testimony, and in his Doctrine was so clear, as frequently to reach the Hearts of the Hearers so effectually, as to convince Opposers.

As he was duly qualified for, so he was a painful Labourer in the Work of the Gospel, which

which his Travels in *England, Scotland, Ireland* and *America* plainly indicate; and therein his Labours were not ineffectual, for many were convinced by his Ministry, and brought not only to a Confession and Acknowledgement of the Truth, but to sit under the Teachings of Christ our Lord, the only Shepherd and Bishop of Souls.

The Concern for the Welfare of the Society engaged his Attendance in Meetings for Discipline, where his Endeavours to promote the Peace and Prosperity of the Churches, rendered him acceptable. He was generally present with us, both in Monthly and Quarterly-meetings, and often attended the Yearly-meeting in *London*.

During the latter Part of his Life, he went not much abroad, but continued, so long as by any Means it was possible, to attend our Meetings for religious Worship, both on First-days and other Days of the Week, and was a punctual Observer of the Time appointed; wherein, as well as in other Respects, his Example was worthy Imitation.

His Decline was so gradual, as scarcely to be perceived, but at distant Periods; and he retained a lively Sense of divine and heavenly Goodness upon his Spirit, which we doubt not continued with him to his last Moments.

He died the Tenth of the Eighth Month 1740, at his own House in *Leeds*.

K 2 *A Testimony*

A Testimony from Brighouse *Monthly-meeting in* Yorkshire, *concerning* BENJAMIN HORNOR.

THIS our dear and antient Friend was born at *Leeds*, in the County of *York*, in the Eleventh Month 1667; descended from religious Parents, who, in early Days, received the blessed Truth, and bore a Part in suffering for the same, whereof he also partook in his Youth; and being strictly educated therein, he soon became zealous for its noble Cause.

His House has been always open for the Reception of travelling Friends, where they found free and generous Entertainment, which he conscientiously communicated to them, as believing it his Duty; and therein was heartily and freely assisted by his Wife and Family.

He was a diligent Attender of our Meetings for religious Worship, and, at times, found himself engaged to bear a publick Testimony. And as he was serviceable, so he was rarely absent, for near fifty Years, from Monthly or Quarterly-meetings, for the Discipline of the Church; and mostly attended the Yearly-Meeting in *London*.

To his Wife he was a tender and affectionate Husband; to his Children a provident and indulgent Father; to his Servants a kind and
generous

generous Mafter. In his Neighbourhood, efpecially to the Poor, he was beneficent and humane; to his Dependants, who were many, he was open and free of Accefs. In a large and extenfive Trade, he ever appeared punctual and ftrictly honeft. His moral Character fhone with peculiar Luftre, and remained unfullied.

He had the general Efteem of thofe who knew him, of every Denomination: So forcibly does the Principle, by which he walked, recommend itfelf to all confiderate Men, that it would be a Bleffing to us, and the Society in general, did all carefully follow fo bright an Example.

He lived to a good old Age, retain'd his Capacity to the laft, left his temporal Affairs in a fatisfactory and commendable Order, and died in ftrict Unity with Friends, and, we hope, in great Peace with the Lord, on the 4th of the Tenth Month 1740. Aged near Seventy three Years.

A Testimony from the Quarterly - meeting of Norfolk, *concerning* JOHN GURNEY, *who departed this Life the 19th of the Eleventh Month* 1740.

HE was descended of worthy Parents, who received the Truth in the Love of it, soon after the first Appearance of Friends in the City of *Norwich*. His Father had no small Share in Suffering, for bearing Testimony to the Truth, in the most severe Persecutions which Friends underwent in those early times, and continued faithful to the End of his Days. They took particular Care in the religious Education of all their Children, and had the Satisfaction to find the blessed Effects thereof in most of them.

This our dear Friend, having seen through the Follies and Vanities of Youth, did set his Heart to seek the Lord, in his young and tender Years; and by submitting to the Guidance of his holy Spirit, he was indued with a good Understanding in the Mysteries of the Gospel; and about the Twenty second Year of his Age, his Mouth was opened in the Assemblies of his Friends, as a Minister, much to their Edification and Comfort; and as he advanced in Years, that excellent Gift was more plentifully bestowed upon him,

being

being an eloquent Man, and mighty in the Scriptures; his Miniftry having often the Demonftration of the Spirit and Power of Life attending it, being delivered with much plainnefs, and fo fuitably adapted, as generally reached the meaneft Capacities, and anfwered to the Witnefs of God in the Auditors; which made him very acceptable to many, who for the moft part delighted to fit under the fame, and fought for Opportunities fo to do: Though it may be faid, he endeavoured rather to be hid, than to appear to gratify the Curious, or only to fatisfy their itching Ears, being careful in attending to the immediate Preffures on his own Mind, before he entered thereupon; and often gave way to others, though perhaps inferior to himfelf in many Refpects, which made his Service more available, and better accepted.

His Life and Converfation well correfponded with his Doctrine; he lived in the Fear of God, and was a Pattern of Sobriety, Chaftity, Moderation and Temperance, as well as of other *Chriftian* Virtues; thereby adorning the Gofpel of Chrift: And we think we may, without Flattery, give this Teftimony of him, *That he was a Workman, who needed not to be afhamed, rightly dividing the Word of Truth.*

He often travelled to vifit the Churches in this Nation, and was well received where he came, and many are the Seals of that Virtue which attended his Labour of Love, for the Good of Souls.

He was a constant Attender of our religious Assemblies, both on the First-days and other Days in the Week, if Health permitted; as also those of Discipline, highly esteeming the good Order established in our Society, which he was well acquainted with; and great Regard was paid to his Judgment, not only in Monthly and Quarterly Meetings, but also in the Yearly-meeting at *London*.

He was a great Lover and Promoter of Peace, and was frequently instrumental in healing many Wounds and Breaches, which have happened in the Churches. He often said, *That he believed our Constitution, respecting Discipline, was preferable to any other now subsisting in the World.*

He was no less remarkable in *civil Affairs*; His Depth of Judgment, and Quickness of Apprehension, joined with a solid and grave Deportment, made him conspicuous, being willing to serve Mankind, when it lay in his Power, which was very frequent: And not only those of his own Society, but likewise other Parts of the Commonwealth, reaped no small Benefit from him; which rendered him generally beloved and esteemed, yet was he not puffed up therewith, but shunned the Opportunities of Applause, which frequently offered.

His Patience and Resignation to the Will of God was great, being afflicted for a considerable Number of Years with grievous Pains, caused by the *Stone* and *Gravel*, which weakened

weakened his Conftitution very much; yet his Soul feemed fupported with *Chriftian* Fortitude through them all, to the Admiration, as well as great Confolation, of thofe who highly efteemed him for his eminent Qualifications and Services.

His Removal appears a very great Lofs to his Family, in which he was a moft loving and affectionate Hufband, an indulgent and tender Father, and a kind Mafter. Amongft his Relations, a faithful Overfeer, a worthy Counfellor, and a fteady Friend to all. His Friends, Neighbours, and Countrymen of all Denominations, reaped no fmall Advantages from thofe free and candid Advices which, as Application was made to him, he generoufly and in a *Chriftian* Spirit communicated.

Thefe Virtues, mixed with a free and affable Difpofition, could not but draw great Love and Refpect from all Sorts of People towards him; and much more fo from us, who were joined in the fame Communion, and Partakers of the like precious Faith with him.

He finifhed his Courfe in unfeigned Love and Unity with his Brethren, and we doubt not, in perfect Charity with all Men.

His Body was attended to the Grave by fome Thoufands, as were fuppofed, of his Friends and fellow Citizens; and a very folemn Meeting we had, his Death being univerfally regretted.

A Teftimony

A Testimony from Norwich *Monthly-meeting, concerning* John Gurney.

AS our Friends in the Country have given you a large and particular Account, concerning our dear and deceased Friend *John Gurney*, we therefore only add,

His Service, as a Minister of the Gospel of Christ, and our Loss, as a Society in general, and in these Parts in particular, must be too well known to require to be mentioned by us; yet suffer us to say, we in this Place do most sensibly experience it; for, although his long Ilness did prevent his travelling much abroad, yet we had frequently his Company in our Assemblies; and the living and efficatious Ministry, which it pleased God to endue him with, did powerfully affect many amongst us, by confirming the Faith of the Weak, and encouraging the sincere Travellers to persevere in the Way of Truth, through this troublesome and afflicting World.

The First-day two Weeks before his last Ilness, he was at our Meeting in the Forenoon, when he appeared in a lively Testimony amongst us: He pressed us to consider, *How our Time passed away!* and to examine, *How far our Minds had been religiously disposed since our meeting together. Some of us,* he said, *seemed to be at the Top of the Mountain, where it*

pleased

pleased God sometimes to remove the Clouds, and give us a clear Prospect into the promised Land, though we were not yet quite arrived, so as to take Possession thereof. It was a melting Time, and an Opportunity that will leave a lasting Remembrance on the Minds of many.

He drank large Draughts of Affliction in this Life; yet he bore them with great Patience and Refignation to the divine Hand which permitted them. He faw clearly they muft foon finifh him, as to this World; and as they did greatly wean him from it, fo they did abundantly encreafe his Faith, in the Dealings and Goodnefs of God, by which, we doubt not, they were fanctified unto him: And though they were permitted to end his Days in this World, yet, we doubt not, they did work for him, through divine Affiftance, a more exceeding and joyful Inheritance in the World to come.

When we look back and confider him through the whole of his Life; when we confider the Temptation of Profperity, and the Kindnefs and Efteem of great Men of this World; and do further confider him, not exalted thereby; we cannot but admire that divine Hand which was his Preferver and Keeper, and did fo eminently fupport him, that nothing was permitted to feparate him from that Truth, which the Lord had eminently convinced him of, and gathered him into.

A Testimony

A Teſtimony from the Quarterly - meeting of Cheſhire, *concerning* BENJAMIN BANGS.

THIS our antient honourable Friend, and eminent Miniſter of Jeſus Chriſt, was born in the Pariſh of *Longham*, in the County of *Norfolk*, the 1ſt of the Tenth Month 1652, deſcended of reputable Parents, and was religiouſly educated, in the Principles of the Church of *England*, by his Mother, his Father dying when he was young.

The Lord was pleaſed, in his young and tender Years, to extend a merciful Viſitation of Love to him, with which he was at times deeply affected; and about the Nineteenth Year of his Age, being then ſettled in *London*, was convinced of the bleſſed Truth, and ſhortly after, he came forth in a publick Teſtimony, and became an able Miniſter of the Goſpel of Chriſt; in which he laboured faithfully and fervently, in divers Parts of this Nation and the Kingdom of *Ireland*, before he came to reſide amongſt us; and was inſtrumental in the Convincement of many.

In the Year 1683, he married our worthy Friend *Mary Lowe*, of this County, and thereupon ſettled amongſt us. After which he viſited many Parts of this Nation and the Principality of *Wales*; and, till Age and Infirmities prevailed, continued to viſit the Meetings of Friends,

Friends, in this and the adjacent Counties, where his Services were always acceptable.

He was an Elder worthy of double Honour, having obtained a good Report; not of Men seeking Glory, nor as a Lord over God's Heritage, but an Enſample to the Flock; not forward to appear in publick Service. In Doctrine ſound, clear, inſtructive and uncorrupt: His Openings were freſh and lively, and his manner of Expreſſion truly amiable. He delighted much to wait in ſilence, for the Diſcoveries of the Word of Life, whereby he became ſtrong in the Lord, and in the Power of his Might, ſounding forth the Word of Reconciliation by Chriſt our Lord, and Salvation through his eternal Spirit.

He was often fervent in Supplication, and drawn forth in a ſweet and heavenly manner, to the great Joy and Gladneſs of the ſincere in Heart. He was ſignally qualified, in our Monthly and Quarterly-meetings, to ſpeak a Word in Seaſon, for the Promotion of Peace, good Order and Diſcipline in the Church; which Meetings he conſtantly attended, when at home and in Health.

He was remarkably compaſſionate to the Poor of the Society, in whom he obſerved a degree of Sincerity and Worthineſs, who were ſure to meet with an Advocate in him.

His Countenance was awful, his Deportment grave, but intermixed with a pleaſant and familiar Manner of Expreſſion, that rendered his

his Company delectable to such as he conversed with; and when old Age and Infirmities attended, his Understanding was clear, and many sweet and heavenly Expressions dropt from him, concerning the Largeness of the Love of God to his Soul, together with sundry seasonable Advices, to the tendering of the Hearts of those present: And he often said, *That his Work was finished, and he was freely resigned; feeling nothing but Peace from the Lord upon his Spirit.* Yea, so plentifully was it poured forth upon him, that, when near his End, he could not forbear rejoicing in the blessed Experience thereof, saying, *Now I know and witness the Saying of our blessed Lord fulfilled,* viz. He that believeth in me, out of his Belly shall flow Rivers of living Water.

Much more might be said concerning this great and good Man; but his sundry Services and diligent Labours, in the Work of the Gospel, for many Years, are so well known, that we need not enlarge thereon. And altho' his Removal be a Loss to the Church, yet we fully believe it is his everlasting Gain, he being gathered home, as a Shock of Corn fully ripe, into the Garner of God, there to enjoy the blessed Reward of the Righteous, in an endless Fruition of Joy and Glory; for as he lived, so he died, a Servant of the Lord and his People, the 6th Day of the Twelfth Month 1741, in the Ninetieth Year of his Age. A Minister about Sixty five Years.

JOHN

JOHN RICHARDSON's *Teſtimony, concerning our worthy Friend and Brother* LUKE COCK, *who died the 29th of the Tenth Month* 1740, *Aged about Eighty three Years*; *and was decently buried in Friend's Burying Place in* Danby Dale.

HE was a Miniſter near Thirty ſeven Years. I have heard him ſay, before he came to the Knowledge of the Truth, he bore the Character of the greateſt Singer, *viz.* of irreligious vain Songs, in all that Part of the Country where he lived. He ſung then the *Babylonian* Song, by the muddy Waters thereof; but having drank of the Brooks of *Shiloh*, that run ſoftly into the newly converted Soul, he could ſing and rejoice in the Lord Jeſus Chriſt. And altho' he met with many Trials and great Tribulations, he witneſſed his Robes waſhed, and in a good degree made white, in the Blood of the Lamb, being, by the good Hand and Arm of Strength and Salvation, brought through all his Troubles, and ſet as upon Mount *Sion*, where he could ſing a new Song, the Song of *Moſes* and of the Lamb.

And being called into the Work of the Miniſtry, he bore a ſound and living Teſtimony for the Truth, which was greatly edifying to Friends. And it being my Lot to follow him

in

in several Parts of *England* and *Ireland*, I heard a good Account of him; Friends speaking very lovingly and tenderly concerning him, greatly desiring to see him again.

He was cautious not to minister, until he evidently felt Truth to open his Way. He was a good Example to Friends, in duly and diligently attending Meetings. A just Man, a good Neighbour, free in Conversation, but solid and instructive. In his Supplication to the Lord, he had great Access to that River which makes glad the City of God.

A little time before his Change I visited him, when he expressed his Mind to me in these Words,—*I am confined at home through Age and Weakness, and cannot get to see Friends, and to Meetings, as I could wish; but the Lord hath been great in his Goodness to me, by comforting and refreshing my Soul with his living Presence, and my Mind is much with* Abraham, Isaac, *and* Jacob; *the Prophets and Apostles; Sufferers and Martyrs for Christ's Sake; with an innumerable Company of Angels, and the Spirits of just Men made perfect: And I hope in a little time to be with them for ever.*

I thought he spoke these Words in that Weightiness and Sweetness of Mind and Spirit, that it would not be well to leave them in Oblivion.

Much might be said concerning this Man of God, our beloved Friend and Brother in Christ, and fellow Labourer with us in the Gospel

Gospel of Peace and Salvation. But now he is removed from us, to our great Loss, but, without doubt, to his everlasting Gain and Rest, in a Mansion of Glory; and that we may follow such worthy Mens Examples, so long as we remain here, *viz.* Such as followed Christ under the daily Cross, in true Humility and Self-denial, as this our beloved Friend did, with many others who are gone before, is the hearty and sincere Desire of your Friend and Brother in the Lord,

<small>Hutton in the Hole, *the* 23*d*
of the First Month 1740.</small>   JOHN RICHARDSON.

A Testimony from Gisborough *Monthly-meeting, concerning* LUKE COCK.

SINCE it hath pleased the Lord to remove from us our antient and worthy Friend, we cannot well but give some Account of his Faithfulness and good Service amongst us.

We believe he was careful not to give any just Occasion of Offence to Friends or others. He was clear, plain, and sound in his Testimony, and of a good Understanding. He travelled several Journeys in Truth's Service, while he was of Ability of Body. He held his Integrity to the End, and died in good Unity with Friends.

L *A Testimony*

A Testimony from the Quarterly-meeting of Durham, *concerning* JEREMIAH HUNTER.

WE think it our Duty to give this Testimony concerning our antient and well esteemed Friend, *Jeremiah Hunter* deceased, hoping it may be of Service to Posterity, and encouraging to hold on in Well-doing.

He was born at *Benfield-side*, in the County of *Durham*, in the Year 1658, and came to *Newcastle* upon *Tyne*, as an Apprentice, and continued there. And about the Twenty fifth Year of his Age, the Lord was pleased to open his Mouth in a publick Testimony for Truth; he grew in the Ministry, and became very serviceable, and his Gift edifying.

We can experimentally say, he was sound in Doctrine, a fresh and lively Minister, great in Understanding, well applying the Matter that opened before him; many times wonderfully filled and divinely furnished with the Spirit of Prayer and Supplication, to the comforting, reaching and tendering of many Souls.

He was an open-hearted Man, ready to help and relieve the Poor, not only amongst us, but to others he gave freely. He diligently attended Meetings for Worship, as also Monthly and Quarterly-meetings, where he had great Service in Discipline; giving seasonable Advice,

encouraging

encouraging the Well-minded, and reproving Evil-doers.

He vifited divers Counties in *England*, and often attended the Yearly-meeting at *London*; his Labour of Love being acceptable to his Brethren.

His Body weakened gradually, which he bore with great Patience, not defiring to ftay much longer here, but rather to be diffolved. After his Strength failed, fo that he was not able to get abroad, feveral Meetings were held at his Houfe, where a degree of divine Favour was often witneffed, and he appeared alive in the Miniftry to our Comfort.

He was entered into the Eighty fourth Year of his Age when he died, which was on the 24th Day of the Twelfth Month 1741, having been a Minifter about Fifty eight Years; and we doubt not but he has laid down his Head in Peace with the Lord, in Unity with his Brethren, and in good Report amongft Men, and is entered into that Reft prepared for the Righteous, where all Crowns muft be laid down, and the Glory and Honour afcribed to him that fits upon the Throne, and to the Lamb, for evermore.

A Testimony from the Monthly-meeting of Wells *in* Norfolk, *concerning* KATHERINE PECKOVER.

WE think it incumbent upon us to say something in Commemoration of so good and valuable a Woman, counting it no small Blessing to the Churches in these Parts, wherein she continued from about the Twentieth Year of her Age, to her Departure out of this Life; and was all along a very serviceable and honourable Member amongst us. Her many excellent Qualifications, attended with a meek, humble, reverent Deportment, in all Respects, rendered her very near and dear to us.

It pleased God to bestow upon her a Gift of the Ministry, which she was faithful to, and very exemplary in waiting for, delivering the Matter she had to say with much Plainness and Brevity, being attended with great Power, to the no small Edification and Comfort of the Churches. Her Life and Conversation well corresponded with her Doctrine, and she was much respected by People of other Societies: She was very charitable and full of good Works; her Delight was to be found in Practices becoming the Gospel; and she was an eminent Pillar amongst us, a worthy Mother

Mother in *Israel*, and a great Ornament to the Society

She received the Truth whilst she was very young; and, with her honourable Mother, was imprisoned for her Testimony thereunto, before she was sixteen Years of Age, and undauntedly confessed the same, and pleaded for it in her Examinations before the Judge in Court, being first called to answer to their *Indictment*, though there were upwards of sixty Persons then present upon the same good Account, and she the youngest of them all; where she conducted herself with such Modesty, giving pertinent Reasons for her joining with her Friends in assembling together to worship God in Spirit, &c. and refusing her Liberty on Terms inconsistent with her religious Profession, as drew from the Court no small Attention and Surprise; and it was so ordered, that she with her fellow Prisoners, were all set at Liberty: Which she would afterwards often mention with great Sweetness and Gratitude of Soul, to the Divine Hand by which she was supported to hold out to the End of her Days, in a constant Dependance on that Arm of Power, which gloriously visited and wrought upon her. She retained the Sense and Savour of Truth in as precious and lively a manner as in the Beginning; it being very frequent with her to express the same in her living Ministry amongst us.

Much more might be said concerning this our worthy Friend, but we study Brevity, being nearly affected with her Removal from us; which though it be our unspeakable Loss, we doubt not but is her great Gain, and that she is centered in the holy Mansions, with Saints and Angels, and the Spirits of the Just made perfect.

She departed this Life at her own Dwelling-house in *Fakenham* in the said County, on the 1st Day of the Eighth Month 1741, and was attended to the Grave by great Numbers of Friends and others. She was born about the Year 1666, and died in the Year 1741, and was a Minister about Forty six Years.

A Testimony from the Quarterly-meeting at Pardshaw-hall *in* Cumberland, *concerning* JAMES DICKINSON.

JAMES DICKINSON of *Green-trees*, otherwise *Moorside*, belonging to *Pardshaw* Meeting in the County of *Cumberland*, descended of honest Parents, was born at *Low-moor*, in the Year 1658. The Lord was pleased tenderly to visit him in his young Years, whereby he became acquainted with his Teachings when but a Child; but for want of keeping a stedfast Eye to his Guidings, he was led forth into those Follies and Vanities of the World

World incident to Youth: But such was the Love of the heavenly Father (as he often declared amongst us in the Spring of the Gospel) that he was met with again and brought back, as a Sheep strayed from the Father's Fold; and, after much Affliction and solitary Exercise, fitted for future Service, and engaged in a publick Testimony about the Eighteenth Year of his Age.

He was shortly after concerned to go to several Meetings of the *Dissenters*, in the County where he lived, and underwent Hardships amongst them; yet Truth crowned his Labours with some Convincement. After which, he travelled in the Service of the Ministry in divers Counties, through *England*, *Ireland* and *Holland*, undergoing Sufferings in the time of Persecution. He visited Friends in *Ireland* Twelve times; Three times in *America*; Once in *Holland* and *Germany*; and laboured much in his native Country of *England*, many being convinced by him. Much more might be said concerning his Labours and Travels in the Work of the Ministry, but we refer to his *Journal*.

He was a diligent Labourer at home, a constant Attender of Meetings, a sincere Traveller therein, very tender over the Youth, a nursing Father to the least, and full of Charity to all rightly anointed; yet not hasty to join with forward Spirits. He was also careful not to join in party Causes, but was greatly concerned

concerned for the Promotion and Unity of the Church; and often expressed his stedfast Faith, that the Testimony of Truth would be exalted in the Nations, and the *antichristian* Oppression of Tithes brought down; and with Concern declared his Sorrow for such as weakly complied therewith.

When his natural Abilities failed, he would speak with Strength apparently beyond his Age and Constitution. He was seized with a *Palsy* near a Year before he died, which detained him from Meetings, and by it his Speech was much taken from him; but would often say, *He was well, he was well, and had nothing but Peace on every hand*; expressing his Care and Concern for the Growth and Preservation of the Church.

He died on the 6th of the Third Month, 1741, and was interred on the 8th of the same, in Friends Burying Ground at *Eaglesfield*, being accompanied by a great many Friends and others. Aged Eighty three, a Minister Sixty five Years.

A Testimony

A Testimony from the Monthly-meeting of Aylesbury *in* Buckinghamshire, *concerning* MARY LARCUM.

THE Time of her Convincement being before our Knowledge of her, we cannot be very particular therein; but some of us have heard from herself, that she going to the Goal at *Reading* in *Berkshire*, (the Place of her Abode) to visit a Relation, a Friend then a Prisoner there, was at a Meeting of Friends, many being then Prisoners; among whom was our eminent Friend *Isaac Pennington*, by whose Ministry she was then convinced of Truth; which she receiving in the Love of it, became willing to yield Obedience to the Requirings thereof, in taking up a Cross to the Vanities her youthful Age might be inclined to.

For many Years past, some of us were well acquainted with her, and in remembrance of her Service in the Church, and exemplary Conduct in general, we are engaged to give this brief Memorial of her: That her Conversation, while single, was sober and religious; and when engaged in a State of Marriage, she was a true Helpmeet to her Husband, being very industrious in her temporal Affairs, and diligent in attending Meetings both for Worship and Discipline. She was very compassionate

passionate and liberal in extending Help to the Needy among Friends, and others as occasion offered.

About the Fiftieth Year of her Age she appeared in Testimony for the Truth; in which Service she was often made an Instrument of Comfort and Edification to the Faithful, as well as of Reproof and Exhortation to the Careless and Indifferent. While Ability of Body continued, she often travelled in the Service of the Ministry, visiting the Churches in several adjacent Counties. When Age and Weakness rendered her uncapable of going far abroad, she did not decline in her Zeal for Truth, but was diligent in attending Meetings, and often livingly opened in tender Advice and Exhortation to Faithfulness; sometimes expressing the Satisfaction and Peace she enjoyed, in that she had been diligent in serving the Lord in her known Duty.

We have good Cause to believe she died in Peace with the Lord, and is entered into everlasting Rest. She departed this Life the 23d of the Fifth Month 1741, about the Eighty fifth Year of her Age, and was interred the 28th following, in Friends Burying Ground at *Wiccomb* in the County of *Bucks*. A Minister Thirty five Years.

A Testimony

A Testimony from the Mens Meeting in Dublin, *concerning* JOSEPH GILL.

HE was educated by his Parents *William* and *Margaret Gill,* of *How* in *Cumberland,* in the Profession of Truth, and came into *Ireland* in the Year 1697, but resided mostly in the Country until the Year 1702, when he settled in this City, and gained Love and Esteem among Friends and others.

He was religiously inclined from his Youth, and a diligent Attender of Meetings for Worship and Discipline; and concerned, when there, to wait for that divine Power, that strengthens and encourages the Faithful, to travel on in the Way that leads to everlasting Happiness.

About the Year 1711, he was called to the Work of the Ministry, wherein he was, in a good degree, attended with that Life and Power, which made it comfortable and edifying to the well disposed Hearers. He several times visited Friends in *England* and *Scotland,* as also in this Nation; and many times attended the Yearly-meeting in *London*; to answer which Service he was freely given up.

In the Year 1734, he visited Friends in many Parts of the Continent of *America,* and the Islands adjacent; in all which Visits, we we believe his Labour of Love was ferviceable and acceptable.

He was well gifted for Difcipline, and of great Help to Friends of this Meeting. He was zealous againft the undue Liberties taken by too many profeffing Truth. His Life was exemplary, adorning the Doctrine he preached by a good Converfation. He arrived to the State of an Elder in the Church, and was a nurfing Father to fuch as he thought religioufly inclined. He was given to Hofpitality, and his Houfe was open to entertain Strangers.

Some time before his laft Ilnefs, he acquainted us of his Concern to vifit *Ulfter* Province, in order to have our Concurrence and Certificate, without which he was careful not to travel on Truth's Account: He was but in a poor State of Health when he fet out on his Journey, in which he vifited moft of Friends Meetings in the faid Province; but his Indifpofition increafing, he returned home, where he continued weak about five Weeks, and departed this Life, in a fweet Frame of Mind, the 28th of the Eleventh Month 1741, and was buried the 30th of the fame, at Friends Burying Ground in *Cork-ftreet*. And although we may fay, we are forrowfully affected for our Lofs of him, yet we are perfwaded it is his great Gain, being, we doubt not, entered into everlafting Reft and Peace.

Aged Sixty feven Years, a Minifter about Thirty Years.

A Teftimony

A Testimony from the Monthly-meeting of Montrath *in* Ireland, *concerning* JOHN ASHTON.

HE was born in *Cheshire*, near the Forest of *Delamere*, and when a Child, was brought by his Parents into *Ireland*, who educated him according to the Way of the Church of *England*, wherein he continued until near the Fortieth Year of his Age ; but being desirous of farther Discoveries of the Knowledge of God and Way of Salvation, he with his Wife went to a Meeting of Friends at *Birr*, where a Marriage was solemnized, and both of them were convinced that Day, by the powerful and efficacious Ministry of that faithful Servant of Jesus Christ, *Thomas Wilson*, and was obedient to the Manifestations of Truth in his Heart ; and, soon after his Convincement, was cast into Prison on account of his faithful Testimony against paying of Tithes, where he remained about six Months ; not repining, shrinking, or in the least giving way ; and may be likened to the Faithful of old, who overcame by the Blood of the Lamb, and Word of their Testimony : And as he grew in the Knowledge of Truth, so his Love encreased towards his Neighbours, frequently inviting them to Meetings, going to their Houses early and late on that Occasion.

He

He was inſtrumental in gathering and ſettling a Meeting at his Houſe, which remains there to this Time. He was a conſtant Attender of Meetings both at home and abroad.

About the Sixty ſecond Year of his Age, his Mouth was opened in a publick Teſtimony for Truth; in which he faithfully laboured for the ſtirring up the pure Mind, and encouraging that which was good in all; and was zealouſly concerned againſt Pride and vain Faſhions; the Increaſe of which is too manifeſt among the Youth of our Society of late Years.

In the Year 1733, he, with another Friend, went to the Yearly-meeting at *London*, and from thence viſited ſeveral Meetings in ſundry Counties in *England*; as alſo the Meetings of Friends in *North-Britain*.

He was helpful and ſerviceable, with other Friends, in viſiting the Families in this Monthly-meeting, and was conſtant in Friendſhip, his Heart and Houſe always open to receive Friends; a Mourner with the Afflicted, and full of Compaſſion to the Poor, by whom his Death is greatly lamented.

He died the 14th Day of the Third Month 1741, Aged about Eighty, and a Miniſter about Eighteen Years.

Though our Loſs of him is great, we are perſuaded he now reaps the Gain of all his *Chriſtian* Labours, and remains with the Juſt in a Manſion of eternal Happineſs.

A Teſtimony

A Testimony from the Quarterly - meeting of Birmingham *in the County of* Warwick, *concerning* JANE BRISCOE.

JANE BRISCOE, late of *Warwick*, was born the 30th of the Ninth Month 1654. In her youthful Days, she was under Convictions for some time before she frequented our Meetings, which was about the Twenty first Year of her Age; for which she endured a great deal of hard Speeches from her Father and other Relations; yet this did not daunt her religious Courage and Resolution to suffer Affliction for the Truth's sake, rather than enjoy the sinful Pleasures of this momentary Life. And this her steady Conduct in the Path of Truth, gained such an Ascendency over her Father, that upon his Death-bed he was reconciled to her, and desired, *that God would direct her for the best.*

Her great Respect for *William Dewsbury* was very conspicuous, with whom she lived as a Servant for many Years, waiting upon him very dutifully in his Confinement, and faithfully managing his Business, which was entrusted to her, while he was a Prisoner on Account of Religion: She attended him in his last Ilness, and has been heard to say, *She thought she had reason to bless God, that her Lot was to live with him:* Whose good Example encouraged her in Faithfulness to the divine Discoveries received, wherein she made such Advances, that it pleased the Divine Being, about the Year 1677, to bestow on her a Gift in the Ministry, which she faithfully discharged, not by enticing Words of Man's Wisdom, but in the Demonstration of the Spirit and of Power.

She mightily desired, that Truth might prosper in the Hearts of the Youth; and had a frequent Concern in Meetings, to pray to the Almighty for a Blessing upon the Children of his People. She was zealous in the Discharge of her Duty in the Ministry. Her Doctrine was enforced by a sober Life and godly Conversation, which made her Ministry the more acceptable to her Hearers. She was a diligent Frequenter of Meetings, as long as she was able to attend them; and many times, when bodily Weakness would not permit her to go on foot to Meeting, in the same Town where she resided, she used to be carried on Horseback. She would often say, *I love to go to Meetings;* and very much desired, that all Friends would be as diligent as might be in attending them, while they had Health and Strength.

She was charitably disposed towards the Poor, whom she liberally relieved. She had a great deal of Illness some Years before her Death, which she bore with *Christian* Fortitude; and would

would often say, *She should be very willing to die;* but desired, *she might patiently wait the Lord's Time.* One time in her last Ilness, she said, *If these bodily Afflictions were over, all would be well, and I shall be where the Weary are at Rest.* She several times said, *I wait for my Change;* and often signified, *the Lord was good to her, and refreshed her Soul in the Night-season, when she could not sleep.* She often pressed her Children and Family to seek the Lord, and to live in his Fear, and to wait for the Guidance of the Spirit of Truth, which is able to preserve out of every evil Way, and will certainly lead them, who truly follow and obey it, through the Troubles of this Life, to Peace and Rest for evermore.

Thus this our worthy Friend, having patiently waited for her Change, and surmounted the Difficulties of Mutability, was gathered, like an Ear of Corn fully ripe, into the Garner of Eternity, in the Eighty eighth Year of her Age, and has left behind her a Memorial of a good Report and sweet Savour, worthy to be followed by her Survivors.

She departed this Life the 31st of the Fifth Month, and was interred in Friends Burying Ground in *Warwick*, the 3d of the Sixth Month 1742.

A Testimony from the Quarterly - meeting at Birmingham in the County of Warwick, *concerning* JOSEPH FREETH.

HE was Son of our worthy Friend *Jonathan Freeth*, of *Birmingham* deceased. The pious godly Care and Counsel of his Parents in his Education, though not strictly adhered to in his Youth, yet, as he grew in Years, made very deep Impressions upon his Mind, which he hath often expressed with great Thankfulness, both to the Lord and them.

When he left his Parents, he settled at *Coventry*, about the Twenty fifth Year of his Age, when it pleased the Lord to afford him a fresh Visitation of his Love, so that he became very religious, diligently seeking after the Way of Life and Salvation; and, by yielding Obedience, through Faith, unto the Gift of God, he was made Partaker of Life and Peace in our Lord Jesus Christ.

About the Twenty eighth Year of his Age, it pleased the Lord to call him to the Work of the Ministry; and he being faithful to the heavenly Vision, preached the Gospel with Zeal and Fervency. In his Ministry he was plain, sound and powerful; in Supplication fervent. He visited some Meetings in several Counties

Counties in this Nation, and lately in our own County and the Counties adjacent, much to the Comfort and Satisfaction of Friends.

He was very diligent in attending Meetings for Worſhip and Diſcipline, in ſettling the Affairs of the Church, in which he was of excellent Service, being often cloſely exerciſed in Spirit, that he might witneſs a degree of that Power which Friends were ſo eminently favoured with in their firſt Settlement; in the Senſe whereof, his Counſel was ſolid and weighty. He was particularly inſtrumental, when any undue Warmth appeared, to the reſtoring Calmneſs and Quiet in the Meeting; being earneſtly concerned, that Friends might be influenced by nothing but Love and Zeal for the Truth.

He often viſited both Friends and others, when under Affliction; and in ſuch Opportunities was frequently divinely favoured, to the great Comfort and Conſolation of the Afflicted. He was endued with a good Underſtanding, both in the Things of God, relating to the Good and Welfare of the Soul, and alſo in the Affairs of this Life; ſo that he had great and good Service in both, and many received Benefit thereby.

He was endued with excellent Virtues, being found in admoniſhing, circumſpect and gentle in reproving, tender in adviſing, abounding in Charity, given to Hoſpitality, liberal in communicating, free and careful in Diſtributions,

tions, willing to do Good to all, especially to the Houshold of Faith, labouring earnestly for the Prosperity of *Sion*; and, being a Partaker of the like precious Faith with the Elders of old, hath obtained a good Report, being universally esteemed, and his Loss lamented.

He was a faithful and loving Husband, a tender Father, a kind and compassionate Master, a sincere Friend and good Neighbour.

He had but a few Days Ilness, in which he signified to some Friends about him, *He felt Peace within.* We doubt not but he finished his Course with Joy, died in Favour with the Lord, and is at Rest with the Faithful.

He departed this Life on the 3d Day of the Sixth Month 1742, and was decently buried in Friends Burying Ground, in the City of *Coventry*, the 5th of the same. In the Fifty third Year of his Age, a Minister about Twenty five Years.

A Testimony

*A Testimony from the Monthly-meeting at
Carlisle, concerning* THOMAS STORY.

BEING exhorted, in holy Writ, to count those Elders worthy of double Honour, who rule well, and labour in the Word and Doctrine; we think it our Duty, in Love and Esteem, as well as Justice, to the Memory of this our antient, eminent and worthy Friend, to give forth this brief Testimony; and that others also may be encouraged, by such pious Examples, to embrace the Truth, and persevere in the Way of Life and Salvation.

He was born at *Justice-Town*, near *Carlisle* in *Cumberland*, descended of reputable Parents of the Church of *England*, who gave him a liberal Education: But for a farther Acount of this and several other Particulars, we refer to his *Journal*, and shall only signify in general, that in the Year 1689, he was convinced of the Truth, and of the inward and spiritual Appearance of Christ in the Souls of Mankind, for the Completion of their Redemption and Salvation; and about the Year 1693 had a Testimony given to bear to the same, in the Demonstration of the Spirit and of Power.

He travelled much, in the Service of the Gospel, in *England*, *Scotland*, and *Ireland*; and also in the *English* Plantations in *America*, where he was very ferviceable in fettling and confirming the Churches, and remained there many Years.

After his Return to *England*, he was often concerned to vifit Friends in divers Places in this Nation, and more particularly at *London*; for being a Man of great Qualifications, and thefe fanctified, and made inftrumental by Divine Wifdom, rendered his Miniftry very convincing and edifying; fo that he was acknowledged, not only by our Society, but alfo by other People, to be a truly great and evangelical Minifter.

When he found it his Place, after fuch Vifits, to return to us, we received him in fincere Love and good Unity; being often comforted and refrefhed under his Miniftry.

Some time before his Death, he was taken with a *Paralytick* Ilnefs, which affected his Speech; after which, he feldom appeared in the Miniftry, fignifying, *that his Day's Work feem'd to be near over*. He continued in a fweet Frame of Spirit, and attended Meetings when able.

He departed this Life, at *Carlifle*, the 21ft of the Fourth Month 1742, and was buried in Friends Burying Ground there the 23d of the fame.

Aged near Eighty, a Minifter about Fifty Years.

A Supplement

A Supplement to the foregoing Testimony, from the Quarterly-meeting of Cumberland.

THE foregoing Testimony, concerning our worthy Friend *Thomas Story* deceased, was read, duly considered and approved. We could freely add, of his Convincement, Travels, Labours and Service in the Ministry, and Discipline in the Church, but for Brevity's sake shall conclude, and refer to his said *Journal*; only signifying, *that he died in good Unity with us.*

A Testimony from the Monthly-meeting of Charlecot *in* Wiltshire, *concerning* JOAN CALE.

HER Memory is very precious among us, she having been one whom the Lord reached to in her young Years, and visited with his blessed Truth; unto which she gave up in Faithfulness, soon after her Convincement, which was about the Eighteenth Year of her Age; and, by the Goodness of the Almighty, was early brought off from the many deceitful and pleasing Vanities of the World, to which, she had been before much addicted.

And as she experienced a Growth in the Truth, she soon became very serviceable in the Church, by her exemplary Virtue, pious Deportment, Plainness of Speech, Habit, and Houshold Furniture. And she was a real Mother in *Israel*, in her Care and Support of the Lord's Servants, who travelled in the Service of his blessed Truth.

In her Ministry she was eminent, and travelled much in this Kingdom; she was very zealous, and laboured earnestly in recommending Friends and others, to the inward experimental Knowledge of the Life and Power of Religion; and therein, as well as in private Conversation, was fervent in exhorting Friends against the Growth of those Thing among us, which tend to weaken and lessen us as a People; particularly, against Superfluity and Gaudiness of Apparel: And continued lively and edifying in her Testimony, when under the Weakness of Body that attended her in old Age.

We are fully persuaded she finished her Course well, and that she is at Rest with the Righteous. She died the 12th of the Second Month 1742, and was buried the 16th of the same, in Friends Burying Ground at *Caln*.

A Testimony

A Testimony from the Province-meeting at Lurgan *in* Ireland, *concerning* MARY GREER.

SHE was a Woman much esteemed amongst us, being of an exemplary Life and Conversation; a Pattern of Plainness and Humility; diligent in attending Meetings for the Worship of God, duly observing the Hour appointed. And although she was not large in Declaration, yet what she had to offer, by way of publick Testimony, was often to the Comfort of the Well-minded. She was also a good Example in attending our Province-meetings, whilst of Ability of Body.

She travelled through *Scotland*, and some Parts of *England*; also visited some Parts of *Leinster* and *Munster* Provinces, and we believe her Visit was well accepted. She was of a sweet Temper, and laboured much in her own Family in Gospel Love, that her Children and Servants might be preserved out of Pride and Idleness, and live in the Fear of the Lord; so that we fully believe she was faithful in discharging her Duty, according to the Gift bestowed on her. We may truly say, she was nearly united in Spirit to us, and generally beloved.

She was a loving Wife, a good Neighbour, being much given to Hospitality, and her Heart

Heart and House were open to entertain Friends.

Having but a few Days Sickness, she spoke little; but some short time before her Departure, her Children being about her, she desired *they might live in Love one with another*. And although her Removal be a Loss to her Family and Neighbours, and to the Meeting to which she belonged, yet we are fully satisfied it is her great Gain, having done her Day's Work in her Day.

She departed this Life the 9th of the Tenth Month 1742, in the Seventy third Year of her Age, a Minister about Thirty seven Years.

A Testimony concerning GEORGE ROOKE, *from the Quarterly-meeting of* Leinster *Province in* Ireland,

GEORGE ROOKE, Son of *Thomas Rooke*, was born in the Parish of *Bolton* in *Cumberland*, in the Third Month, in the Year 1652. He was educated in the National Profession; but, about the Twentieth Year of his Age, he was convinced of the Truth, preached by that able Minister *John Graves*, and joined himself in Society with the People called *Quakers*; and proving faithful to the Call of God, was enabled by him to embrace the Cross, not conforming himself to the vain Customs

Cuſtoms and Faſhions of the World, but endeavouring to be transformed by the Renewing of his Mind: To which End, he was very diligent in attending Meetings for divine Worſhip, being encouraged thereto by the ſpiritual Refreſhment he there met with. And about the Twenty fifth Year of his Age his Mouth was opened, to declare unto others his own Experience of the Lord's Goodneſs, though attended with great Difficulties, Fears, and the Conſcioufneſs of his own Weakneſs; but the good Hand of God, and the Countenance of his ſympathizing Friends, was a great Support to him under that Exerciſe.

He became early engaged in travelling in the Work of the Miniſtry, zealouſly and chearfully devoting his Strength and youthful Days to the Propagation of the Goſpel, and Promotion of Truth and Righteouſneſs in the Earth; being greatly encouraged in theſe Services by the Conſolation that attended them.

In the Year 1679, he went on this Account to *Scotland*, accompanied by *Peter Fearon*, though in a troubleſome and dangerous Time, *viz.* a little before the Fight at *Bothwell-bridge*, the King's Troops, and the Rebels, in ſeveral Places poſſeſſing the Towns through which they paſſed. They travelled on foot, by the Advice of that eminent Elder *George Fox*, becauſe their Horſes might, in all Probability, have been taken from them by one Party or the other, if they had rode; and ſo following
their

their Master's Business in the Innocency of the Truth, they were preserved, and visited the Meetings of Friends without much Interruption or Disturbance, and had comfortable Opportunities with them, who were glad of their Visit, having suffered greatly by the Armies.

In the Year 1681, he visited Friends in all their Meetings in *Scotland* a second time, and the same Year came to *Ireland*, and visited most of the Friends through the Nation, and had many satisfactory Opportunities with them, who were very loving and respectful to him, though he was but young.

In the Year 1684, he visited Friends in *Ireland* a second time. In the Intervals of his Travels he usually wrought at his Trade, being a *Carpenter* and *Joiner*, to supply his Necessities, that he might not be burthensome to the Church. After his Return from *Ireland* this Year, finding Drawings in his Mind, he visited Friends in *Westmorland* and *Durham*, and at *Stockton*, where he was brought before the Mayor, and the Oaths of Allegiance and Supremacy were tendered to him; and because for Conscience-sake he refused to swear, he was by him committed Prisoner to *Durham* Goal, and detained there about two Months.

In the Year 1685, he visited Friends in *Ireland* a third time, accompanied by *John Bowstead*, and had many comfortable Meetings here, finding a great Openness among the People

People to receive Truth's Teſtimony, and ſome were convinced by Means of their Miniſtry.

In the Year 1686, he came to *Ireland* the fourth time; and after having viſited moſt of the Meetings of Friends in the Nation, he took to Wife *Joan*, the Daughter of *John Cooke*, and ſettled at *Limerick*, ſtill continuing diligent in the Exercife of his Gift, to the Edification of the Churches. He went to the next Half-year's Meeting, and from thence to *England*, viſiting Friends in the North and Weſt Parts thereof, and *London* and *Eſſex*.

He continued at *Limerick* in the Year 1689 and 1690, in the troubleſome Times of the Wars between King *William* and King *James*, and during the firſt Seige; but in the Year 1691, before the ſecond Seige, while King *James*'s Army had Poſſeſſion of the City, he removed himſelf and Family to *Cumberland*, having been wonderfully preſerved through great Dangers from the *Rapparees*, who then harboured much in the Way to *Dublin*.

But notwithſtanding all theſe Troubles, he ſtill continued laborious and fervent in Spirit, in viſiting the Meetings of Friends; and in the Year 1692, again viſited the Brethren in *Scotland*. And in the Year 1693 he returned to *Ireland*, and ſettled and continued his Reſidence in *Dublin* the remaining Part of his Life; during which time, whilſt of Ability, he frequently viſited Friends in the three Provinces, and ſometimes had Meetings in Places where

no

no Meetings of Friends were settled. He also sometimes visited Friends in divers Parts of *England* and *Wales*, and was frequently at the Yearly-meeting at *London*.

He was a very diligent Attender, not only of Meetings for divine Worship, where he was particularly careful in observing the Hour appointed, but also of those for Discipline, and was scarce ever absent, (unless when engaged in travelling elsewhere on Truth's Service) from the Province and Quarterly-meetings, until disabled by Infirmity of Body.

He was a Man of good Understanding, though but little School Learning, of a sweet Temper, in Conversation pleasant and affable, an affectionate Husband and Father, a frequent and sympathizing Visiter of the Sick: He was a diligent and faithful Minister, and his Labours were often crowned with Success to the Convincement of many, some of whom proved serviceable and eminent in the Church, and to the Edification and Establishment of others.

In the Exercise of his Gift he was clear, solid and lively, even unto extream old Age. In Prayer, living, reverent, weighty and concise; in his Deportment, meek and humble, not elevated by his Gifts and good Services; a diligent Reader of the holy Scriptures, and, in his Preaching, a faithful Quoter of them; tender of the Glory of God, and of the Honour of our holy Principle.

He

He retained his Integrity, as well as Understanding and Memory, to the laſt. And expired the 7th of the Twelfth Month, and was buried in Friends Burying Place in *Dolphin's Barn-lane*, *Dublin*, the 10th of the ſame, in the Year 1742, being the Ninety firſt Year of his Age, and about the Sixty ſeventh of his Miniſtry.

A Teſtimony from the Quarterly - meeting of Birmingham, *concerning* ELIZABETH HANDS.

ELIZABETH HANDS, Wife of our worthy Friend *John Hands* of *Warwick*, was born on the 3d Day of the Third Month 1667. Her Father and Mother were both convinced of the bleſſed Truth when ſhe was very young; her Mother being ſoon removed by Death, her Father took Care to educate her in the Principles of Truth, which being attended with a ſteady walking in Faithfulneſs to the divine Diſcoveries made known to her, ſhe was well eſteemed when young.

In the Year 1687 ſhe was married to the aforeſaid *John Hands*; and in the Year 1705 ſhe came forth in publick Miniſtry; in which ſhe faithfully laboured, to the Exhortation, Edification and Comfort of the Church of Chriſt; and though ſhe had a large Family, was

was sometimes drawn forth, in the Love of Truth, to visit Friends in divers Parts of the Nation: And in her own Family was a good Example, not only of Frugality and Industry, for the Support of the same, as becomes the Professors of Truth, but also of Piety, Virtue and Zeal for the Promotion thereof. Her Stability, Patience and Chearfulness, in the closest Exercises and Trials, were very remarkable. She was a true Sympathizer with those in Afflictions, and often visited such, both among Friends and other Societies, to great Satisfaction and Comfort.

She was frequent in secret Retirement, and steady in waiting for the Renewal of Strength from above; examplary in diligently attending Meetings both for Worship and Discipline, in which she was not an indifferent or lukewarm, but a lively Member; and was often attended with Tokens of Fervency in Spirit, and of one travelling in the Deeps, even when bodily Weakness and Infirmities lay heavy upon her; which still encreasing, prevented her going much abroad for some considerable time before her last Ilness, which she bore, about two Weeks, with much Fortitude of Mind, and Resignation to the divine Will, and was gathered like a Shock of Corn in due Season; and is, we doubt not, entered into the Mansions of eternal Rest and Bliss.

She departed this Life the 2d Day of the Third Month 1743, and was interred, the 5th
of

of the same, in Friends Burying Ground in *Warwick*, in the Seventy sixth Year of her Age. A Minister about Thirty eight Years.

A Testimony from the Monthly-meeting of Kendal *in the County of* Westmorland, *concerning* WILLIAM WILLIAMSON.

HE was the Son of our Friends *Thomas* and *Agnes Williamson*, of *Bannerig* in the Parish of *Windermore*, and County of *Westmorland*; born the 7th of the Tenth Month 1684. His Parents were religious, and careful of his Education, which, through divine Aid, had that Effect on him, that as he grew in Years, he grew in Grace, and the saving Knowledge of our blessed Lord Jesus Christ; for, when but a Child, he witnessed the Influence of divine Virtue so to operate on his Mind, that about the Seventeenth Year of his Age, he came forth in a publick Testimony to the Truth, and laboured faithfully therein; travelling through *Cumberland* and *Scotland*, in Company with our Friend *Isaac Thompson*, in 1704; and, in the Years 1708 and 1709, with our Friend *Thomas Wilson*, visited the Western and Southern Parts of this Nation; frequently attending the Service of the National Meeeting.

He was an able Minister of the Gospel, and a worthy Elder in the Church; his Doctrine was sound and clear, distinguishing and dividing the Word aright, according to the various States of those to whom he had to minister. In Discipline he was strong and weighty, and in the Execution thereof impartial, which procured him considerable Regard in the Church. He abounded in Charity and Benevolence, not only to the Society, but his Neighbours and Acquaintance, to whom he was singularly useful in Advice, and very instrumental in helping to accommodate Differences, thereby preventing many injurious and litigious Law-suits.

He was devoted to serve the Church and his Neighbours, which gained him Esteem among all sorts of People; an excellent Example in a diligent Care to attend Meetings, both for Worship and Discipline, wherein he was grave and solid; and when concerned to speak in either, it was with Authority, his Words being seasoned with Grace.

In Conversation he was free and open, without Levity, which gained on all who had the Pleasure of being intimately acquainted with him; the Consideration whereof, renders our Loss the greater, and affects us with Sorrow, though not without Hope, being fully satisfied it is his eternal Gain: And therefore are engaged to travail in Soul, and breath forth earnest and strong Desires, that the great Lord

Lord of the Harveſt, who hath raiſed up and qualified many of our antient Worthies in their Day, to preach the everlaſting Goſpel, and promote good Order in the Churches, may raiſe up and qualify many more, to fill up the Places of thoſe who are gone to their Reſt; that the great Work of Reformation may ſtill be carried on, and Righteouſneſs be exalted and cover the Earth.

Our ſaid Friend was ſeized with *Stitches,* and a *Pain in his Breaſt,* in the Fifth Month laſt, which continued and increaſed on him, ſo that he gradually declined; and, being ſenſible that his Departure drew near, frequently expreſſed his Reſignation to the Divine Will; and that, *He found his Love to continue and remain as ſtrong to the Cauſe of Truth as ever;* in which he often deſired to be remembered to his Friends.

He departed this Life, in great Quietneſs, the 21ſt, and was interred in Friends Burying Ground at *Kendal* the 24th of the Ninth Month 1743, in the Fifty ninth Year of his Age, his Corps being attended by a great Concourſe, both of Friends and others, where ſeveral living Teſtimonies were born to the Truth, to the Information and Edification of many. And as he was generally reſpected, ſo the Loſs of him, as appeared by the Countenances of moſt preſent, was as generally lamented.

A Miniſter about Forty two Years.

A Testimony from the Monthly-meeting of Richmond *in* Yorkshire, *concerning* JOHN FOTHERGILL.

ALTHOUGH our dear and well esteemed Friend *John Fothergill*, removed himself and Family from within the Compass of our Monthly-meeting, about eight Years before his Decease, and that most of our ancient Friends, who were of the foremost Rank, and knew his Birth and Education, are removed; yet inasmuch as divers of us (though the greatest Part of a younger Generation) have been well acquainted with him for many Years, and favoured with sitting under many powerful and living Testimonies, delivered by him when amongst us, we have good reason to believe he was one whom the Lord, in his Wisdom, saw good to make use of for the Work of the Gospel, and fitted and qualified him by his holy Spirit, and called him forth, when but young, to publish the glad Tidings thereof in many Places; to which divine and inward Call and holy Requiring, he readily gave up, and answered in Obedience, and suffered not the Things of this World to take up his Mind and Time, but in true Fervency of Zeal, and Love for the Cause of God, he spent the Prime of his Time in visiting the Churches, when

and

and where he was pleafed to draw him ; and by his Faithfulnefs and unwearied Labours, he improved in his Gift, and grew eminent in his Service, and more and more in Favour with God, and efteemed by his People ; always having a Regard to the well approved Practice of duly acquainting his Friends, and having their Unity and Approbation made known by Certificate. And right careful he was to perform the Service required with as much Expedition as poffible, choofing rather to take Hardfhip to himfelf, than to be burthenfome to Friends.

And in the Procefs of Time, he was brought under an Engagement of Soul to vifit divers of the *American* Plantations ; which, through the Goodnefs and favourable Support of that divine Power which influenced his Heart, and required the Service, he was enabled to perform three feveral times ; and good reafon we have to believe, that in them all he difcharged himfelf honeftly ; his Chearfulnefs, and comfortable Accounts at his Returns, feemed to manifeft it fully.

He alfo found it his Concern to vifit Friends in *Scotland* and *Ireland* feveral times, and had good Service for the Lord.

His Teftimony was living and found, delivered in Demonftration of divine Authority ; for he handled not the Word deceitfully, nor endeavoured to pleafe itching Ears, or high and airy Difpofitions ; but like a fkilful Workman

man and true Servant of Jesus Christ, waited to be renewedly endowed with Power from on high, by which he was directed to divide the Word aright, and speak home to the States and Conditions of the People; whereby he approved himself faithful and just both to God and Man.

He was one that shewed his Moderation in using the Necessaries of Life, which, together with his Plainness, Humility and Sincerity, rendered his Ministry the more acceptable and convincing. He was a Man zealously concerned for good Order, and keeping up the Discipline of the Church, and had a good Understanding respecting the Management of its Affairs in our Monthly, Quarterly and Yearly-meetings; of all which, he was a diligent Attender when at home or in this Nation, and we believe had good Service therein. He was a Man kind and assisting to his Friends by good Admonition, &c. He was pleasant and helpful to his Neighbours when Occasion required; also a Man of Skill and Industry in managing his temporal Affairs for the Benefit of his Family, over which he had a true Paternal Care; so that it may well be said, he was a kind Husband, and tender Father. His Prudence and Discretion gained the Esteem of Persons of superior Stations in the World.

More might be added concerning the Goodness of God manifested to him in several Respects,

Respects, and his Faithfulness and Diligence in the Performance of the Work of his Day; but having nothing in View, but that his Memory may remain amongst the Righteous, for an Encouragement to Faithfulness, and that the worthy Name of the Almighty may be praised and magnified for ever and ever, shall conclude with Desires, that the great Lord of the Harvest may be pleased to raise up and send forth many more such faithful Labourers in his Power.

A Testimony from Knaresborough *Monthly-meeting, concerning* JOHN FOTHERGILL.

PRECIOUS in the Eyes of the Lord is the Death of his Saints, who are delivered from the Evils and Dangers of Mortality; and precious also, in the Eyes of his People, is the Remembrance of them, and of their Labours and Services for promoting the Good of Souls, and the shewing forth of the divine Glory; of which Number was our worthy and much esteemed Friend *John Fothergill,* who was religiously educated by his godly Parents; but in his early Years, being made sensible that neither Tradition, outward Regularity, nor any thing short of inward Purification of Soul and Spirit, would render him acceptable in the Sight of the Lord, he gave up his Heart to him, who, through the effectual

Operation of his divine Grace, baptized and gradually purified his Spirit, and prepared and qualified him to be an able Minister of the Gospel of Peace and Salvation, who could tell to others, what the Lord had done for his Soul; which he did with an holy Zeal and Fervour, becoming such as have a deep and weighty Sense of the Value of Souls, the Dangers and Snares they are environ'd with in this State of Probation, and the awful Majesty of the divine Being; by the blessed Teachings of whose holy Spirit, he grew in Experience in the Mysteries of the heavenly Kingdom; and also discovered the mysterious Workings of Satan in Opposition thereto: Thus qualified, he was frequently employed in detecting his Snares, in pointing out and directing to the Way that leads safely to eternal Rest. He was quick of Apprehension, and of an extensive Capacity and deep Judgment, and could express himself aptly and strongly. That holy Power which cut *Rahab*, and wounded the Dragon, made him, at times, as a sharp Sword against Hypocrisy and Wickedness, and those that held the Truth in Unrighteousness.

He was a near Sympathizer with the Afflicted, a steady Way-mark to those that were travelling towards *Sion*, having frequently suitable Advice and Consolation to administer unto such; so that he might be truly called a nursing Father over those he believed were born of God. He turned not his Back in the Day

Day of Battle; was a Son of Thunder, and
alfo of Confolation; had an awakening, living
and edifying Teftimony, wherein he laboured
diligently and faithfully, from his firft being
anointed in his young Years, to the Conclufion
of his Days.

He travelled much in this Nation in the
Service of the Gofpel, fometimes in *Scotland*,
feveral times in *Ireland* and *Wales*, and thrice
in *America*, to the Comfort and Edification of
the Church, leaving Seals of his Miniftry in
many Places; though in the latter Part of his
time attended with great bodily Afflictions,
under which he vifited feveral Places in this
Nation.

He was indeed a Man remarkably qualified
and furnifhed, both for Church Difcipline and
the preaching of the everlafting glorious Gofpel; and of very peculiar Service in Monthly,
Quarterly, and General-meetings, wherein he
approved himfelf a wife and able Counfellor,
and was alfo a diligent Attender of the fame.
He was exemplary in Converfation, Plainnefs,
Temperance, Vigilance and Fortitude, endur-
ing Afflictions, doing the Work of an Evan-
gelift, making full Proof of his Miniftry, being a Workman that needed not to be afhamed,
rightly dividing the Word of Truth. In fhort,
he was a fincere hearted *Chriftian*, a living
Minifter, a faithful Friend, a loving Hufband,
an affectionate Father; and it is our Faith and
firm Belief, he died in the Lord, hath refted
from

from his Labours, and his Works do follow him, who being dead yet speaketh.

He departed this Life at *Knaresborough* aforesaid, the 13th of the Eleventh Month 1744, and was honourable buried in Friends Burying Ground at *Scotten*, near the said Town, the 15th of the same. Aged Sixty nine Years, having been a Minister near Fifty Years.

A Testimony from the Monthly-meeting of Norwich, *concerning* THOMAS WHITE.

HE was born, in or about the Year 1676, in this City. His Parents being of the Church of *England*, educated him in that Way; but as he grew up to Man's Estate, finding still a Want in himself, and a Desire after a nearer Acquaintance with God, his Mind was disposed to look into several religious Societies, and at length became convinced of the Truth.

After some time, having walked in an exemplary manner, it pleased God to give him a Dispensation of the Gospel to preach, and indeed he became excellently gifted; and what made him appear the more so, his Education was so low, that he could scarcely read; yet he afterwards attained to a great Knowledge of the Scriptures; and this, accompanied with sound Judgment, and a good Experience of

God's

God's Dealings with his Soul, made him eminently ferviceable in the Church, to the building up of many in the moft holy Faith, and likewife in convincing feveral; fo that many were the Seals of his Miniftry. And we have to fay of him, that he was a faithful Labourer, whilft his Strength remained, in the Caufe of God, nothing delighting him more than the Profperity of Truth, and beholding the Children of Friends coming up in the Nobility thereof; to whom he was often drawn forth in a very affectionate manner, both in our publick Meetings, and in private Converfation.

When he faw any running out into fuch Liberties as our holy Profeffion did not allow of, being afhamed of the Plainnefs and Simplicity thereof, and thereby fhunning the Crofs, he would labour with fuch in great Love and Affection, that they might fee their Miftake, and the Tendency thereof.

He was zealoufly concerned, that Love and Unity might be preferved amongft us, and that Friends would watch againft every thing that might have a Tendency to the contrary, knowing our Strength is therein; and fo far as that Knot becomes loofed, fo far we become weakened: To the laft of his Minifterial Service he was very preffing thereunto, and that all might be concerned to end where they began, *in Love*.

He

He was often drawn forth to visit the Churches in this Nation, and once through *Scotland*, in Company with our dear Friend *Isaac Pickerell*; he also visited the Meetings of Friends in *Wales*; in all which Places, we have reason to believe, from the Accounts received, his Labours were both acceptable and serviceable.

He was always careful, before he undertook any Journey, to have his Affairs in good Order at home, that every Thing in that Respect might be savoury and of good Report amongst his Neighbours; and when his Service was over, he hasted back to his Family again, and applied himself with great Industry for the Support thereof.

Some few Years before he died, a very close Trial befel him in his own Family, which much affected his Spirits; and though Friends were very tenderly concerned for him, and that he might be preserved in his Service as before, yet his Weakness rather increased, till his Health became very much impaired, and his Understanding weakened; so that we suffered the Loss of him in our Meetings some time before his Death, of which we were very sensible.

His last Ilness was short; an Alteration appearing, that threatened his Dissolution, on the 26th of the Eleventh Month 1744, and the Night following he breathed his last. And we are well satisfied he now enjoys the Reward
of

of his faithful Labours, his Soul being at Peace with God in his Kingdom, where the Righteous rest, and Sorrowing is no more.

Aged about Sixty nine, a Minister upwards of Forty Years.

A Testimony from the Monthly - meeting of Gisborough *in* Yorkshire, *concerning* MARY SNOWDEN.

SHE was a Woman of a tender and affectionate Spirit, much given to Hospitality ; charitably disposed to the Poor ; often visiting and sympathizing with those under Affliction ; and was industrious to keep up good Order in the Church, amongst her own Sex, often shewing her Dislike of *Self-righteousness* in religious Performances.

In the Ministry she was not large, yet sound and edifying ; not being forward to appear in a publick Way, but waiting till she found herself under a Necessity.

In her last Illness, which was long and tedious, she was deprived of the Use of her Limbs for a considerable time, and attended with great Pain and inward Weakness, yet she behaved with much *Christian* Patience ; often gave good Advice to Friends and others, and was many times favoured with divine Consolation,

tion, which was her greatest Support in times of Distress.

Near the time of her Departure, being in full Resignation and Tranquility of Mind, she expressed, in much Sweetness, a great Regard *for the Prosperity of Truth*; and seemed to be satisfied, *it would yet stand, though some of its Professors were in a declining Way* : And added, *I am now in some measure favoured with a Taste of eternal Joys; and whether Life or Death, it will be well* ; with many more Heavenly Expressions. So we are induced to believe, she had a firm Hope of a glorious Change, and is now at Rest with the Lord.

She died on the 10th of the Sixth Month 1745, and was decently buried in Friends Burying Ground at *Kirkby-moor-side*, in the Fifty seventh Year of her Age. A Minister about Twenty Years.

A Testimony

A Testimony from the Monthly - meeting of Brighouse *in* Yorkshire, *concerning* TABITHA HORNOR.

OUR dear and worthy Friend *Tabitha Hornor*, was Daughter of the late *Benjamin Hornor* of *Leeds*, Merchant, and *Christiana* his Wife, by whom she was favoured with a religious Education; during which, it soon appeared that she was endowed with an extraordinary Capacity, and in a short time, made considerable Advances in sundry Parts of useful Learning; which Abilities, in process of time, were greatly improved by the blessed Work of Religion upon her Mind; having in her early Days embraced the Tenders of divine Love, and undergone sundry Dispensations of Almighty God, in order for her farther Growth and Experience in the great Mystery of Godliness, she became well qualified to perform the great and good Work whereunto she was called.

About the Year 1722, she was first engaged in the Work of the Ministry, wherein she soon approved herself a Workwoman that needed not to be ashamed, and laboured amongst us with considerable Openness and Acceptance. And as she increased in the Gift, by the Increase of God, she became a living and

and powerful Inftrument, and was often called forth to vifit the Churches; once in *Ireland*, once into *Scotland*, twice in *Wales*, and feveral times through moft Parts of this Nation. In all which, we have good reafon to believe her Miniftry was well received, being in the Demonftration of the Power and Spirit of our Lord and Saviour Jefus Chrift, and often had its intended Effect: The Gainfayers were reproved, the Carelefs and Negligent admonifhed, the Babes replenifhed, and the Weak confirmed: For indeed the Spirit of the Lord God was renewedly upon her, and fhe was gracioufly anointed to preach the Gofpel to the Poor.

Nor was this her only Province in the Church, being fingularly ferviceable in the Preparitive, Monthly and Quarterly Womens Meetings; in which fhe laboured to promote good Order, with a Difpofition truly *Chriftian*, which rendered her Services therein not only acceptable, but oftentimes effectual.

Her private Life was fo worthy of Imitation, that fhould we take no Notice of it, we fhould be wanting to Friendfhip and Gratitude. She was affectionately dutiful to her Parents, a kind and fympathizing Sifter, and particularly ferviceable in managing fundry Affairs which, after her Father's and Brother's Deceafe, principally fell to her fhare. In Friendfhip fhe was warm and fincere; and as fhe was juftly prudent in the Choice of her Intimates, held

the

the Unity in the one Spirit. She was not only capable to advife in difficult Cafes, but ready to affift when fhe found it neceffary; and very liberal to the Poor: All which, with a prudent and virtuous Life and Converfation, did not a little inforce her many great and publick Services.

We cannot therefore avoid being deeply affected with the Lofs we, in particular, and the Church in general, have fuftained, humbly imploring Almighty God, the great Lord and Mafter of our Affemblies, to raife up and qualify many more fuch able and faithful Inftruments, for the Honour of his Name, and a Bleffing to his Church; that all in the End might receive the welcome Commendation of *well done*, and become intituled to a Crown of immortal Glory, as we doubt not, but this our dear and worthy Friend is called hence to inherit.

She departed this Life the 16th of the Twelfth Month 1746, and was buried in Friends Burying Ground in *Meadow-lane, Leeds*, the 19th of the fame, whither her Remains were accompanied by a great Number of Friends and others; and after the Interment a Meeting was held, which was very large, and attended with a Stilnefs and Gravity well becoming the Solemnity of the Occafion, and feveral Teftimonies born to general Satisfaction.

Aged near Fifty two, a Minifter about Twenty four Years.

A Testimony from the Monthly-meeting of Brigflats *in* Sedbergh, *concerning* CHRISTOPHER MASON.

HE was born in the Parish of *Sedbergh*, and County of *York*, descended of honest religious Parents, who carefully educated him in the Way of Truth; and as he grew in Years he grew in Grace, being obedient thereto, by which his Understanding was opened and enlarged; and about the Twenty fifth Year of his Age he appeared in a publick Testimony, to his Friends Satisfaction; and often visited Friends in the said County, as also several adjacent Counties.

His Ministry was fresh and living, and well esteemed where he travelled. He was a Pattern of great Humility, and adorned his Testimony with an holy self-denying Life and Conversation; of a meek and quiet Spirit, labouring much to promote Peace in the Churches of Christ; extensive in Charity, yet far from countenancing undue Liberty in any; constant in attending First and Week-day Meetings; often saying, *that to feel the Enjoyment of the Lord's good Presence, was his greatest Delight.*

He often visited his Friends and Neighbours in Affliction, and was of great Strength and Encouragement to such as were ready to droop under

under their Troubles, having passed through many himself. It may well be said, he was strong in true Faith; for though his Circumstance was narrow, as to the Things of this Life, he would often say, *I have enough, and shall never want.* His great and constant Care was for Heavenly Treasure; and he had as much of the Treasure of this World as gave him full Content in that Respect; for which he was thankful to God the Fountain of all his Mercies.

A Testimony from the Quarterly - meeting of Stourbridge *in the County of* Worcester, *concerning* HENRY PAYTON.

HE was born in the Town of *Dudley*, in the County of *Worcester*, and educated according to our Principles, his Father being a publick Friend. He was early visited of the Lord, and faithfully gave up to bear a Testimony for his Truth, dedicating the Flower of his Age to the Service of God and his Church.

He was endowed with a good natural Capacity; and, by the supernatural Illumination of the divine Spirit in his Soul, became an able Minister of the Word of Life. He travelled much in his younger Years, visiting Meetings in this Kingdom, as also in *Scotland, Ireland,* and the *American* Plantations, with the Unity and

Approbation of Friends here; and what he had to deliver was well accepted, his Conduct corresponding with his Preaching.

In his Conversation he was rather reserved than talkative; and, in Proportion to his Ability, extensively charitable to the Necessitous, whether Friends or others. He was an affectionate Husband, a tender Father, a good Neighbour, and a sincere and valuable Friend. And though in his latter Years he was much afflicted with bodily Infirmities, so that his publick Service in the Church was thereby prevented, yet he retained his Integrity to his Maker to the last; and would often exhort his Family, above all Things, *strictly to regard the internal Dictates of the Divine Monitor, which can never be removed into a Corner; which would be a Guide to them in all the Duties of their several Stations:* And then, *to observe all the good Orders established in our Society; by which they would come to enjoy that Peace and Serenity of Mind which the Righteous possess, in this present Life, as an Earnest of that eternal Felicity, which the great Lord and Governor of the World hath prepared for all them who truly love and fear him.*

Much more might be related of this our worthy Friend, but we rather chuse Brevity, and only further inform you, that he departed this Life, in a quiet resigned Frame of Spirit, the 29th of the Seventh Month 1746, aged near Seventy five Years. His Body was interred

in

in Friends Burying Ground in *Dudley*, the 1ft of the Eighth Month, being attended by a great Number of Friends and others, when divers living Teftimonies were delivered.

A Teftimony from the Monthly-meeting in Monmouthfhire, *concerning* EVAN BEVAN.

Mark the perfect Man, and behold the Upright, for the End of that Man is Peace. Pfal. xxxvii. 37.

THE 17th Day of the Second Month 1746, departed this Life our dear, worthy, innocent Friend, Minifter and Elder, *Evan Bevan*, aged about Sixty feven Years. His Father's Name was *Charles Bevan*, of *Lantwit Vardre* in *Glamorganfhire*, who gave him a liberal Education at *Oxford*, where he made a great Progrefs in various Parts of Literature.

After he left *Oxford*, being duly qualified, he practifed the Law in *Glamorganfhire*, where he ferved and executed the Office of Deputy-Sheriff with much Reputation; yet, after fome time, it pleafed Divine Providence to vifit our faid Friend in an extraordinary manner, he being caft down, as into the Deep, in Anguifh and Sorrow, until after long Mourning and various Baptizings, the Lord was pleafed in Mercy to bind up the bruifed Reed with Strength,

Strength, so that he seemed to be brought forth pure as Gold seven times refined, and made a chosen Vessel. And finding Unity in his Spirit with those of the Society called *Quakers*, he joined himself in Fellowship with them; as appears more fully by an Epistle of his, published in *Sewel*'s History of the *Quakers*, page 705, under the Name of *Evan Jevens*.

He was concerned as a Minister about Twenty Years, not made so by Man, altho' he was brought up in the Languages and Sciences of Men, but by a real Experience of the Power of Truth, and through the Demonstration of the Gospel.

Oh! in what an awful weighty Frame of Mind we have seen him sit in Meetings, solidly feeding on the Bread of Life, which the World knows not of; and when Words flowed from his Lips, they were sweet as the Honey-comb, and seasoned with the divine Salt; which, with his innocent Deportment, affected the Hearts of the Hearers, unless grown cold through the Love of the World.

He was pressing with Friends, *to be faithful towards God, in the various Branches of our* Christian *Testimony*; especially, *to keep clear from that* Antichristian *Yoke of Tithes; the upholding whereof, is an indirect Denial of the Coming of our Lord and Saviour Jesus Christ, who, by the one acceptable Sacrifice of the offering himself upon the Cross, made Atonement to God*

the

the Father, brought Mankind from under the Law, and put an End thereto, with all Types and Shadows. He would often remind Friends to be thankful to God, for the manifold Mercies received and enjoyed; more especially in this time of our uninterrupted meeting together, *in* order to perform divine *Worſhip*; and likewiſe, to conſider what *Hardſhips and Sufferings* our worthy *Antients* were expoſed to on this *Account.*

His Words were few and ſavoury, his Teſtimony ſhort; which was a Wonder to ſuch as knew him, and expected long Diſcourſes, and eloquent Orations; yet he, through divine Aſſiſtance, confounded the Wiſdom of the Wiſe of this World, who therein know not God. He would moſt Nights wait in ſilence, together with his Family, and the Scholars who lodged with him, and would adviſe them to that Practice, laying before them *the Benefit thence accruing.*

He kept a School in Friends Meeting-houſe in *Pontimoyle,* for about Thirty five Years, and conſcientiouſly refuſed to teach any of the *Heathen* Authors; however, he brought up many in the uſeful Parts of Literature, as *Latin, Greek,* and *Geography,* with various Branches of the *Mathematicks*; moſt of which time he was Clerk to our Meeting, and was a tender nurſing Father in *Iſrael*; very condeſcending and forbearing with thoſe who, by undue Meaſures, had juſtly deſerved the Cenſures of the Church. Sometimes his mild

Behaviour has reached and convinced the Difobedient, and brought them to a Sense of their Out-goings.

We do not remember, that he mist the Opportunity of one Meeting, unless through Sickness. He had a great Love for Friends, and would visit those who were indisposed. We had intire Love and Goodwill to him, as a cordial, sincere Friend, and as an Elder and Pillar in the Church, who was worthy of double Honour. His Memory is dear to us, and, being dead, he yet speaketh. He did not lord it over the Church, although his Knowledge and Wisdom, both spiritual and natural, might have entituled him to bear rule; but being clothed with the Spirit of Meekness and Patience, he would condescend to the weakest Member, in Charity, Goodwill and pure Love; thereby plainly demonstrating whose Disciple he was: Yea, a noble Pattern and Example was he: His Conduct kept pace with his Doctrine, and with the Principles he made a Profession of. He was no Respecter of Persons, yet his Conversation was free and agreeable, chiefly tending to Instruction and Edification.

He having denied himself, and taken up the Cross, to the Riches, Honours and Preferments of this World, with the Pomps and Pleasures thereof, despised the Shame, looking forward, in Patience, to the Prize of the high Calling in Christ Jesus, which is the Recompence of Reward; in Hope of which, the humble contrite

contrite Soul is enabled to perfevere in Fear unto the End.

We queftion not, but our Lofs is his great Gain; and that now his Spirit enjoys the Crown of Reft and Peace, which is laid up in ftore for the Righteous in the Manfions of Glory, where there needs not the Light of the Sun or Moon, for the Glory of God is the Light thereof.

His Body was interred in Friends Burying Ground at *Pontimoyle*, and was attended to the Grave with Decency and Gravity, by a great Number of moft Perfwafions and Degrees.

A Teftimony from the Yearly-meeting at Aberdeen, *concerning* ROBERT BARCLAY.

ROBERT BARCLAY, of *Ury*, eldeft Son of the Author of the APOLOGY, was born at *Aberdeen* the 25th of the Firft Month 1672.

As he had the Advantage of the Precepts and Example of his worthy Father and Mother, as well as that of his Grand-father, fo it made a fenfible Impreflion upon him, in his early Years, much to their Comfort. He was fcarce out of his Infancy, when he difcovered an Heart devoted to Religion. After he had been a while educated at home, in the Eleventh Year of his Age he accompanied his

Parents

Parents to *London*, where he became acquainted with *George Fox*, and other eminent Friends, who rejoiced to see so hopeful an Appearance in the Son of so worthy and honourable a Father. He was, at that time, left to the Tuition of *George Keith*, to be educated with him at his School at *Theobalds*, where he remained about a Year, and then returned to *Scotland*.

In his Sixteenth Year, he went again with his Father to *London*: Having been a considerable time at *Windsor*, at the King's Court, where, on Account of his Father's Interest, which created many Dependents, he was much caressed; yet then, as well as through his whole Life, his Conversation was clean and void of Offence; and he may be truly said, *to have remembered his Creator in the Days of his Youth*.

It was especially observed, after his Father's Death, that as he grew in Years, he dedicated himself more particularly to the great Work of Religion; which Concern ever remained with him.

About the Twenty second Year of his Age, his Mouth was opened in a publick Manner to praise his Maker, and to preach the everlasting Gospel; which he continued to do to the End of his Time, being upwards of Seventy five Years old.

As he had a serious and living Sense of Religion, so he laboured to propagate the same

in

in others; and his humble, meek Behaviour, his remarkable Charity to the Poor, and other amiable Qualities, corresponded well with his Doctrine. His Testimonies were not tedious to the Hearers, nor unseasonably delivered; what he said, being the Effect of his Duty, knowing he was answerable for the Talents received.

He often visited Friends in *London*, and several Parts of *England* and *Scotland*: Once he went with *Andrew Jaffray*, by *Inverness*, to the *High-lands*, having Meetings as they passed along, where no Friends had ever been before. He never flinched from what he was convinced was his Duty; particularly, at the publick Meeting-place of the Parish where he lived in, where he was concerned, *to warn the People to come out of their Forms, and turn to Jesus Christ, whom, if they did look unto in Faith, they should as certainly be healed, as those of old were, who looked in Faith towards the brazen Serpent which* Moses *caused to be lifted up in the Wilderness.*

In the Year 1708, one *Garden*, a learned and much followed Preacher at *Aberdeen*, tainted with *Bourignonism*, having in his Writings inveighed against Friends Principles, *Robert Barclay* wrote a notable Answer, intituled, *A serious Address to the well-meaning Followers of* ANTONIA BOURIGNON; which had so good an Effect, being printed and dispersed among a great many, that the Sect afterward dwindled much away.

About

About the Seventieth Year of his Age, he wrote a small Treatise concerning FAITH; and after his Death there was found about a Sheet of Paper, wrote with his own Hand, upon CHARITY. It was thought his Sickness prevented his enlarging upon so good a Subject; for about two Years ago he contracted a Weakness, from which he never quite recover'd; though, when he was able, was diligent in visiting the Meetings of Friends, in the adjacent Places, and in a sincere meek Frame of Mind waited for his Change; and when much afflicted with Sickness, he used to repeat,—*Not his, but the Lord's Will be done in every Thing:* And a short Space before he was Speechless, one standing by his Bedside whispered to another, thinking he had not heard it, that *she was surprised to feel such a Sweat upon him;* he answered, as with a strong Voice, *This is the Sweat that comes before Death; and I shall now soon be among the Spirits of just Men made perfect.* Which was among the last of his Expressions; for he afterwards slept away, and expired about the seventh Hour in the Morning of the 27th of the First Month, at his House of *Springhall*, and was interred on the 1st of the Second Month 1747, in the Family's Burying Place, in the Presence of most Friends in the North of this Kingdom, with several of the Gentry who were his Relations, and also his own Tenants, in the plain decent Manner he himself prescribed.

A Testimony

A Testimony from the Monthly-meeting of Leominster in Herefordshire, *concerning* WILLIAM OSBORN.

HAVING a Concern to say something in remembrance of our worthy deceased Friend and Elder, *William Osborn,* we hope it will be edifying to others, as he was well known to be a sound and powerful Gospel Minister; and so careful not to move without, or exceed his Commission, as rendered him truly a good Example.

He was also of such an exemplary, sweet, inoffensive and self-denying Life, as demonstrated him to be a true Follower of the holy Lamb of God; and made an intimate Acquaintance with him very pleasant, as several of us can witness; to whom, in his last Ilness, he spoke very incouragingly *of the Goodness of God,* and expressed a particular Satisfaction in bearing a faithful Testimony *against the Payment of Tithes*; on which Account he had been a great Sufferer.

He is, we doubt not, entered into eternal Rest with the Blessed, and his Memory remains dear to us. He departed this Life the 15th of the Eighth Month 1747. Aged about Seventy eight, a Minister upwards of Forty Years.

A Testimony

A Testimony from the Monthly-meeting of Hitchin *in the County of* Hertford, *concerning* MARY RANSOM.

WE think it incumbent on us to give in this Testimony concerning our dear and worthy Friend *Mary Ransom* of *Hitchin*, deceased, who was educated, and rested in the meer Profession of the Truth, till about the Twenty first Year of her Age; when it pleased the Lord to awaken her by the powerful Visitation of his Love, by which she became inwardly convinced of Sin, feeling the Terrors of the Lord for it; and being made sensible that the Axe must be laid to the Root of the corrupt Tree, and that every Plant, which was not of the Heavenly Father's planting, must be rooted up, became willing, in the Day of his Power, to deny herself of those captivating Baits of youthful Pleasure and Vanity, which had before but too far betrayed her, into a Conformity to the vain Customs and Fashions of this present evil World.

But when it pleased God to reveal his Son in her, and to give her an effectual Touch and Call by his Grace, she plainly saw, no Fig-leave Covering of a formal Profession, no Excuse nor Delay, no Reasoning with Flesh and Blood, would avail in his Sight, before whom all
Things

Things are open and naked, who is a jealous God, and will not admit of any Rival in the Minds of his Servants; so that being brought into the Obedience of the Cross, she knew it to be an acceptable Time, and a Day of Salvation to her Soul; so that those Things which had been taking to the natural Part, now became to her as Dross and Dung, that she might win Christ, and be espoused to him, the Bridegroom of her Soul, in the Covenant of Life and Peace. And as the Lord was thus pleased to reach and visit her, in her young and tender Years, it appeared by her future Progress, that the Grace of God was not bestowed on her in vain; for as she was faithful in the little received, it was blessed with an heavenly Increase; so that having her Candle lighted, her House swept and set in order, she was then able to call to others to rejoice with her, saying, *Come and feel the Weight of that Power, and see that Light that has shewed me all that ever I have done, is not this the Christ?*

She soon became skilful in the Word of Righteousness, and an able Minister of the everlasting Gospel; being of strong natural Faculties, and these truly sanctified by the Heavenly Gift, render'd her Ministry the more acceptable. Her Ministry was plain and powerful, and had often a very great Reach on the Meeting, and tended very much to gather the Minds of People to the Gift of God in themselves.

She

She had a Gift of Discerning surpassing many; so that the Wolf in Sheep's Clothing scarcely escaped when it came in her Way; which was manifested by her reprehending and detecting many Impostors, in the Authority of the Truth.

She travelled in the Labour of the Gospel, when young, into the North of *England* and *Scotland*; also into the West and Eastern Parts of this Nation, and into divers adjacent Counties; and often to the City of *London*: In which Visits we believe she had good Service.

She was an excellent Example in attending Meetings for Worship, both on First and other Days, and a diligent Promoter of wholsome Discipline and good Order in the Church; for which she had a peculiar Talent; being as careful to prevent Differences, as she was to heal and compose them. She was valiant for the Truth upon Earth, and not afraid to face its Enemies; yet although she was bold in the Lord's Cause, in this she manifested herself a Disciple of Jesus, in that she was clothed with a meek and quiet Spirit.

She has often refreshed the Lord's Servants in their Travels, being always desirous, in Concurrence with her Husband, to entertain Strangers, and always to assist and help them.

She was an affectionate Wife, a loving Mother, and a kind Neighbour; so that her Removal will be sensibly felt by many, in whose whofe Minds her Memory is fweet, and her Teftimony ftill lives.

Towards the latter Part of her time, fhe laboured under many Infirmities and great Afflictions of Body, which fhe bore with a becoming Refignation of Mind; often commemorating the Goodnefs and Mercy of God to her in her young Years, and continued to her till the Decline of Life; expreffing her great Satisfaction, *that fhe had done her Day's Work in the Day time.* So quietly departed this Life in Peace with the Lord, and in Unity with his People, the 4th Day of the Tenth Month 1747, and was buried in Friends Burial Ground at *Hitchin* the 9th Day following. Aged about Sixty five, a Minifter about Forty Years.

The Teftimony from the Monthly - meeting of Edenderry *in* Ireland, *concerning* MONGO BEWLEY.

A Teftimony lives in our Hearts, to the Memory of this faithful Elder and Minifter of Chrift, his Removal being a great Lofs to the Church in general, and to us in particular; having devoted himfelf to the Service of Chrift our Lord, leaving all for his fake when called thereto, and freely giving up
himfelf

himself to spend and be spent for the Promotion of Piety in the Earth.

He was Son of *Thomas* and *Margaret Bewley*, of *Woodhall* in *Cumberland*; born the 3d of the Fourth Month 1677. He was favoured in his young Years with a tender Visitation of the Love of God: And so great became his Concern to get out to Week-day Meetings, that we find, among his Papers, one which was written by him, in the time of his Apprenticeship, to his Master; earnestly requesting, *either to know his Work, that he might make Preparation against the Meeting-time, or be allowed to pay for the Time, after his Apprenticeship expired.*

He came over into this Nation, and settled within the Compass of this Meeting; and as he farther grew in the saving Knowledge of the Truth, he received a Dispensation of the Gospel, not long after his coming hither, whereof he became a living and powerful Minister; being made instrumental to the Exaltation of the Testimony of Truth, the Honour of his great Lord, the Edification of his Church and Heritage, the tendering of the Spirits of the Honest-hearted; and many times, with consolating Sweetness, to the reviving and healing the afflicted and wounded in Spirit.

He was diligent in attending Meetings for Worship and Discipline, at home and abroad; and concerned, that others might be so too;
often

often lamenting the Lukewarmnefs of fuch as could neglect this Duty, and that declined a due Attendance of Week-day Meetings.

He feveral times croffed the Sea, to vifit Friends in *England*, *Scotland* and *Wales*; once to *Holland*, and once to *America* ; in which latter Journey he was abroad about two Years, and wherein we find, by Accounts from feveral Parts of that Continent, he had good Service for the Lord, and was very acceptable to Friends, and left a good Savour behind him, both in his Miniftry and Conduct. For indeed we may fay, his grave, folid, weighty Behaviour, adorned his Miniftry.

He always travelled in Truth's Service with the Unity and Approbation of Friends ; and was careful, when abroad, not to make the Gofpel chargeable or burthenfome ; nor to over-ftay the time of his Service. And, when at home, was induftrious and careful in Bufinefs ; wherein the Lord profpered his Undertakings, and enabled him, not only to provide plentifully for his Family, but alfo to do Good in his Neighbourhood, and gain Efteem by his confcientious and upright Dealings in Commerce and Converfe. Thus he preached well at home divers Ways. He was careful to train up his Children in the Nurture and Admonition of the Lord ; and was of good Service in vifiting the Families of Friends, wherein he was often drawn forth in great Love, particularly to the Youth, to exhort and encourage them *to make choice of that good Part, which would be an everlasting Portion to them who retain it to the End.*

He was helpful to Friends in this Nation, in the Discipline of the Church; for which Service he was well qualified, and furnished with a good Understanding and sound Judgment, being also zealous for good Order, the Peace of the Church, and maintaining the Testimony of Truth, against wrong Things and undue Liberty; having often a Word of Advice and Counsel, pertinent and suitable to the Matter, in the Authority of Truth, to deliver in those Meetings; wherein he seemed in his elder Years, to be somewhat of an Awe and Check on forward Spirits, but an Encourager of that which was of the right Birth.

He was of a noble Mind and chearful Disposition; pleasant and edifying in Conversation; liberal and open-hearted to Friends and others; a tender Sympathizer with the Afflicted, the Widows and Fatherless; a nursing Father to young Travellers in the Way to *Sion*; yet not hasty to lay Hands on those *who were more in Shew than Substance*, being endued in a good degree with the Spirit of Discerning. He was a Man of Integrity and Firmness, like a fixed Pillar; deliberate and careful in forming a Judgment of Things that concerned the Good of the Society, and not apt to be tossed to and fro, or easily turned aside therein; and yet we have particularly to remark, that he

was

was an humble-minded Man, often fignifying his own Fears refpecting himfelf, and his earneft Defire, *that he might hold out to the End; and that he might not die, or decay, as to the Truth, in old Age.* And we have no Doubt of his Defire being anfwered, for his Candle burned bright to the laft ; being very fweet and lively in his Teftimony in our Week-day Meeting, the Day before he took his laft Ilnefs, which held not quite three Days, wherein he departed quietly out of this Life, and, we doubt not, is entered into the Habitation of the Righteous, there to fing high Praifes to the Lord God and the Lamb, who is worthy for ever.

He departed this Life the 3d of the Third Month 1747, and was buried in Friends Burying Ground near *Edenderry*, accompanied both by his Neighbours and Friends, from many Parts of *Linfter* Province, the 6th of the faid Month. In the Seventieth Year of his Age, having been a Minifter about Forty Years.

A Testimony from the Monthly-meeting of Colchester *in the County of* Essex, *concerning* Elizabeth Dennis.

ELIZABETH DENNIS, of *Layer-Bretton*, near *Colchester*, was descended from honest Parents. She was visited in the early Part of her time, and made willing to bend to the powerful Work of the Cross of Christ, when she was very young; by Virtue whereof, she came to be so fitted and prepared, as to be made a Vessel fit for the Use of him who had visited her.

About the Twentieth Year of her Age, it pleased the Lord to call her to the Work of the Ministry; to which Call she gave up in Faithfulness, and discharged herself of the Talent committed to her Trust, in the Innocency and Simplicity of the Truth, to the Edification and Comfort of many, and to the stirring up of some who were negligent.

She travelled several times through the Western and Northern Parts of this Nation, as well as the Counties adjacent; and once through *Scotland*, as far as is inhabited by Friends; in all which her Travels she was very diligent in hasting forward, with as much Speed as possible, notwithstanding she was attended with much bodily Weakness; and
great

great was her Care, that she might not make the Gospel chargeable.

She was innocent and inoffensive in her Conversation, and had but low and mean Thoughts of herself; by reason of both which Qualifications, she gain'd the Favour of many, and had a great place in the Hearts of honest-minded Friends.

She was an Example of Plainness and Humility, as also of Frugality and Industry; when at home in her Business, using Diligence, both early and late, that she might have wherewith, by the Work of her own Hands, to administer to her own Necessities, and not be burthensome to any: And although her Income, by her Labour, was but small, yet would she cast in her Mite, according to her Ability, for the Relief of others, and was a constant Attender of the Meetings settled for that Purpose. And although her Company was much desired by many, yet she could not be free to leave her own home, unless of Necessity, either to visit the Churches, or upon the Account of her Business.

Towards the latter Part of her time, she was seized with the *Palsey*, losing wholly the Use of one Side, and her Speech in great measure, and was a great Part of her Time confined to her Bed; yet notwithstanding her Confinement and Pain was hard to bear, she was supported and carried through it with *Christian* Patience and Resignation; although she could not, sometimes, but earnestly desire to *be removed hence from her painful Afflictions;* yet *willing to submit to the Will of the Almighty.*

She departed this Life, in a quiet Frame of Spirit, the 3d of the Third Month 1748, and was buried the 8th of the same, in Friends Burying Ground at *Coptford.* Aged upwards of Sixty three, a Minister Forty three Years

---

A Testimony from the Monthly - meeting of Oustwick *in* Yorkshire, *concerning* THOMAS SMITH.

THIS our dear Friend was born at *Groundhill-house,* in the Parish of *Oldborough,* a Place within the Compass of this Meeting, on the 27th of the Sixth Month 1670, and died at *Owstwick* the 2d of the Second Month 1749, and was buried the 3d of the same, in Friends Burying Ground at *Owstwick,* aged Seventy eight Years, seven Months and three Weeks.

He was descended from believing Parents, had a religious Education, and was, we believe, from his Childhood, inclined to that which is good; and in due time it pleased the Almighty, in his great Love to Mankind, to fit and qualify him for the Work of the Ministry, in which he laboured diligently, and, we believe faithfully, according to the Gift received,

for

for the laſt.Twenty ſeven Years of his Life; and was often made inſtrumental in ſtirring up the pure Gift in many, and had frequently a Word of Encouragement to all thoſe whoſe Faces were turned *Sion*-ward, adviſing them to Faithfulneſs and Perſeverance, wherein their Reward would be ſure. He was alſo compaſſionately tender, and frequently concerned to call to the backward and backſliding Ones to repent, ſhewing them the Neceſſity of Regeneration, and the abſolute Need of Holineſs, without which, none ſhall ſee God to their Comfort: And it may, with great Juſtice be ſaid of him, he was an Ornament to his Profeſſion; being particularly concerned to adorn his Doctrine by a true *Chriſtian* Converſation, wherein he did ſhine more conſpicuouſly than in Words: His Doctrine was ſound, tender, and to Edification. Much more might be wrote on his Behalf, but as we don't deſire to write long Encomiums, ſhall only add, he was a tender Father, a very affectionate Huſband, and kind Friend; and in his Dealings amongſt Men remarkably juſt. To thoſe in Diſtreſs very humane; one of the beſt of Neighbours; and in all Things ſeem'd to do as he would have others do to him.

Some Account of the Sickness and Death of THOMAS SMITH, *with some of his Expressions in the Time of his Ilness.*

"IN the latter Part of his time, he often
" laboured under divers bodily Infirmities,
" and was sometimes afflicted with the *Stone*
" or *Gravel*; and on the 21st of the First
" Month 1748, in the Evening, had a Fit of
" an *Ague*, and about Midnight was seized
" with an entire Stoppage of Urine, which,
" notwithstanding he had the Advice of a
" Physician, continued till he died, being
" above eleven Days; in all which time
" he was endued with singular Patience, to
" undergo so great Affliction, *in a State of*
" *Contentment and Resignation to the divine*
" *Will*, as he divers times expressed to those
" about him.

" On the first Day of his Ilness, to a Friend
" who sat by him, he signified, that *He was*
" *under great Affliction ; and if it were the*
" *Lord's Will to remove him by it, he was well*
" *content, having not been short in plainly ad-*
" *vising and warning those he had been among;*
" *that as the Lord had in some degree made*
" *him as a Watchman, he had faithfully dis-*
" *charged his Trust therein, and had then Peace*
" *in it, being clear of the Blood of all Men;*
" *and*

" and that, through the Lord's Mercy, his Life
" and Conversation had been such, that he could
" recommend, as a Pattern to follow, to those
" amongst whom he had laboured in the Ministry.

" The next Day, some Friends coming in
" to see him after the Week-day Meeting,
" and one saying, *He had thought him not well
" by his not being there* ; he replied, *That he
" had not been short in attending Week-day
" Meetings, while the Lord gave Ability* ; but
" he believed his Day's Work was now done ;
" and he was freely resigned to the Lord's Will,
" whether in Life or Death ; but, as his Af-
" fliction was great, he rather chose to be releas-
" ed, if the Lord saw meet.

" On the First-day following, many Friends
" being in the Room in Stilness by him, he
" raised himself on his Bed, and spoke a few
" Words of Exhortation, in a very solid and
" weighty manner, advising *To dwell near the
" Lord, in order to be truly prepared for their
" Change* ; and when they took Leave of him,
" he signified *his Sense of their Kindness in
" visiting him*; desiring *the Lord might reward
" them when they came to such a Time.*"

A Testimony

A Testimony from the Monthly-meeting of Thirsk *in* Yorkshire, *concerning* RACHEL PROUD, *formerly* KENDERAH.

SHE was descended of believing Parents, near *Bilsdale* in the Parish of *Kelmsley* in *Yorkshire*; and having a religious Education, and an early Visitation, she came to be religiously inclined, and was concerned, in Sincerity, to seek the Lord in her young and tender Years, in order to be acquainted with him and his Truth; and in this Condition it pleased him, who is the Father and Fountain of all our Mercies, and the Giver of every good and perfect Gift, who is full of Compassion, and will not with-hold from those who seek him in Sincerity, to open her Understanding, by which she came acquainted with him and his Truth, and by taking heed thereto, she witnessed a Growth in the same; and before she was Seventeen Years of Age, she was concerned to bear a publick Testimony for him who had thus visited her in Mercy; and although her Appearance at first was but small, yet her Innocency was so great, that it was greatly edifying to Friends; and being faithful thereunto, she experienced an Improvement therein, like the profitable Servant; and found that Saying of Christ to be true, *Unto every one that hath*

hath shall be given, and they shall have Abundance: Thus was her Gift enlarged, until she became a living and powerful Minister.

In her publick Service she was not wont to appear, unless she evidently felt Truth to open her Way. She was a good Example to the Youth, her Life and Conversation agreeing with her Ministry; a constant Attender of Meetings, both on First-days and other Days. She was one who greatly desired the Prosperity of Truth, and was zealously concerned for the propogating of the same, and travelled much, towards the latter End of her Time, upon that Account. She visited most of the Meetings in *England*, and was once in *Ireland*; in which Journeys we had a good Account of her and her Service, Friends speaking very lovingly and tenderly of her, and greatly desiring to see her again.

Much might be said concerning this our Sister and Labourer in the Vineyard of the Lord, who is now taken from us, to our great Loss, but, we trust, to her eternal Gain.

She departed this Life, we believe, in much Peace with the Lord, the 9th of the Sixth Month 1749, and was buried at *Thirsk* the 11th of the same. Aged Thirty one, a Minister Fourteen Years and upwards.

An Abstract of the Testimony from the Mens-Meeting of Cork *in* Ireland, *concerning* GEORGE BEWLEY.

HE was the Son of *George* and *Mary Bewley*, of *Ive-gill* in *Cumberland*. The Lord was pleased early to visit his Soul, and incline his Mind to seek after Purity and Holiness; and about the Thirtieth Year of his Age he received a Gift of the Ministry. His Appearance therein was to our Edification and Comfort, he being sound in Doctrine, and an humble Waiter upon the Lord in our religious Meetings; and zealously concerned, that good Order and Discipline should be maintained in the Church, the Lord having gifted him for that Service.

He was a loving Husband, a tender Father, a good Example in his Conversation and Conduct, of few Words in his Dealings, and just therein; faithful to his Word and Promise, and careful to keep out of the unnecessary Incumbrances of this Life.

He was a frequent Attender of our Quarterly and Province-meetings, also the National Half-year's-meetings, as they fell in course, whilst of Ability of Body; and sometimes attended the Yearly-meeting at *London*. He also several times visited most of the Meetings of Friends in this Nation, and some Parts of *England, Scotland*

Scotland and *Wales*, in the Work of the Miniftry.

He was feveral Years afflicted with great Weaknefs of Body, which he bore with great Patience; and fignified to Friends who vifited him, his Concern *for the Welfare of the Church*; and reminded them *of the great Zeal and Care that was upon Friends formerly, that all Things might be kept clean*; and *of their Diligence in attending Meetings for Worſhip and Difcipline*; with Sorrow obferving, *great Coolnefs, in this Refpect, to prevail in thefe Days*; and that *it was his great Comfort, now in his Affliction of Body, that he had been in the Practice thereof*; which, he faid, was all little enough, having done but his Duty therein.

He was preferved in a refigned Frame of Mind to the Will of God, waiting for his great Change; yet, with Submiffion thereto, defired *to be removed to where the Wicked ceafe from troubling, and the Weary are at reſt.* He departed this Life, in great Peace and Quietnefs, the 11th of the Twelfth Month 1749, in the Sixty fixth Year of his Age, having been a Minifter Thirty fix Years.

And though we are forrowfully affected with the Removal of fo fteady an Elder, and ferviceable Man, yet it is a Comfort to us, that we have Caufe to believe he is gone to eternal Reft, among the Spirits of juft Men made perfect, to praife the Lord God and the Lamb, who is worthy for ever. *Amen.*

A Teſtimony

A Testimony from the Monthly-meeting of Hartshaw *in the County of* Lancaster, *concerning* William Taylor, *of* Manchester.

HE was descended of believing Parents, near old *Meldrum* in *Aberdeenshire* in *Scotland*; from whence, about the Twenty first Year of his Age, he removed to *Stonehive* near *Urie*, where he resided a few Years; during which time, he appeared in a publick Testimony, which was acceptable to Friends, as appeared by the Recommendation given by them to this Monthly-meeting, when he came to settle amongst us; and, as he advanced in the Improvement of his Gift, he was concerned to visit Friends in his native Country several times, in *Ireland* once, and likewise some Parts of this Nation, we hope to his own Peace, and the Advantage of those among whom he laboured. We esteemed him an honest and faithful Minister; his Life and Conversation were in a good degree blameless and inoffensive. He was, when at home, diligent in his Business, that he might not make the Gospel chargeable; and exemplary in the Attendance of Meetings, and often therein gave Exhortations to the Comfort and Edification of Friends.

During his laſt Ilnefs, which continued fome Weeks, he was conducted with much Patience and Reſignation to the divine Will, though his bodily Pain was great. And from the Aboundings of divine Love, which often fill'd his Soul, he was concerned fervently to adviſe many of thoſe who viſited him, *to maintain the Unity of the Spirit in the Bond of Peace*; and, *to avoid an inordinate, or over anxious, Purſuit of worldly Things, that they might be preſerved to his Glory*; with many other lively Exhortations at ſeveral times. And not long before his Death, ſignified, *his great Satisfaction, under a Senſe of the divine Preſence and Favour*; and ſaid, *He had ſeen clearly, and would have it known, that the true Miniſters of God muſt not ſeek or deſire any Gifts, Rewards, or Honour from Men, nor any Thing in lieu thereof; but in true Humility wait in the pure Fear of God, and under the Exerciſe of their Gifts, if ever they obtained his Approbation.* He ſignified likewiſe his Satisfaction, *in having done his Day's Work*, and that *his Peace was ſure in the Lord*; in which comfortable Aſſurance, he quietly departed this Life the 3d, and was decently buried in Friends Burying Ground in *Mancheſter*, the 6th Day of the Firſt Month 1749, the Solemnity being evidently favoured with that divine Preſence which had been his Strength in the Time of Health, and Comfort in the Decline of Life, to the ſolid Satisfaction of many preſent, and Succour of his neareſt

Q Friends,

Friends. Aged Thirty eight, a Minifter Sixteen Years.

An Account of fome Expreſſions and Advice, given by William Taylor *aforeſaid, not long before his Death,* viz.

One Evening, feveral Friends being come to vifit him, he faid, "Some of them had feen
" him very weak at times, but never fo much
" reduced as then; that, confidering his pre-
" fent Situation, he could not but fay, it had
" feemed defirable to have continued a few
" Years in the World, but was now ready to
" think his time would not be long." He was going to fay fomething further, but was interrupted by the Enterance of more Company.

The next Evening, feveral Friends being again fitting by him, he expreffed his Gladnefs and Satisfaction in their Company, and that he was never more united in Love to his Friends than at prefent; he fometimes thought, he had a new Heart given him to love them; and faid, " As I had it on my Mind to ex-
" prefs laſt Evening: I have feen there is a
" Vanity which vexeth the Soul, that more or
" lefs lurketh about moſt of us, even about
" well-minded People, which in the time of
" Health and Strength, would boaſt itfelf, and
" be thought well of by others; but when the
" Hand of God is upon us in Affliction of
" Body,

" Body, we see it to be Chaff, that must be
" winnowed away, before we can be fitted for
" that pure Rest: For, Oh! Friends, it is a
" pure holy Rest; and none but purified and
" refined Souls can ever be admitted to enter
" into it. It hath of late been a searching
" Time to me; I have had to recollect some
" Passages of my Life, which have long been
" unthought of, but they have now been
" searched out, and brought to Judgment:
" For, Oh! I have seen so much of the Purity
" of that Rest, that I have often been afraid
" of late, lest I should not be enough refined
" to obtain an Admittance into it; and have
" earnestly desired, that nothing might remain,
" but what might bear the divine Hand in
" Judgment: And though I have been pre-
" served in a good degree of Sincerity, accord-
" ing to my Measure, so that I have nothing
" to charge myself with on that Account; yet
" I know and see all this is nothing to trust in,
" nothing but divine Mercy; and I see clearly
" the great Need I have of a Mediator, in
" whom I have a comfortable Hope: To look
" upon the Separation of Soul and Body by
" Death, seems a dark shady Thing: I have
" often remembered those Expressions of
" *David,—Though I walk through the Valley of*
" *the Shadow of Death, I will fear no Evil:*
" Death seems a gloomy Thing to human
" Nature, which is ready to shrink at the
" Prospect of it; but Oh! the Hope that

" *David*

" *David* had is a fine Thing: If the Guardian
" Angel of his Prefence do but conduct us
" through it, all will be well; and this I
" think I may fay, I have a fixed and com-
" fortable Hope in. I have no certain Senfe,
" whether I fhall at this time be removed, or
" not; that I leave to infinite Wifdom, and
" hope I can truly fay, I am entirely refigned
" to the divine Will. My greateft Concern
" on my own Account is, left I fhould not
" bear the Sharpnefs of my Pain with fuch a
" Degree of Submiffion and Patience, as I
" have defired to do; and am afraid it fhould
" unhinge my Thoughts from looking fo fted-
" faftly to the divine Object, as I hope I have
" done of late. It is a fine Thing for thofe
" that are young, to remember their Creator
" in the Days of their Youth, before the evil
" Day come, and the Time in which the Soul
" knows no Pleafure: The *evil Day*, I take
" to be the Time of Affliction or Pain of
" Body; Health and profperous Circumftances
" in Life, feem like Days of Sun-fhine, wherein
" we are too apt not properly to confider our
" latter End; but a Day will come, when all
" will find the World to be a Cheat, a meer
" Shadow, a Delufion, and not to be trufted
" in or relied upon.

" I remember the laft time I had any Con-
" cern to fpeak in a publick Meeting, I had
" to mention this Expreffion, which was then
" very much illuftrated in my View, — *The*
" *Righteous*

"*Righteous hath Hope in his Death*; little apprehending, at that time, it would so soon be my Lot, to think so much about it; however, I find it to be a comfortable Truth. I have laboured, I think I may say, honestly amongst my Friends in this Meeting, according to the Understanding given; and can truly say, with one formerly, *I have coveted no Man's Silver or Gold*, but, if possible, that I might be instrumental to gather Souls to God."

At another time he said, "Our worthy Friends might well recommend it, that *all might endeavour to keep the true Unity of the Spirit in the Bond of Peace*; and we who sometimes are concerned to advise others, what Need have we to be careful to maintain this pure Unity, and to be watchful left any Thing of Self get up, that would appear something, and be thought well of by Man, and would boast itself, and be thought to exceed others? If this be given way to, it will consequently lead to insinuate Things to hurt and lessen the Service of others. All this I have seen to be meer Chaff that must be winnowed away, if ever we be approved of by the Almighty.

"I have of late been very much united in Love to my Friends, and have looked with great Compassion and Tenderness towards those who have been drawn aside; and earnestly desire that those, who are concerned

"cerned to labour with such, may do it in
"the Spirit of Love and Tenderness, which
"only can gain upon them, in order that they
"may be restored into the Unity of the Body,
"wherein is received that Nourishment which
"preserves alive the Members thereof; and
"that none may look at the Weakness of
"others, with an Eye that would seek and
"fish for Faults. I have seen so much of my
"own Weakness, and the great Need I have
"had of the compassionate Regard of the
"Almighty, that I have been induced to look
"with great Pity and Tenderness, even to-
"wards Transgressors; and I believe, if we
"be truly sensible of our own Weakness, it
"will lead us to look after this manner one
"towards another; and if we hear or observe
"little Faults, we shall not delight to expose
"or aggravate them, but rather seek to help
"and watch over one another for Good.

"I have often observed with Grief, and so
"have some of you, the great Loss which our
"Society hath suffered, by a too anxious Pursuit
"and grasping after the World and the Things
"of it, in many, in order to appear great, and
"that their Posterity might have large Pos-
"sessions. Some who have even tasted of the
"Love of God, by suffering their Minds to be
"ensnared and entangled, have insensibly lost
"ground in Religion, and gone on, by degrees,
"till they have almost lost the Relish of it.
"I very much desire that this may never be the
"unhappy

"unhappy Circumstance of any of us; for we
"have tasted of this divine Sweetness, and it
"has at times been far more precious than any
"of these fading transitory Things."

And having been still for some time, he said,
"In the Lord's Presence there is Quiet indeed!
"I could scarcely have thought, that such a
"Foretaste of divine Favour could have been
"enjoyed whilst in these Bodies, and I could
"have been glad to have gone in it; but not
"my Will, but thine O Lord be done."

At another time he said, "I have often
"considered the great Advantage that those
"have had, who have been religiously educated
"in our Society; and happy will it be for such,
"who make a right Use of it. Many and
"great Favours we receive, by the Ministry of
"those whom divine Providence hath qualified
"to labour amongst us; and, in a particular
"Manner, we in this Meeting have been emi-
"nently favoured of late; notwithstanding
"which, if any should be satisfied with hear-
"ing and professing, and with having the
"Name of Religion, and appearing orderly
"amongst Men, and yet be Strangers to the
"Life and Virtue thereof in their own Hearts,
"they will find themselves miserably disap-
"pointed at last. Oh! it is a fine Thing to
"have Religion so near us, as to have our
"Hearts rooted and grounded in the Fear of
"God: I have, through Mercy, found the
"Comfort and Advantage of it, in this Time
"of

"of Bodily Affliction: It hath administered
"more Relief than all my Friends could do.
"What could it avail me now, if I had a
"House full of Silver or Gold to look at? It
"could not afford the least degree of that
"Comfort and Peace of Mind I now enjoy.
"I have many times thought, that I am more
"at liberty, and my Mind more composed
"and easy, to leave the World, than if I had
"a great deal in it. I have wanted nothing;
"but have had every Thing necessary and suit-
"able for me, and am much more free from
"Cumber than if I had abundance to leave
"behind me.

"When I have at times, for some Days
"past, been concerned to speak a little to my
"Friends, by way of Advice, I have been
"much refreshed both in Body and Mind. It
"seems to alleviate my Pain and Affliction of
"Body; and if it please divine Providence to
"number me to my Grave, nothing seems to
"lay in my Way; I have nothing but Peace
"of Mind, and doubt not but his merciful
"Care will be extended, and be my Conductor
"through the shadowy Prospect of Death;
"and I have a fixed Hope, that divine Good-
"ness will visit this Meeting in an extraordi-
"nary Manner. And though there may be
"some whose Views are much confined, and
"their Pursuits strongly after the Things of
"this Life; a Time will come, when such
"will be shaken, and have a clear Sight of
"the

"the Vanity and Emptiness of the World,
"which is really a Cheat and a Delusion; a
"Shadow, and not worth grasping after, nor
"to be relied upon. I know it is necessary and
"lawful to provide for the Accommodation
"of these Bodies, for a little time; and if I
"recover, it will be my Care; but I hope I
"shall always look upon it in such a Light, as
"to prefer what I know and see to be my
"greatest Interest."

At another time he said, "I have of late seen
"more clearly than ever, the Advantage and
"Excellency of dwelling in true Love and
"Unity; that pure Unity of the Spirit, the
"Bond of Peace: Oh! Friends, endeavour to
"keep in it, and out of that which would
"divide in *Jacob*, and scatter in *Israel*; and
"then Satan, with all his Craft, can never sap
"the Foundation, but it will stand for ever.

"Though it hath of late been a trying and
"searching Time to me, it hath been the most
"profitable Time of all my Life: And I fully
"believe a Time is approaching, that will try
"the Foundations of Men; and it is well for
"those who are prepared to stand through it;
"but much more happy those, who may be
"landed safe *before that Time overtake them.*
"I do not only think so, because several of
"our Friends have been concern'd to mention
"it, but from a full Persuasion and fixed
"Evidence of it in my own Mind."

Taking

Taking Leave of a particular Friend, he said, "We have been long acquainted; and I know thou haft been favoured with the Experience of the Love of God, and haft been a good Example to thy Family. I wifh thou mayft ftill endeavour to live near Truth; feel after the Virtue of it more and more in thy own Heart, and then thou'lt be concerned to bring up thy Children in the Fear of God, and that they may have Portions in the Truth, which will far exceed all the great Things in this vain World."

He faid to his Wife, who he faw very forrowful, "My Dear, moderate thy Grief on my Account; let us not mumur at the Cup that is handed to us; but remember him to whom it was given for our fakes: To him it was adminiftred with great Scorn and Derifion, but to us in great Mercy."

At another time he faid, "My Dear, do not grieve fo much for me; I have obtained the utmoft Wifhes that ever I had, with regard to any Profpect of Happinefs in this Life, by having thy Company; and though it hath been but a fhort time, it hath tended, in degree, to prepare me for my latter End: I am quite eafy to refign my Spirit to him who gave it. Thou wouldft have had much more Caufe of Sorrow, if thou hadft been joined to one who, in the fame Situation, had been weighed down with Horror and Guilt of Confcience. Sorrow not for me, I
"fhall

"shall soon be centered into that Rest which
" good *Abraham* long ago entered into, as a
" Reward of his Faithfulness. What! though
" these poor mouldring Bodies must be dis-
" solved and returned to their original Dust,
" there is a glorious Assembly of the Spirits of
" just Men made perfect, even the Church of
" the First-born, which I am going to join,
" and which all redeemed Souls must join,
" when they quit these Tabernacles of Clay;
" then all Sorrow and Tears will be wiped
" away, and uninterrupted Rest and Tran-
" quility will be their Portion for ever; even
" the Portion of all those who resign them-
" selves in Faith, Body, Soul and Spirit, to
" their great Creator: Then there is no Will,
" no Desire, either of Life or Death, but an
" entire Submission to the divine Will. They
" dare not desire to live a Year, a Month or a
" Day, longer than he sees meet; neither to
" die before his Time."

At several times he acknowledged the great Care and Concern of his Wife and Brother for him. He said, " Your Care for me is quite
" compleat; you having sympathized with me
" and born part of my Burthen; you can do
" no more; and I fully believe you will be
" rewarded when I am gone: It will, like the
" Prayers and Alms-deeds of *Cornelius*, go up
" as a Memorial before Almighty God."

At another time he said, " Thou art, *my*
" *Dear*, exceeding near to me; so near I
" cannot

"cannot exprefs it. I never loved thee more
" than now, and I fully believe, if I am taken
" away, the Lord will blefs and comfort thee,
" beyond what I could do for thee if I live ;
" therefore endeavour to refign me entirely to
" the Divine Difpofal. We muft be parted
" fome time, and I can never leave thee with
" lefs Incumbrance than at prefent. If Nature
" muft fometimes have a little Vent by Sorrow,
" take Care to moderate it, fo as not to offend
" divine Providence, nor hurt thy Health: He
" will, I truft, help and fupport thee beyond
" what thou canft now fee. I once thought it
" had been fcarce poffible for me to have been
" fo eafy to part with thee fo foon ; but divine
" Mercy is great to me. I am as happy, as
" thou canft wifh me, and far more fo than I
" have deferved. When thou haft any fenfible
" Intereft with divine Goodnefs, join my Spirit
" in Prayer, that he may be pleafed to eafe
" my Pain of Body, or renew and ftrengthen
" my Patience to bear it his Time, without
" repining ; and alfo that he may be with me
" to the laft, and favour me with an eafy
" Paffage."

Not long before his Death, having been very ftill for fome time, he expreffed the great Satisfaction that he had, in a Senfe of the divine Prefence and Favour, and faid, *He wanted his Brother* ; who being called, he faid, " I have lain with great Satisfaction, even as if " upon a Bed of Rofes ; and though I have
" great

"great Pain of Body, it has been chained
"down, and I have feen beyond all Pain. I
"I have had a View of the Tree of Life, that
"ftands in the Midft of the Paradice of God;
"and have feen how far that Satisfaction ex-
"ceeds all fenfual Pleafures. It is likely I fhall
"die foon, and if I do, I hope I fhall die well.
"I have feen clearly, and would have it to be
"known, that the true Minifters of God muft
"not feek or defire any Reward, Gifts or
"Honour from Men, nor any Thing in lieu
"thereof; but, in true Humility, wait in the
"pure Fear of God, and under the Exercife
"of his Gift, if ever they obtain his Appro-
"bation: I would have this to be known,
"and that is all."

After which he continued about two Days;
and though his Pain was great, he was preferved in much Patience and Refignation to
the divine Will: And the laft Words he was
heard to fpeak, were, *It is now over; I am
juft going. Farewel, my dear Love, the Lord
blefs thee, and be with me now.*

Some Friends being called in, he continued
about Half an Hour, and departed very quietly.

A Teftimony

A Testimony from the Monthly-meeting of Norwich, *concerning* JOSEPH GURNEY.

HE was descended of religious Parents, who not only professed the Truth, but were great Sufferers for their faithful Testimony thereto in this City. They took great Care in the Education of their Children, which, by the Blessing of God, they lived in great measure to see the good Effects of, as well in others of them, as in this our dear Friend, who was visited with the Day-spring from on high, in his very young and tender Age; and by closing in therewith, as he advanced in Years, he grew in Sobriety and Virtue; and, in the Twenty first Year of his Age, it pleased God to dispense to him a Gift of the Ministry, in which he was very acceptable, it being attended with Life and Power.

In the Year 1717, he visited Meetings in *Ireland*, and afterwards in *Wales*, and several Parts of *England*; and we have good reason to believe, that his Services in all these Visits were acceptable.

After the Year 1732, he was rendered incapable, by bodily Infirmity, to ride on Horseback, which confined his Service more to our own Meeting and County; wherein he was of great Service, by endeavouring to stir up
the

the pure Mind in all, both by Example and Precept.

He was a Man of great Humility; a Pattern of Benevolence, Moderation and Temperance, as well as of moſt other *Chriſtian* Virtues; by which Behaviour he greatly adorned the Goſpel of Chriſt, and obtained the Eſteem of all Ranks and Degrees of People here, by whom he was univerſally beloved and reſpected. He hath left a ſweet Savour behind, ſo that it may be truly ſaid, his Memory is bleſſed, and being dead, he yet ſpeaketh.

He dearly loved Peace and Unity in the Church, and any Thing that wounded its Reputation, very deeply affected him. He was a conſtant Attender of Meetings, both on Firſt and other Days of the Week; and when he obſerved a Lukewarmneſs in any thereunto, it gave him great Sorrow.

It pleaſed the Almighty, in the Courſe of his Providence, to permit this our dear Friend to be tried with much Ilneſs, being for the laſt Eighteen Years of his Life greatly afflicted with the *Stone* and *Gravel*, hardly in that Space having enjoyed one Day of perfect Health; which, though naturally of a weak and tender Spirit, he bore with great Patience; but ſeemed very ſenſible it would ſoon finiſh him, as to this World.

His laſt Ilneſs was very ſevere and afflicting, being not able, for near a Month before he died, to keep in Bed; which he ſuſtained

with

with remarkable Refignation, not uttering one impatient or difcontented Word, during the whole time; but expreffed great Satisfaction *in his inward State,* and that *he made it the Bufinefs of his whole Life, to be prepared for fuch a Time:* And fome of the laſt Words he fpoke to be underſtood, a few Hours before his Departure, were, that *He was happy.*

Much might be mentioned of this our dear deceafed Friend; but we fhall conclude with faying, he was a moſt indulgent Hufband, a kind and tender Parent, a good Maſter, and a fincere Friend.

Our Lofs of fuch an Elder and Miniſter is very great, and greater than we can exprefs, not only in our publick Meetings of Worſhip, but alfo in thofe for Difcipline and good Order; in which he was particularly ferviceable, being as a Father in the Churches in thefe Parts.

This our dear Friend departed this Life the 5th of the Third Month 1750, and was buried the 8th of the fame, in Friends Burying Ground, accompanied to the Grave by a great Number of Friends and others.

As he lived beloved, fo he died lamented, and is, we doubt not, entered into that Reſt prepared for the Righteous; there, with Saints and Angels, and the Spirits of juſt Men made perfect, giving Praife and Honour to him who lives for ever.

He was Aged Fifty eight Years and fix Weeks; a Miniſter about Thirty eight Years.

A Teſtimony

A Testimony from the Monthly - meeting of Brighouse *in* Yorkshire, *concerning* JOHN HORSFALL.

THIS our well esteemed Friend and approved Minister, was a Man of a good Understanding; his Conversation and Deportment was solid, grave and weighty: And tho' his Service was within a narrow Compass, in comparison of many others of the Lord's Messengers, who are called to distant Parts, his Concern being mostly in his own and some few neighbouring Meetings; yet he was zealous for the Cause of God, and the Promotion of his Truth upon Earth. He was a diligent Attender of Meetings, and careful to observe the Time appointed; often concerned to stir up others to the like decent and orderly Practice. His Ministry was clear, sound and edifying; not consisting in a Multitude of Words, especially in his latter Years, the chief Tendency thereof being rather to turn People to the Gift of Grace in their own Hearts, that in the Ability thereof they might labour for themselves, to witness the experimental Work of Sanctification, and not settle in a bare Form and Profession of Religion, or have their Dependance upon Instruments,

Nor was he less careful to discharge his Duty in the other Stations and Relations of Life, being a loving and affectionate Husband, a tender Father, a kind and peaceable Neighbour; and, by his sober and *Christian* Conversation, obtained a good Report, and has left a sweet Savour behind him. And though his Substance was not great in the World, yet did he readily and chearfully administer thereof to the Necessities of the Poor, and those who were in Distress; and with Freedom and Open-heartedness received and entertained his fellow Labourers in the Work of the Ministry.

His declining Age was attended with Exercises and Afflictions of various Kinds; all which he endured with exemplary Patience and Resignation. Nor was his Zeal for the Cause of Truth in the least abated; but he continued to attend Meetings almost constantly as formerly, though many times with great Difficulty, having his Eye to the Recompence of Reward: And the earnest Desire and Travail of his Soul was; *that he might finish his Day's Work in the Day-time; that whenever he should be called to give an Account of his Stewardship, he might be prepared to do the same with Joy.*

May we, under the Consideration of our great Loss of him, and many other faithful Labourers in the Lord's Vinyard, now removed from us, be excited so to follow their Footsteps, that with them we may be Partakers of that

that incorruptible Inheritance which is referved for the Righteous, when time here fhall be no more.

He departed this Life the 28th of the Eighth Month 1748, in the Seventy fifth Year of his Age, having been concerned in publick Teftimony upwards of Forty Years.

A Teftimony from the Monthly-meeting of Settle *in* Yorkfhire, *concerning* THOMAS CARR.

THIS our dear, worthy and well-efteemed Friend, was defcended of honeft Parents, at *Longrig* near *Settle*, in the Third Month 1670; and, when very young, the Lord was pleafed *to vifit him*, as he often declared, *with the Inbreakings of divine Virtue*; under which Vifitations, he was very folicitous to find out a People under the fame Influence he experienced; and after going from one Society to another, he found not, as he thought, any under fuch a Heart-melting Work as the Lord was pleafed to exercife him with; under which he remained difconfolate, till one time, when alone, the Lord's Power tendered his Heart to that degree, that he was willing to be as paffive Clay in his Hand; and defired to know what he fhould do, or to what People he fhould join himfelf, as Companions to his tribulated Soul. It then appeared to him, that the People called *Quakers* were favoured with the same Truth, Life and Power, that he had a Sense of; though it was more contrary to his own Will to join with them, than to any other Perswasion.

In the Year 1690 he joined Friends, and soon after came forth in Testimony for the Truth, being then about Twenty one Years of Age; in which he continued a faithful Labourer till his Death. He travelled in the Work of the Ministry, and visited the Meetings of Friends in *Scotland, Ireland,* and most Parts of *England,* approving himself a sound and able Minister of the Gospel.

He was a large Experiencer of the Work of God, and the deep Mysteries of the Heavenly Kingdom, having clear Openings in Meetings to declare of and unfold the same, in the Demonstration of the Spirit, to the comforting and establishing of Friends in their Journey *Sion*-ward. He was not only an Asserter of the true Faith and Doctrine of our Lord and Saviour Jesus Christ, in a sound and intelligible Testimony, but also one who, through a long Course of time, was careful to adorn the Doctrine of our holy Profession, by a circumspect Life and godly Conversation; wherein the Fruits of the Spirit, *to wit,* Love, Joy, Peace, Long-suffering, Gentleness, Goodness, Faith, Meekness and Temperance, did shine forth to the Praise and Glory of God. Being thus qualified, and of a meek and peaceable Disposition,

Difpofition, he was well efteemed by Friends and others.

He was very exemplary in attending religious Meetings for Worfhip, and the Difcipline of the Church, at the Time appointed; and in our Monthly-meetings eminently ferviceable, being zealous to fupport good Order therein. His Advice was folid and weighty, feafoned with Grace; fo that when any Differences appeared, he was very helpful, by endeavouring to compofe the fame in an amicable Manner; not leaning to any Party through Favour or Affection, but laboured that the Affairs of the Church might be eftablifhed, to the Honour of him who hath not only laid the Foundation, but crowned the Labour of the Faithful with Peace.

Our dear Friend, for fome Years before his Departure, was violently afflicted with the *Stone* and *Gravel*, which often rendered him incapable of getting to Meetings; but when he had a little Eafe he diligently attended; and, when there, frequently opened in a living and powerful Teftimony, being frefh and lively in old Age, to the comforting and refrefhing thofe prefent, and earneftly concerned to ftir up Friends to Faithfulnefs.

In the laft Meeting he attended, he was in a fweet Heavenly Frame of Mind, faying,— *Oh! the Melody that is in Heaven:* Then, or at another Time, fervently praying, *That the sweet*

sweet Sound of the Gospel might be heard in that Place.

Two Days before his Departure he broke forth in a lively Manner, uttering many comfortable Expressions in praising and glorifying his Creator, many times repeating these Words, *The Goodness of the Lord endures for ever*; adding, *The Tongue and Pen of Man cannot declare it to the full:* Which caused Brokenness of Heart in the Hearers.

He departed this Life the 17th of the Third Month 1750, we trust, in Peace with the Lord, and in perfect Unity with his Brethren, and was decently interred in Friends Burying Ground at *Settle,* the 20th of the same.

Aged Eighty, a Minister Fifty nine Years.

A Testimony from the Monthly-meeting of Lancaster, *concerning* ELIZABETH RAWLINSON.

SHE was a Branch sprung from a pious Stock; her Father and Mother, *William* and *Dorothy Beck,* gave her a sober careful Education, and lived to see their Labour and Prayers for her were blessed with Success; for it pleased the merciful Lord to reach her Heart by divine Love, and to lay his gracious Hand upon her, to prepare and qualify her for his Work, when she was very young; and about the Seventeenth Year of her Age, she came forth

forth in a publick Testimony for the Truth, which she held, and was fruitful in to the End.

She travelled much, and went many Journeys, in her Youth, before she married; visited Friends Meetings in *Scotland,* and many Parts of *England* and *Wales*; some Counties divers times over; and after she was married to *Abraham Rawlinson,* she had her Liberty, with suitable Encouragement from him, to discharge the Trust her great Master reposed in her, and which she preferred above her chiefest Joy in this World, being made willing to leave an affectionate Husband, and several tender Children, to visit the Churches both in this Nation and *Ireland,* several times over; and feeling her Mind drawn by divine Love to visit Friends in divers Parts of *America,* she was not disobedient to the Heavenly Vision, but when she believed her Time was fully come, left all and went forth in that Journey, visited the Meetings fully in *New-England, Rhode-Island, Nantucket, Long-Island, New-York, Pensilvania,* the *Jerseys, Maryland, Virginia* and *North Carolina*; in all which, notwithstanding the Extreams of the Seasons, her Age, and the Tenderness of her Sex, she was enabled to surmount the Difficulties, and perform that Service to the Honour of Truth, the Satisfaction of Friends, and the Peace of her own Soul: So that it may be truly said, she lived and walked in the Faith which made her valiant

valiant in Fight, subdued Enemies, and gave Victory over evil Spirits; abounding in that Charity which is the Bond of Perfectness, so that her Soul did often magnify the Lord, and her Spirit rejoiced in God her Saviour, who made her fruitful in old Age, her Ministry being found, living, and truly acceptable to the Conclusion of her Days.

She departed this Life in full Unity with Friends, and the general Respect of those who knew her, the 5th Day of the Fifth Month 1750, in the Eightieth Year of her Age, having been a Minister about Sixty three Years, and was decently interred in Friends Burying Ground in *Lancaster* the 7th of the same; upon which solemn Occasion the glorious Truth, in which she lived and died, was evidently manifested to the Comfort of many.

" Our dear Friend *Elizabeth Rawlinson*,
" before mentioned, was on the fourteenth and
" fifteenth Days of her Ilness reduced to a State
" of such outward Weakness, that those who
" attended her, scarcely expected she would be
" able to open her Mouth any more; yet, the
" following Day in the Morning, she seemed
" somewhat to revive, and expressed a Desire
" *her Children should be called*; who being
" come, she was in a wonderful Manner filled
" with inward Strength and Comfort, and
" brake forth, saying, *Death is no Terror to*
" *me: It is no Surprize to me. My Heart*
" *is*

" is full of the Joy of God's Salvation; yea,
" full of the Comforts of the Holy Ghost.
" The Lord visited my Soul when I was very
" young, and often broke in upon my Spirit by his
" Heart-melting, bowing and tendering Power,
" preparing me for that Work which he shew'd
" me was to be required at my Hand; telling
" me, if I was faithful, I should be a Mouth
" for him; which Word brought great Awe
" and Dread over my Mind, and I said, Lord,
" who is sufficient for these Things! But as I
" have steadily kept my Eye to him, I have still
" found sufficient Ability for every Service that
" ever he required of me; yea, I can say, he
" hath been with me all my Life long, and made
" hard Things easy to me; and now I can say,
" Come Lord Jesus, come quickly, thy Servant
" is ready: I have fought the good Fight of
" Faith, I have finished my Course, my Day's
" Work is done; henceforth there is laid up
" for me a Crown of Righteousness: Yea, I
" feel it is sure to me, and will be to all who
" love Truth above all, as (blessed be the Lord)
" I have done. I have served him in Sincerity,
" and left all that was near to me in this World,
" to run the Ways of his Commandments, which
" have not been grievous, but joyous to me.

" Oh! that you, my dear Children, may
" give up your Hearts to serve the Lord, and
" join freely with those gracious Visitations he
" extends to you; I pray God bless you all, and
" prosper his Truth in you, when I am gone to
                                            " the

"the silent Grave, that you may be valiant for
"the Cause of God; for I can truly say, that
"since I gave up to serve the Lord, I have
"never been an idle slothful Servant, neither
"have I played the Coward, nor turned my
"Back in the Day of Battle; but have laboured
"for my Penny, and now I have it in a plen-
"tiful Manner: Oh! the Highth, and Length
"and Breadth of the Comfort and Joy that flows
"in my Soul! My Tongue is too short to set
"forth one Half of the Goodness of my God."

A Testimony from the Monthly-meeting at Brigflats in Yorkshire, concerning ALICE THISTLETHWAIT.

SHE was convinced of the blessed Truth when young; not by instrumental Means, but by the immediate Manifestation of the Grace of God, powerfully operating in her Heart, which caused her many times to retire into secret Places, to put up her Supplications to Almighty God, that *If he would please to shew her the Way to Life and Salvation, then she would serve him*; which, in good degree, he was pleased to make known to her, by manifesting himself in the Secret of her Soul, whereby she came to know her Heavenly Father's good Pleasure concerning her. Then she consulted not with Flesh and Blood, but
gave

gave up to the Heavenly Vifion, whereby fhe became a chofen Veffel to place his Name in; and had the Gift of the Miniftry beftowed upon her, in which fhe faithfully laboured, being concerned to travel abroad, into feveral Parts of this Nation, to vifit the Churches of Chrift at fundry times. And when her Service on that Account feemed to be over for a time, fhe entered into a Marriage State of Life, and it pleafed God to give her nine Children, whom fhe carefully nurfed and brought up, not in Pride and Idlenefs, but in good Subjection; and when they came to Years of Underftanding, fhe often admonifhed them *to live in the Fear of the Lord, and be mindful of the Day of their Vifitation, fo that they might become an Honour to his worthy Name.* Eight of them are living, and thankful to Almighty God, on her Behalf, for fuch good Education, and tender Regard towards them, in Things that concerned their eternal Welfare.

We can do no lefs than, with great Sincerity and Affection, remember the many good Qualifications that Truth endued her with; her Teftimony was powerful, to the Edification of many; and it was her Lot to call to the Loofe and Difobedient, amongft Friends and others, in order to reclaim them from the Evil of their Ways.

She was very diligent in vifiting the Sick, amongft Friends and others, by which fhe obtained a good Report. She was likewife of a

quick

quick Apprehenſion, and of a ſolid and ſound Judgment, to the confounding and putting to ſilence the Mouths of Gainſayers.

In her declining Years, ſhe had a Concern on her Mind to viſit Friends in ſeveral Counties of this Nation, and in *London*, having *Agnes Maſon* for a Companion ; and, notwithſtanding her many Infirmities of Body, ſhe undertook her Journey with great Reſignation of Mind, being freely given up in Heart and Soul to obey her great Lord and Maſter, whom ſhe knew was worthy above all to be obeyed and ſerved, in whatſover he might require at her Hands.

When they found themſelves clear of thoſe Parts, they returned homewards, having been abroad about ſeven Months in the Service of Truth. Her Health became farther impaired through the Fatigue of this painful Journey, ſhe being about ſixty eight Years of Age when ſhe undertook it, and having travelled upwards of nine Hundred Miles in ſo ſhort a time.

After her Return, ſhe conſtantly continued to attend Meetings at home, and often abroad, though it was with great Difficulty to her Body; and on the 1ſt Day of the Firſt Month 1750, it pleaſed God to viſit her with Sickneſs that proved unto Death, in about ſeven Days from the time ſhe was taken. Her Pain of Body was great, which ſhe endured with much Patience ; the Love of God was ſo prevalent upon her, that ſhe was often made to

ſing

sing Praises to his Name, for his continued Goodness towards her Soul, tho' under great Affliction of Body. Many Friends and Neighbours came to visit her when she lay upon her sick Bed, and it pleased God to open her Mouth, by way of Exhortation and good Advice, to the tendering the Hearts of many. And now the time drawing near that she must give up this natural Life, could appeal to the Beloved of her Soul, that *she had done her Day's Work in the Day-time, and was at Peace with the Lord*; desiring *to be dissolved, and freed from this earthly Tabernacle.*

She departed this Life the 7th Day of the First Month 1750, in the Seventieth Year of her Age, having been a Minister upwards of Fifty Years.

A Testimony from Thirsk *Monthly-meeting in* Yorkshire, *concerning* MABEL BARKER.

ABOUT the Year 1741, it pleased the Lord, in the Riches of his Love, to raise up our well-beloved Friend *Mabel Barker* to bear Testimony to his blessed Truth ; in which Service she manifested her Love and Zeal for the Prosperity thereof, by her frequent Exercise and Labour amongst us. Her Concern was great *for the Welfare of our immortal Souls,* and that *we might demean ourselves so, as to give*

give no just Occasion for the Truth to be evil spoken of; advising us *to be very careful in all our Deportment among Men*; sometimes expressing *the great Need there was for her to be careful, upon her own Account, lest she should offend in Thought, Word or Deed*; and that she believed *all had the like Need, but was afraid all did not see their Need to be so great as it really was*; and so would tenderly advise, to the Comfort and Consolation of her Friends; for the Lord blessed her in her Labour, and often eminently attended her in her Ministry with his divine Power, whereby the Hearts of many were reached, and the Heritage of God watered by the divine Showers, that, through her, as an Instrument in the Hand of the Lord, fell upon them. Oh! the bedewing Seasons, and comfortable Opportunities, which we have had with this our Friend, the Impressions whereof at times still revive upon our Spirits, and makes us sensible our Loss of her is great; but as we are well satisfied it is her eternal Gain, we dare not murmur, but say, as one of old, *The Lord gave, and the Lord hath taken away, blessed be the Name of the Lord:* Desiring, that others may be raised up, and made willing to labour faithfully in the Lord's Vineyard, as we believe this our Friend hath done; for it was her great Concern, that his Work might be done to his own Praise: And she was willing to lend a helping Hand to the Weak, that so all might be encouraged therein.

She

She laboured much, and was very ferviceable to our Women Friends, for the promoting of good Order amongft them, that the Church might be kept clean from the Defilements of the World, and that it might be fo, fhe fpared no Pains or Advice, which fhe thought would tend to the Glory of God, or the Good of her Friends, being willing to fpend and be fpent, according to her Ability, for his Caufe, as fhe fometimes would declare. She travelled not much abroad in the Service of Truth, fave in our own County, and the County of *Durham*, or Meetings adjacent, for her Labour was much about home.

She vifited the Families of Friends in our own Monthly-meeting, in which Service we have Caufe to believe, fhe was an Inftrument of Good to thofe whom fhe fo vifited, being one who, we doubt not, was rightly qualified for fuch a Work, and did advife from her own Experience.

She was exemplary in the Courfe and Conduct of her Life, meek, gentle and courteous to all, a great Lover of Peace, Concord and Unity, which fhe laboured much to promote amongft us, being an Example of Good to thofe fhe was converfant with; a loving Wife, an affectionate Mother, a good Neighbour and kind Friend: And as fhe lived, fo fhe died, a Pattern of Meeknefs and Innocency, and no doubt is at Reft from her Labours, and her Works follow her. And that it may be fo

with

with us, and all the Lord's People, is the fervent Desire and Breathing of our Souls to the Lord; that we, like her, may be concerned to work the Work of our Day, fight the good Fight of Faith, and hold out to the End, as she has done; that we may be entituled to that immortal Crown that will never fade away.

She departed this Life the 14th of the Third Month 1751, Aged Fifty four Years, a Minister upwards of Nine Years. Her Corps was interred in Friends Burying Ground at *Thirsk* the 16th of the said Month, being accompanied by a great many Friends and others.

A Testimony from the Quarterly-meeting of Wiltshire, *held at* Chippenham, *concerning* JOSEPH STORRS.

BY Accounts received, he was born on the 13th of the Third Month 1670, at *Chesterfield* in *Derbyshire*, of honourable and religious Parents, by whom he was carefully and religiously educated: His Father *William Storrs* being a very great Sufferer for Truth's-sake, and his Mother's Father and Mother, *William* and *Grace Sykes*, both died Prisoners for the same.

Notwithstanding

Notwithstanding which, as he grew up towards Man's Estate, his Mind was too much led out after the Vanity and Gaiety of Life, and drawn away from the Simplicity of the Truth, till he was mercifully visited and reached to by an immediate Touch from God; to which being faithful, he became an Example of Religion and Virtue: And, about the Thirtieth Year of his Age, was concerned in a publick Testimony for the same; and soon after married *Katharine*, Daughter of *Henry Frost* of *Bridlington*, who having, very young, a large and excellent Gift in the Ministry, exceeding most of her Age, she found it her Duty after Marriage, as she had done before, frequently to travel, in the Exercise thereof, in this Kingdom, *Ireland, Scotland, Holland* and *Germany*, but more especially in these three Kingdoms; in all which he freely gave her up, and affectionately accommodated her for her Journies and Voyages, saying, *When the Lord required her to run of his Errands, she was not his, nor at his Disposal.* He was a frequent Attender of the Yearly-meeting at *London*, and visited Friends Meetings in sundry Counties, and especially in the North and West Parts of this Nation, in which his Visits were very acceptable to Friends.

He was lively in his Ministry, strict in Discipline, zealous in supporting the respective Testimonies of Truth, and careful in the Education of his Children; and often expressed his Thankfulness to the Lord, for their Preservation and comfortable Settlement in the World; and as they were mostly married from him, when it pleased the Lord to remove his dear Wife by Death, with whom he had lived in great Unity and Affection near Forty two Years, he soon after inclined to remove and live with his Daughters in this County, producing a Certificate from the Monthly-meeting at *Chesterfield*, of Friends Unity with him, and his many acceptable Services among them. He spent the Residue of his Days among his Children, and in visiting Meetings in divers Parts of this County, *Bristol*, &c. But when Age rendered him incapable of travelling, he very frequently appeared in his own Meeting, to encourage Friends in their great Duty of Waiting upon the Lord; he was fresh and edifying in his Ministry to the last, and remarkable for his instructive and affecting Conversation, being, by his Faithfulness to the Gift received, rendered fruitful in the Things of God. And though his Memory and Understanding very much decayed some time before his Death, yet he retained a good Sense and Savour of divine Things; and, the Evening before his Departure, gave some tender Advice to his Grand-daughter *Katherine Fry*, (*John Fry*'s Daughter) and very sweetly departed this Life in the Presence of divers Friends, who were then made sensible of his happy End, the 27th of the Second Month

Month 1751, and was buried the 1st of the Third Month at *Hullington* in this County, being attended by many Friends and Neighbours.

Aged near Eighty one, a Minister about Fifty one Years.

A Testimony from the Monthly - meeting of Chesterfield *in* Derbyshire, *concerning* ELIZABETH FLETCHER.

SHE was born in the First Month 1708, at *Low Park* near *Kendal* in *Westmorland*. Her Parents were *Simon* and *Ann Crosfield*, whose chief Care for their Children was to train them up in the Fear of God.

This our deceased Friend was visited by divine Grace when young, and giving heed thereunto, the Work of Regeneration was happily begun in her Soul. While this great Work was perfecting, many sore Engagements and Baptisms of Spirit she underwent, but at length overcame, and was made more than a Conqueror, through him that had loved and laid down his Life for her.

In the Twenty fourth Year of her Age she was married to *Joseph Fletcher* of *Wessington*, a Member of this Meeting, and soon after was called to the Work of the Ministry, which laid her under deep Exercise of Mind; but, by the Almighty's chastising Rod, was made willing to obey his holy Call, and from the State of a Child, or Babe therein, became an able Minister of Christ Jesus.

She travelled pretty much in this Nation, in the Service of the Gospel, having twice visited the Meetings in and about *London*, the last time in the Year 1748, when she had a Sight that her Service was over in those Parts. She was an Instrument in the Lord's Hand in gathering several from the barren Mountains of empty Profession, some of whom yet remain in this County; but was more particularly sent to the Sheep strayed from *Israel*'s Fold, Persons born and educated amongst us, who for Want of taking due Heed to the inward Teacher of Souls, had run much out into the Spirit and Evils of this World; some of whom, it is probable, will at times remember her with the tenderest Love; because for their Sakes, to her the Word of Reconciliation was richly dispenced, and her Labours therein, we trust, have not been in vain in the Lord; for in sundry Places where she travelled in Truth's Service, a living Testimony remains in the Hearts of many on her Behalf.

She was a Person of a good Capacity, much sweetened and improved by Religion, a tender nursing Mother in the Church of God, as well as in her own Family, and had a deep and excellent Gift in the Ministry. To the Proud and Lofty she was, in the Power of God, as a sharp Sword, smiting at the very Foundation of *Babylon*; yet a true Mourner and Simpathizer
with

with such as were awakened to see their Condition.

In the latter Part of her time she was much afflicted with Indisposition of Body, and often travelled in great Weakness and Difficulty, but her Spirit was so wonderfully born up, that she was carried on in her Labours and Travels beyond human Expectation.

She was a diligent Attender of Meetings, and therein a fervent Labourer in Spirit; her Heart was set to serve the Lord, whom she loved with all her Soul, and spared no Pains to be helpful to her Friends and Neighbours, inwardly and outwardly, as she had Opportunity or Ability. In her last Ilness she was often heard to bewail *a Self-righteous, Pharisaical Spirit*, which she saw was crept into the Churches.

She was confined to her House the far greater Part of the last Year of her Life. Her bodily Complaints were many, and her Pains often very acute; but the Lord supported her through all with singular and exemplary Patience and Resignation to his holy Will.

Two Weeks before her Death, she bore her last publick Testimony at *Furnace*, and concluded the Meeting in Prayer; after which, growing daily weaker, she said, in the Presence of some Friends, a little before her Death, *That she was willing either to die or live; that she had left nothing undone she had to do, and had nothing but Peace, and the Truth was over all.*

The 20th of the Eighth Month 1751, she quietly departed this Life, Aged Forty three, a Minister near Nineteen Years, and was interred the 23d at *Furnace*, the Meeting to which she belonged, her Body being attended to the Grave by many Friends and Neighbours, by whom she was loved and her Loss lamented. A solid and living Testimony was there born to the Truth, and her unwearied Labours therein. May the great Lord of the Harvest, who is removing many eminent Ministers from his Churches, be pleased to raise up and qualify others, to stand faithful Witnesses for his Name and Truth in the Earth.

A Testimony from the Quarterly - meeting at Witney *in the County of* Oxford, *concerning* BENJAMIN KIDD.

HE was a Man much beloved and esteemed, not only by Friends and amongst his Neighbours, but by People in general of different Ranks and Perswasions. He was naturally chearful, open and free in Conversation, which rendered his Company both profitable and very desirable, being deep and sound in Judgment, and of great Sincerity and Integrity; a diligent Attender of Meetings, and exemplary in his Conduct amongst Men; eminently qualified, by the supream Dispenser of of all Good, for great and singular Services in the Church, not only in Discipline, in which he was excellent, exerting himself in great Wisdom; but through the lively and powerful Influences of divine Grace, conspicuously arrayed with Beauty and Brightness in his Ministry, rightly dividing the Word of Truth, and unfolding the Mysteries of the Gospel, to the informing and convincing many who before were unacquainted therewith, and to the Comfort and Encouragement of such as were under Affliction and Distress of Mind in their religious Progress.

Much might be said of his excellent Qualifications, Services and diligent Labours in this Nation, *Ireland,* and *America*; in all which Places he travelled under the Influence of that divine Power and Authority, by which he was enabled to turn many from Darkness to Light, and from the Paths of Disobedience to the Wisdom of the Just.

A more full and exact Account we must suspend giving at present, not being supplied with Materials to be more particular, but which we hope in a little time to be furnished with, by which we may give a more full and ample Account of the Labours and Services of this great and good Man our deceased Friend; the Removal of whom is not only a great Loss to us, but likewise to the Church in general. But not to dwell much upon that, we sincerely desire that the great Lord, who so eminently

qualified

qualified him, would raise up many more such bright Ornaments in the Church, that *Zion* may become a beautiful Habitation, and *Jerusalem* the Praise of the whole Earth.

He departed this Life on the 21st of the Third Month 1751, Aged about Fifty nine, a Minister about Thirty eight Years.

A short Testimony remains upon my Mind to add, concerning my dear and entirely beloved Husband BENJAMIN KIDD, *deceased, whose Memory remains and is very precious, and as a sweet Savour in his Family, and to those that were near and dear unto him.*

HE was a tender Husband, an indulgent Father, and a true Friend to all Mankind; early called into his Master's Vineyard to labour, and indeed made great Improvement in the same. In his last Ilness he was afflicted with great Pain and Sickness, which was hard to bear, yet he underwent it with abundance of Patience, without murmuring or repining, being freely resigned to the divine Hand which supported him, and gave him a grounded Hope and Assurance of his Well-being.

When the *Hickcough* first seized him, he was full of Joy, saying, *This is a welcome Messenger, it is one Step nearer.* And I standing by him said, *Why, my Dear?* He answered,

It

It will be a glorious Change; I am not afraid to die, and to put on Immortality: That will be durable, yet I leave it; though of Choice I had rather be diffolved, but the Lord's Time will be the beft Time. Often faying, *Death would be the moft welcome Meffenger he ever met with.*

Now he is gone to his Reft, to reap the bleffed Fruits of his Labour: May thofe that are left behind follow his worthy Example, that they may enjoy the fame Bleffing, is the ardent Defire of my Mind for all.

MARY KIDD.

A Teftimony from Moate *Monthly-meeting in* Ireland, *concerning* WILLIAM SPROULE.

HE was born at *Toberet* in the County of *Weftmeath* in *Ireland,* in or about the Year 1674; defcended of honeft and religioufly inclined Parents, who educated him in the Way of the Church of *England*; and (as at times he has, in a tender and fweet Frame of Mind, related to fundry of us) the Lord was pleafed, in Mercy, to vifit him in his early Days, and by the Operation of his divine Grace and good Spirit in his Heart, did incline him to a Search after, and Hunger for, that Bread which only and truly fatisfies the hungry Soul; yet not meeting therewith, though a
clofe

close Attender of Time and Place appointed for publick Worship, it caused him much Trouble of Mind; which his Father observing, and understanding the Reason, recommended him to the Notice of the Bishop, and others of the most eminent Clergy, with whom he had many Opportunities, but to little Satisfaction, finding them all Strangers to the Way and Workings of that divine Spirit which, in degree, was at work in him; and also the Emptiness of their Recommendations to the Observance of *outward Performances*; the Practice whereof he had experienced would no way contribute to true Peace, but rather the contrary: He therefore betook himself to reading the Scriptures, Meditation, and solitary walking about the Fields; in which, at times, the Lord was pleased, in Mercy and Goodness, to enlighten his Understanding, and afford of his Life-giving Presence, to his inexpressible Joy and Comfort; and having some little Acquaintance with, and liking to Particulars of the People called *Quakers*, Desires were raised to know more of them, and the Principles professed by them; and accordingly he got to some Meetings, and conversed with them; and believing it to be his Place to join in Society with them, acquainted his Father therewith, who tenderly answered, *That if he really thought it his Duty so to do, he gave him his free Consent, and wished it might contribute to his Peace of Mind*; or Words to that Import.

Some

Some Years after, he married amongſt Friends, and ſettled in the Town of *Athlone*, where his *Chriſtian*-like Life and becoming Deportment gained him the Love and Eſteem of all Ranks of People, both in the Town and Neighbourhood.

His ſitting in Meetings appeared to be under much Weight and Exerciſe of Spirit. In or about the Year 1730, his Mouth was opened in the Miniſtry. While of Ability of Body, he often attended Half-year's, Quarterly and Province-meetings; and viſited ſome Meetings in the neighbouring Provinces. In his publick Appearances he was weighty and tender, much to our Edification and Comfort. He was freely given up to every Service of the Society, and particularly ſerviceable in Family Viſits, wherein he was well accepted.

For ſome time before his Deceaſe, he laboured under a painful Diſorder of the *Stone* and *Gravel*, which he patiently bore with much Reſignation, being ſenſible to the laſt. He quietly departed this Life, the 23d of the Third Month 1751, and was buried in Friends Burying Ground at *Moate* the 25th of the ſame.

The Testimony from Mountmelick *Monthly-meeting, in* Ireland, *concerning* JONATHAN BARNES.

HE was educated in the Profession of the *Presbyterians*, and in his Youth addicted to Gaiety in Dress. He was convinced of Truth in the City of *Dublin*, about the Twenty third Year of his Age, and by it was led into Plainness and Circumspection. He afterwards became a living Minister, sound in Discipline, and serviceable in the Church on divers Occasions, yet neither assuming nor forward; chearful, but not talkative; weighty in Spirit, and reaching in Silence; a lowly minded Seeker of divine Notice and Help; and firm, as a Stake in *Sion*, for the keeping up our ancient Testimony in all its Branches. In Family Visits he was often eminently favoured with an Heart-tendering Power and Energy. He ruled well in his own Family, was esteemed in his Country, was industrious and prudent, charitable and benevolent. His House was freely open for the Lord's Messengers, when in that Part, and to receive them, he counted a great Privilege.

He frequently visited Friends in divers Parts of this Nation; and of *England* and *Scotland* once, in 1733, with his worthy Kinsman *John Ashton*.

Of late Years he was afflicted with bodily Infirmity, and often went to Meetings in great Pain. The Day he died, being in a sweet and tender Frame of Mind, he said, *The God of Abraham, Isaac and Jacob, is my God; he called me when I was in the Wilderness. I have often read, O Death, where is thy Sting? But now I can speak of it by Experience;* — with more of the like Import: After which, he departed in great Stilness the 18th of the Fifth Month 1751, Aged about Fifty five, a Minister about Thirty one Years.

He was buried the 22d, in Friends Burying Ground in *Kilconenmoor*, in the County of *Tipperary*; many Friends of several Meetings, and other People, present; to whom the Efficacy of Truth was declared, as it had been manifested in the Conversion, Life and Ministry of this our dear Friend.

A Testimony from the Monthly - meeting of Carlisle, *concerning* JONATHAN OSTELL.

OUR ancient worthy Friend *Jonathan Ostell*, of *Moorhouse* in *Cumberland*, was descended of Parents well esteem'd amongst us, who were concerned to give him a sober and religious Education. But as he advanced in Years, he found his Mind strongly inclined to the vain Customs and Fashions of the World; and

and, as he sometimes said, *was resolved to cast off all Restraint, and to gratify his Heart's Desires*; but the Lord, who is rich in Mercy, was graciously pleased to visit him, in a powerful Manner, by his Grace and good Spirit, so that, by taking heed thereto, he not only witnessed a happy Change in himself, and a passing from a State of Condemnation to that of Justification and Peace, but was eminently favoured with a Gift in the Ministry; in the Exercise whereof he experienced a Growth, and became an able Minister of the Gospel. In Prayer he was remarkably fervent and powerful.

His Service and Labour of Love was great, not only amongst Friends, but also with People of other Persuasions, with whom he had divers Meetings. He also, at different times, visited the Churches in North and South *Britain*, and *Ireland*; which, we hope, tended to their Edification and his own Peace.

His Heart and House were open to Friends and others. He was plain and humble in Deportment, visited the Sick, relieved the Poor, was of a loving and free Disposition, and generally beloved.

He was remarkable in his Testimony against Tithes, not only as to paying them, but even against receiving the same. In his Life-time, and by his Will, so much as in him lay, he invested the several Owners of the Estates, out of which he, as Impropriator, had formerly been

been paid, with the Right and Property he believed he had or could have claimed, in an impropriate Tithe; which evidently demonſtrated the Sincerity of his confcientious Scruple about Tithes.

In the Seventy fourth Year of his Age, he was concerned to go to *London* to the Yearly-meeting (which was the laſt time he attended that Meeting) where we believe he had good Service; and at his Return expreſſed much Peace and Satisfaction.

Though he was of a pretty great Age, and laboured under Infirmities of Body, particularly *Want of Sight*; yet he attended Meetings diligently, and frequently appeared in publick Teſtimony and Supplication, in much Devotion and Tenderneſs of Spirit. In his laſt Sickneſs he ſignified, that *Death was no Terror to him*; and that *he was reſigned to the Will of the Almighty, and could ſay in the Sight of Heaven, that he deſired no Man to do otherwiſe to him than he had done unto them*. And adviſed Friends, who came to ſee him, *to maintain the Teſtimony of Truth in every Branch thereof*. He deſired his Wife, *not to be uneaſy at his being removed, for he believed he ſhould die well; for the Lord was good to him*. And a little before his Death, ſaid, *His Heart was full of Praiſe, though he could not utter it much in Words*. And ſo continued in a ſweet Frame of Mind, ſenſible to the laſt.

He departed this Life the 12th, and was buried the 15th of the Tenth Month 1752, Aged Seventy seven, a Minister Fifty three Years.

A Testimony from the National Half-year's Meeting in Dublin, *concerning* ABIGAIL WATSON; *the first Part of it wrote by her Husband.*

Some Account concerning my dear deceased Wife, *Abigail Watson,* who departed this Life the 11th of the Eleventh Month 1752, in the Sixty eighth Year of her Age, having been a Minister Forty Years: In which Service she faithfully laboured in this Nation; five Times in *England,* and once in *America*: In all which Places, by Accounts received, she had acceptable Service, and many were comforted and edified by her Ministry, which was in the Demonstration of the Power; in which she was made as a sharp threshing Instrument against all undue Liberty; yet comfortable to the Mourners in *Zion.*

About a Year before she died, she was sensible her Departure drew nigh; for she found no Engagement on her Mind to travel abroad, as she frequently had done, when of Ability, but said, *She found her Work was done, and nothing in her Way;* so was made quite easy, and

and only waited for the Salvation of God, *who*, she said, in a reverent, thankful Frame of Mind, *had been with her all her Life long; and now I shall sing, sing, sing.*

During the time of her Weakness, whilst of Ability to get down Stairs, she attended the Meeting, which was held in the House, where she frequently appeared in a living Testimony for her Lord and Master, to the tendering many Hearts; and when not able to come down, I brought her down in my Arms; and I may say, that although her outward Strength decayed, she was daily renewed with the Heavenly Oil, which made her Lamp to burn; and she, under the Anointing that was upon her, often ministered to our Comfort, and was enabled to triumph over Death, Hell and the Grave, as I heard her express herself, — *O Death, where is thy Sting? O Grave, where is thy Victory?* And indeed, she was wonderfully favoured with the Renewings of Life, in her Weakness; and the last time she spoke to us, in a Meeting in her Chamber, Oh! the Tenderness that was felt, and Counsel that was dropt, *for all to take Care of themselves, and the Education of their Off-spring, to bring them up in the Fear of God, out of the Pride, vain Customs and Fashions of this World.* As at many other times, it was great Grief to her to see the Prevalence of undue Liberty; against which libertine Spirit she often had a Testimony to bear for her Lord and Master; and indeed,

indeed, great was her Concern for the rising Generation.

Some little time before she died, she was visited by some Friends, to whom she tenderly expressed herself, and spoke of the Saying in the *Revelations*, Chap. iii. 21. — *To him that overcometh, will I grant to sit with me in my Throne, even as I also overcame, and am set down with my Father in his Throne.* And spoke sweetly on that Subject, advising to *Continuance in well-doing, in order to obtain that blessed End.*

And although she was much afflicted with Weakness, and her Body and Limbs so swelled, that she could not help herself, the Patience and Resignation of Mind she bore it with, was great ; often longing and desiring to be dissolved, yet would say, *The Lord's Time is the best* ; so that I could not but often admire, how wonderfully she was supported in Patience, until her Dissolution came. She sensibly prayed about two Hours before her Departure, and then closed her Eyes, and quietly departed this Life without any seeming Uneasiness, but as one falling asleep.

And I have many times since admired the continued Goodness of God to her, in the daily Renewings thereof, and the steady Hand of Love which supported her through her long Infirmity, with so free a Resignation to the Divine Will ; and the Rememberance of her is sweet. And thankful I am to the God of all

our

our Mercies, for his divine Support, having, I think, juft Ground to conclude, that fhe died in the Lord, refts from her Labours, and now receives the Reward of her faithful Services.

To the above I may add, fhe was exemplary in her Family, in Diligence and Induftry, helpful to the Poor, a tender affectionate Wife to me, and Mother to my Children; and fuch a fweet Harmony fubfifted to the laft, that I do not remember ever any Difference between them, nor an angry Word. I may truly fay, fhe was made a Blefling to me and mine, and many more; and as we were truly united together in the Bond of Love and Life, we were many times made one anothers Joy in the Lord, fo that her Lofs to us is great, but her everlafting Gain.

Killconner, the Firft Month, 1753.   SAMUEL WATSON.

The foregoing TESTIMONY being communicated to us, we have true Unity with it; being deeply affected with the Lofs of fo ferviceable an Inftrument: A truly humble Woman indeed; preferved in Simplicity of Heart, and Nothingnefs of Self; not forward, nor defirous of the Applaufe of Men, but ready to give Way to and prefer others. A conftant Attender of Meetings, and a diligent Waiter in them, for the fpringing up of divine Comfort; being often enabled, through the Arifings thereof,

thereof, to minister to the hungry and thirsty Souls, inviting to the Table of the Lord, and often saying, in the Aboundings of Life, *Eat, O Friends, drink, yea, drink abundantly, O Beloved.* Cant. v. 1.

She was a nursing Mother to the young and tender Plants, fervent and powerful in Prayer for their Prosperity; and that it might please the Lord to raise up a living and baptizing Ministry in his Church, which she saw to be in a low Situation; yet she was comforted, in a divine Sense, that the Lord would remember *Zion,* and turn her Captivity as the Streams of the South.

And, in the Openings of the Heavenly Vision, she saw into, and was made to declare of, *a glorious Day approaching;* which, though she said, *she might not live to see, yet should die in the Faith thereof.* And did believe the Lord would first visit with his Judgments, and purge away the Dross from among the Professors of Truth, in order for a Preparation thereunto; saying, *That if our Society did not keep their first Love, and be a separate People out of the Vanities and Corruptions of the World, the Lord would set many of them aside, and call in others; and have a People to shew forth his Praise, and stand for his Truth and Testimony on Earth.*

Her Desire, in Brokenness of Spirit, was to the Almighty, who had mercifully reached to her in her Youth, and preserved her all her Life long, and accompanied her with his divine Presence,

Presence, in the Course of her Service for his Name and Church's Sake, that he might preserve her living in old Age: *Oh!* said she often in Fervency, *that I may not dwindle in old Age.* And we may say, in Thankfulness to the Lord, who does not forget to be gracious to his poor Servants, that her Request was granted; for her Ministry was to the last much attended with Life, which she was often made instrumental to raise in Meetings, to the comforting the Hearts of the Lord's People, amongst whom he was pleased to exalt her in a good degree, though preserved in herself in true Humility and Nothingness, even to the Conclusion of her Time, and finishing her Testimony amongst us.

And now, that the Eye and Expectation of all, both Old and Young, may be unto the Lord alone, whose Care is still extended over his Church, and who is all-sufficient of himself, and can raise up and qualify, even as he removes and takes away, at his Pleasure, is the Desire of a Remnant amongst us.

A Testimony from the Monthly-meeting of Worcester, *concerning* John Corbyn.

OUR ancient and well beloved Friend was born in the aforesaid City, and was convinced of the blessed Truth about the Eighteenth Year of his Age; and, by a diligent and and fervent waiting thereon, he grew strong in Faith, and zealous for the Propogation of the Gospel of our Lord and Saviour Jesus Christ; and, when about the Thirty fourth Year of his Age, he came forth in a publick Testimony, in great Tenderness and Gospel Simplicity, and continued fresh and lively in the Exercise of his Gift, until a few Days before his Death, to the general Satisfaction and Comfort of the Sincere-hearted.

He travelled, as a Minister, divers times into several Parts of *England* and *Wales*, in the Unity and with the Approbation of the Meeting to which he belonged; and, we believe, had good Service in his Labour of Love, and that it had a Tendency to strengthen the Weak, comfort the Afflicted, and stir up the Indolent, to Diligence in religious Concerns, both at home and abroad.

He was very exemplary in attending Meetings, both for Worship and Discipline, and solicitous to maintain Love and Unity amongst Friends;

Friends; and when he apprehended any Thing of a contrary Nature like to prevail, it gave him great Uneasiness and Conflict of Mind, till he saw Peace restored, and that pernicious Weed, *Discord*, extirpated. In Contributions of Charity he was liberal, and in Hospitality remarkably generous. He retained his Integrity, Understanding and Memory, to his End.

Much might be said of this our worthy Friend, but we shall only add, that we rest well assured he finished in Peace, and a well grounded Hope of an immortal Crown of Righteousness, which is laid up for all those who love the Appearing of our Lord and Saviour Jesus Christ.

He departed this Life the 30th of the First Month, and was interred the 1st of the Second Month 1752, in Friends Burial Ground in *Worcester*, in the Eighty third Year of his Age.

A Testimony from the Quarterly-meeting at Coggeshall in Essex, *concerning* ELIZABETH BOWING.

SHE was born, as we are informed, in the County of *Suffolk*; and, being convinced of the Truth in the early Part of her Life, passed through many Exercises, on that Account, from her Mother, who was of a different Perswasion.

Some time after her Convincement, she received a Gift of the Miniſtry. She married a Friend whoſe Name was *Appleyard*, a Practitioner in *Phyſick*, who not many Months after was removed from her by Death.

During her Widowhood, ſhe devoted herſelf to the Work of the Miniſtry, and in the Exerciſe thereof became very acceptable to Friends; whoſe Meetings ſhe was concerned to viſit in many Parts of *England*, as alſo in *Ireland* and *Holland*. Her Teſtimony was lively and convincing, miniſtering Comfort and Edification to the Hearers, ſhe having a Readineſs of Utterance, adorned with a becoming Modeſty in all her publick Appearances. She was well known among Friends by the Name of *Elizabeth Appleyard*, until the Time of her ſecond Marriage.

In the Year 1711, ſhe was married to *Edward Bowing*, an honeſt Friend and Shopkeeper at *Boreham* in this County, where they dwelt together many Years. They were loving and open-hearted to Friends, and well reſpected by their Neighbours, being beneficent and liberal to the utmoſt of their Ability.

The laſt of her Travels, in the Service of Truth, which we have an Account of, was in the Year 1736, when, with the Approbation of her Monthly-meeting, ſhe viſited the Meetings of Friends in ſeveral Counties in *England*.

Both her Huſband and ſhe, when at home, ſo long as Ability of Body continued, were
constant

constant Attenders of the Meetings for Worship to which they belonged, and remarkably exemplary for their exact Observation of the Time appointed. They continued united in the Exercise of Faith and good Works till he died, about seven Years since.

A few Years after his Decease, she being very aged and infirm, was removed to *Chelmsford*, where, after about two Years Continuance, in a constant Expectation of her approaching Dissolution, and in a lively Hope of Rest and Peace hereafter, which she would be often expressing to those who visited and attended her, she departed this Life on the 25th, and was interred the 28th of the Sixth Month 1753, in Friends Burying Ground at *Chelmsford*, being about Eighty eight Years of Age, and having left a good Savour behind her.

A Testimony from the Monthly - meeting of Kendal, *in the County of* Westmorland, *concerning* DEBORAH WILSON.

SHE was descended of religious Parents, and had her Education in the Way of Truth; the divine Influences whereof, made early Impressions on her Mind, by which she was preserved in a sober, exemplary Conversation, and became a serviceable Member in the Church.

She

She was a constant Attender of Meetings, though much engaged in Business, in which she acquired a good Character, and was instrumental in supporting a numerous Poor.

About the Year 1733, she received a Gift in the Ministry, wherein she all along acquitted herself with great Sincerity and Plainness. She travelled through many Parts of *Great Britain* and *Ireland*, gaining much Respect, where she came, by her innocent Freedom in Behaviour, and the great Satisfaction she gave, in being always content with the meanest Entertainment she met with; though, when at home, had Plenty of the good Things of this Life, whereof she communicated to her Friends with Openness of Heart. Her Humility and compassionate Regard for those under Affliction, rendered her amiable to such as were acquainted with her.

Her last Sickness, which was long and severe, she bore with much Patience and Resignation of Mind, frequently saying, *That she found nothing to do but to die; having an Evidence that it would be well with her, when the extreme Moments were past through.* So that without doubt we conclude, our Loss is her great Gain.

She died the 29th of the Fourth Month 1754, in the Sixty sixth Year of her Age, having been a Minister about Twenty Years.

A Testimony

A Testimony from the Monthly-meeting of Horslydown *in* Southwark, *concerning* SIMEON WARNER.

THE affectionate Esteem and just Regard we bear to the Memory of this our ancient and worthy Friend, obliges us to accompany the Notice of his Removal with a brief Testimony concerning him.

He was, in the more early Part of his Life, an useful and reputable Member of the Church; afterwards, for about the Space of Fifty Years, an able and serviceable Minister therein.

When he was about Thirty four Years of Age, he found himself under a religious Concern, from the Movings of the Spirit of Christ, the Sanctifier and Preparer to every good Word and Work, to testify in the publick Assemblies of the Lord's People, somewhat of his own Experience of the Operations of divine Grace in his Heart, for the Encouragement of others; and finding a Return of Peace attended his Obedience therein, became gradually enabled to persevere in that Part of his Duty, and, with all Readiness of Mind, to addict himself to the Work of the Ministry.

His Testimony was sound and edifying, consonant to and corresponding with the holy Scriptures; his frequent Quotations whereof, and Allusions whereto, shewed him to be well instructed therein; a Qualification very agreeable to a Minister of the Gospel: And his assiduous Reading of, and Application to, those sacred Writings, attended with true Conversion to the divine Word in his own Heart, might justly entitle him to the Blessing pronounced by the Psalmist, *On the Man whose Delight is in the Law of the Lord.*

He was a constant Attender of Friends Meetings for Worship, in and about this City; and his Love to his Brethren and Sisters, in the Work of the Ministry, was such, as induced him constantly to attend their Morning-meeting, both on the First and Second Days of the Week, so long as the Continuance of his bodily Health and Strength would permit.

But though the general Exercise of his Ministry was in this City and Parts adjacent; yet was he at some times led to visit the Churches at a farther Distance; for in the Year 1718, he travelled, together with our Friend *Walter Newbury*, into *Holland* and *Germany*, where his Testimony was well received by Friends, and was of good Savour and Service among them.

In the Year 1728, being accompanied by our Friend *Joseph Gurney*, he took a Journey into the West of *England*, as far as the Land's-end in *Cornwall*; and visited the Meetings of Friends through several Counties in that Part of the Nation, to the general Satisfaction of Friends,

Friends, who received their Testimony in a Spirit of *Christian* Love and Brotherhood. He also made several shorter Journeys to visit Friends at *Norwich, Bristol*, &c.

He was a constant Attender of his own Monthly-meeting, the Quarterly, Two-Weeks, and Six-Weeks Meetings; and was generally present at the Meeting for Sufferings; in all which he was very serviceable.

Thus he continued until about the two last Years of his Life, when he became exceeding weak in Body, and unable to go out of his House; in which time, though he had little or no Pain or Sickness, yet the Course of Nature tending to his bodily Dissolution, his Memory became much impaired; yet did the innocent Sweetness and Composure of his Countenance, and the Tenderness of his Spirit, administer Matter of Comfort to such of his Friends as came to visit him.

He departed this Life on the 26th Day of the Eighth Month 1754, and we make no doubt ended his Days in Peace with the Lord; having attained the Age of Eighty five Years: He was interred on the 30th of the same Month in Friends Burying Ground in *Long-lane*, his Corps being attended to his Grave, from *Horslydown* Meeting-house, by a very great Company both of Friends and others.

The

The Testimony from Richmond *Monthly-meeting, concerning* MARY RICHARDSON *of* Burton *in* Bishopsdale.

SHE was one whom the Lord saw meet to visit in her young and tender Years; and as she gave up to the Manifestations of Grace received, it pleased him to open her Mouth in a publick Testimony, and she became cloathed with the Comeliness of the Gospel, and truly valuable in his Church; wherein she laboured diligently the Prime and Flower of her Age, not only in this Nation and *Wales,* but in *North Britain* and *Ireland.*

Her Conversation was pleasant and edifying, being seasoned with a divine Sweetness. Her Conduct was so innocent and blameless, that she gained the Respect of Friends and others, both in her Neighbourhood and elsewhere.

Although, through the Course of her time, divers Trials and Probations of various Kinds fell to her Lot, yet, as she had learned of him who gives Patience in Tribulation, she bore them with a becoming Resignation to his holy Will. More might be said to shew the *Christian* Qualities of this our worthy Friend, but what we have in View is only a short Memorial of her.

Her

Her laſt Journey to viſit Friends was into *Ireland*; and although ſhe was weak in Body, yet the good Hand of Providence enabled her to perform it beyond what could reaſonably be expected. Since that time (which was upwards of Twenty Years) through Weakneſs and Infirmity of Body, ſhe has been moſtly confined to her own Houſe, where the Converſation of Friends was acceptable and pleaſant to her, as hers was alſo to them: At which Opportunities, when drawn into Silence, ſhe ſometimes dropp'd a few Sentences from the Fountain of Life, greatly to the Comfort and Refreſhment of thoſe preſent. Thus ſhe ſteadily ſteered along, until the wiſe Diſpoſer of all Things ſaw meet to cut the Thread of her Life; and we have good Cauſe to believe, ſhe is entered into Reſt with him.

She departed this Life the 26th of the Tenth Month 1754, and was buried the 30th of the ſame in Friends Burying Ground at *Carperby*, being accompanied by a pretty many Friends and others.

Aged Ninety, a Miniſter about Seventy Years.

A Teſtimony

A Testimony from the Monthly-meeting of Marsden *in* Lancashire, *concerning* JOHN ECROYD.

HE was Son of *John* and *Alice Ecroyd* of *Briercliffe* in the Parish of *Burnley* and County of *Lancaster*; was religiously educated by his pious Parents, his Father having been an able Minister of the Gospel, a steady and zealous Labourer therein, a good Example to the Flock of Christ, and a patient Sufferer for the Testimony of a good Conscience.

About the Twentieth Year of his Age, he was favoured with an humbling Visitation of the Day-spring from on high, which brought him into an inward Acquaintance with the Almighty, and in a great measure redeemed his Mind from the Love of the World and its fading Enjoyments: Solitude and Opportunities for religious Meditation were then his chief Delight, that being abstracted from the Tumults and Cares of Life, he might be more at leisure to pursue, without Interruption, the Point he had chiefly in view; and as he was a Man of great Abilities, both natural and acquired, many conceived Hopes, that as they became sanctified by the Power of Truth, he would one Day be made an useful Instrument in the Hand of the Almighty.

But

But in process of time, this Zeal and Fervour abated: For becoming immersed in a Life of Business, and falling into unsuitable Company, he greatly departed from these good Beginnings, became less circumspect in his Conduct, and, at times, was overtaken with the Evil of *Intemperance*. In this State he continued for divers Years; during which time, by Intervals, he was under deep Remorse for his Out-goings, and many times made strong Resolutions to be more careful; *which* (as he often said) *being made too much in his own Will, were of short Duration*.

About ten Years before his Death, he was again effectually awakened, and favoured with such a Sense of his lamentable Departure from his first Love, and that Purity of Heart which he had in his early Years in part attained, as caused him many a sore Conflict; and entering deeply into his own State, he saw the Necessity of bearing the Whip of small Cords, that so his Temple might again be purged.

He now willingly stooped to the Cross of Christ, despising the Shame, and resolving with his whole Heart to endure its Discipline, and to bear the Indignation of the Lord, because he had sinned against him. An eminent Instance of divine Forbearance and Clemency, in thus mercifully sparing Offenders, and reaching forth a Hand of Love for the reclaiming some who have been deemed of the lost Sheep of the House of *Israel*, and, by the Spirit of Judgment

Judgment and of Burning, purifying from dead Works the Consciences of those who submit to the Operation of his pure Spirit and Power, in the Day of Visitation, as did this our departed Friend, who in the Midst of Judgment found that Mercy mixed therewith his Soul longed for; so that as a Brand pluckt out of the Burning, he lived to tell others what the Lord Almighty had done for his Soul, *That he had brought him up out of the horrible Pit, out of the miry Clay, and set his Feet upon a Rock, and was establishing his Goings, and had put a new Song in his Mouth, even* PRAISE UNTO OUR GOD.

His Ministry was lively and powerful, tending to awaken and rouse to Diligence the Careless and Lukewarm; severe, in the Power of the Highest, to the Stubborn and Rebellious, but he had often a Word in Season to the weary Soul; tenderly exhorting the Diffident, but Contrite-hearted, to confide in that merciful Regard himself had so largely experienced: And having known the Terrors of the Lord for Sin, he was earnestly engaged for the Return and Reconciliation of others. He was a zealous Asserter of the Universality of the Love of God in Christ Jesus, in Opposition to that narrow Doctrine of the *Predestinarians*, too much espoused by some of his Neighbours.

The great Duty of Worship, he esteemed of the highest Importance; and his Diligence in attending Meetings, even when almost weighed

weighed down with old Age and Infirmities, and his awful Attention of Mind when there, were truly exemplary: He was frequently engaged therein, in a particular manner, on Account of his Children, *That they might seek to have an Inheritance in the blessed Truth, more than all other Enjoyments.*

He was a Man endowed with uncommon Qualifications for the Good of his fellow Creatures, not only with respect to his serviceable Station in the Church of Christ, which was indeed truly eminent, but also in the Practice of *Physick*; in which Profession he was very successful, obtaining a good Report among People of all Ranks and Perswasions, and being remarkable for his Integrity and Moderation.

In his last Ilness, notwithstanding the Severity of his Disorder, and great bodily Weakness, his Soul was many times as a well watered Garden, and many weighty Expressions dropt from him, to the Edification of those present: Just before his Departure he uttered these Words, *I feel an Evidence of Peace with God: There is Peace through his precious Blood.*

He quietly departed this Life, greatly lamented, at his House in *Biercliffe* aforesaid, the 17th, and was buried at Friends Burying Ground in *Marsden* the 21st Day of the Second Month 1755, in the Seventy seventh Year of his Age.

A Testimony from the Monthly-meeting of Shrewsbury, *concerning* GEORGE BRAWN.

HE had a Gift in the Ministry, to which we believe he was rightly called, and though it was not large, yet he was a sincere-hearted Man, and freely given up to do what was in his Power for the Promotion of Truth. He had been a considerable while declining in his Health; but as his natural Strength abated, he did to our great Comfort grow stronger in the inward Man. He was a good Example to us in diligently attending Meetings, both for Discipline and Worship; and was very much concerned, in those Meetings, to be made Partaker of the true Benefit thereof, and likewise for the Growth of Truth in Friends of our small Meeting, which he constantly attended so long as Ability of Body would permit, (and even till he was hardly able to go) which was about six Weeks before his Departure.

In the time of his Confinement, he expressed himself very much concerned for the Welfare of Friends in general, and that the Discipline might be supported; particularly, that Friends would be careful to see, that our Testimony against Tithes was strictly kept to by every Member concerned therein. He much desired he might be enabled to bear the Afflictions of the Body with Patience, *which*, he said, *he found then were enough to bear, without the Reflection of mispent Time.*

For two Days before he died, he lay seemingly quite easy and free from Pain, and in that Time uttered many sensible Expressions, which are not all remembered; one was, *That we must patiently wait the Lord's Time, which is the best*; by which he appeared to be waiting in Resignation till it pleased the Almighty to remove him hence. Not many Hours before his Departure, he said to a Neighbour, *That his Hearing failed him, his Sight failed him, his Tongue failed him, but the Love of God never failed.* Some time after, he was in a Heavenly Frame of Mind, and continued praising and magnifying the Lord Jesus Christ about the Space of near half an Hour; though the whole of his Expressions could not be perfectly understood, yet the Power that attended him, and was at that Time felt by those that were present, was Cause of Joy. After this he lay quite still till he breathed his last; and we doubt not is entered into that eternal Rest which is prepared for the Righteous.

He departed this Life the 19th of the Second Month 1755, and was buried the 21st of the same in Friends Burying Ground in *Shrewsbury*, Aged Sixty two, a Minister about Thirty Years.

A Testimony from Thirsk *Monthly-meeting in* Yorkshire, *concerning* William Brown.

HE was born at *Camston* in the *East-Riding* of the County of *York*, and descended of believing Parents. He was religiously inclined in his Youth, and came forth in the Ministry about the Twenty fifth Year of his Age, and we believe hath laboured faithfully to the Conclusion of his Days.

He travelled, in the Service of the Gospel, in some Parts of this Nation, but more particularly in some of the Northern Counties, and in *Scotland*; of which Visits we have had acceptable Accounts. He diligently attended Meetings both for Worship and Discipline, though at times under much Difficulty, as he painfully laboured under a severe *Asthmatick* Disorder for many Years, which he was enabled to bear with great Patience.

He was often deeply exercised for the Growth and Prosperity of Truth. He was several times concerned to visit the Families of Friends, where he had to administer suitable Advice to the Refreshment of many; his Testimony was plain, sound and edifying; his Conversation was exemplary, he being of a chearful Disposition, honest and sincere; he was particularly kind and assisting to his Friends,

Friends, especially to the Poor. He was a loving Husband, a tender Father, and a good Neighbour; and as he lived, so he died, in a loving and tender Frame of Mind, being truly resigned, and uttering many tender and comfortable Expressions near his Conclusion.

He departed this Life the 15th Day of the Fifth Month 1755, and was buried in Friends Burying Ground at *Thirsk* the 17th Day of the same Month, Aged about Seventy four, having been a Minister about Forty nine Years.

A Testimony from the National - meeting of Ireland, *held in* Dublin, *concerning* ELIZABETH ASHBRIDGE.

IN the Year 1753, apprehending it required of her to visit the Meetings of Friends in *England* and *Ireland*, she left her Habitation, with the Consent of her Husband, and the Unity and Approbation of Friends, as appears by her Certificate, and performed a religious Visit to many Meetings in this Nation, to the general Satisfaction of Friends; wherein she endured so much bodily Hardship in travelling, and underwent so much spiritual Exercise in Mind, that she fell dangerously ill at the City of *Cork*; and to those two Causes she always imputed her Disease.

After recovering so much Strength as to be able to proceed on her Journey, she left *Cork* and came to *Waterford*, to the House of our Friend *John Hutchinson*, where she remained very much indisposed for the most part of fourteen Weeks; and, in that Interval, was at the Province-meeting at *Clonmell*, where she had extraordinary Service. From thence got to the County of *Carlow*, and to the House of our Friend *Robert Lecky*; whilst there, some Expressions, which she uttered in an affecting Manner, were taken down in Writing, and are as follow.

The 7th of the Fifth Month 1755, *Elizabeth Ashbridge*, being sorely afflicted with Pain of Body, expressed her Fear of not being patient enough under it, but several times desired it, saying, O *dearest Goodness, grant me Patience till my Change come, and then enable me; and do not forsake me, Lord of my Life.* And, speaking of what she had suffered, said, *Words could not express, nor Thoughts conceive, what she had gone through these seven Months; for what Cause, the Lord only knew.* Although it had been so with her, yet she would not have any be discouraged, *for her Master* (she said) *was a good Master, and she did not grudge suffering for him; though he chastises his Children, it is for some good End; sometimes for their own, and sometimes for the Good of others.* And said, *she did not repent coming into this Nation, though she was so tried, being satisfied she was*

in

in her Place, and that it was the Requirings of him who had supported her to a Miracle: And now it looked as if two poor weak Women were sent to lay down their Lives in the Cause of Truth: or to this Purpose; (her Companion *Sarah Worral* having departed this Life at *Cork* a short time before) *And as many faithful Servants had been Sufferers in this Land, as they were not the first, she thought they would not be the last.* She mentioned something of its lying heavy on the Inhabitants thereof, if there was not an Amendment. But for those that had put their Hands to the Plough, she desired such might go on with Courage, and said, *God was on their Side; and that it was happy for those who had remembered their Creator in their Youth.*

Another time, when in extream Pain, she cried out, *Lord, look down upon me;* and begged, *that* Patience, *her old Companion, might not leave her;* and said, *Although Pain of Body was her Portion at present, through the Mercies of a gracious God her Mind was pretty easy.* Though sometimes she feared she was not quite fitted for that glorious Mansion which she aimed at, and into which nothing that is unholy can enter; yet had a Hope it was not in Wrath she was chastised, for she had to acknowledge, *she felt the Touches of divine Love to her Soul:* And said, *She loved the Truth, and those that loved it were precious to her Life, whether Relations or others;* and that *she had fought*

fought it from her Youth, and was thankful for being preserved so, as not to bring a Blemish on it, since she made Profession thereof, but had done what she could for it.

A Friend taking leave of her, she told him, *Whether he heard of her Life or Death, she hoped it would be well.* Some Friends being with her, she said something of the Singularity of her Trials, but that *the Hand that permitted them, had an indisputable Right;* to which she seemed resigned, whether in Life or Death, hoping it would be well. She said, *She loved the Truth, and it had been her Support*; and desired those, that had begun to walk in it, *to keep close to it, and it would never leave them.*

She seemed thankful, *that the Beauty of this World, and the Enjoyments of it, were stained in her View, and she made willing to give up all*; the hardest was her dear Husband, being so far from him; but even that was made easier than she could expect. Being wished *a good Night's Rest*; she said, *She did not expect to be free from Pain, but that every Night, that the Lord sent, was good*; and, though uneasy, hoped they all would be good Nights, and when once the Gulph was shot, she should have Rest.

Speaking to a Friend, she said, *She endeavoured to live without a Will*; and that *she hoped she had born her Afflictions with a degree of* Christian *Fortitude.* Being in great Pain, and asked, *Whether she would be settled?* she said, *None could settle her but one*; and in his

own

own Time, she hoped, he would: Then cried out, *Dearest Lord, though thou slay me, I will die at thy Feet; for I have loved thee more than Life.* She spoke affectionately to a Friend that visited her, gratefully acknowledging the Care and Tenderness shewn to her, and counted it a high Favour, that the Hearts of her Friends were opened to receive and sympathize with her. She spoke something of the Exercises of Mind she went through before her Convincement, and the Time she got Relief out of great Distress, and was enabled to make Covenant with the Lord; *which Time she still remembered, and hoped she should never forget, being desirous often to return to* Bethel, *and to remember the Time of her Espousals.* She acknowledged the Advantage there was *in being deeply tried, and that it was the Way to be enabled to speak comfortably to others.*

Having grown weaker for several Days, she departed this Life, in a quiet Frame, the 16th of the Fifth Month 1755, and on the 19th her Corps (accompanied by many Friends) was conveyed, in a solemn Manner, from our Friend *Robert Lecky*'s to Friends Burying Ground at *Ballybrumhill,* where several Testimonies were born to the Truth.

Thus our dear Friend finished her Course. It remains briefly to add our Testimony concerning her.

She was a Woman of an excellent natural Understanding; in her Conversation chearful, yet

yet grave and inſtructive; ſhe felt the Afflictions of others with a tender Sympathy, and bore her own with Patience and Reſignation.

As a Miniſter, ſhe was deep in Travail, clear in her Openings, plain and pertinent in her Expreſſions, ſolid and awful in her Deportment, and attended with that *baptizing Power*, which is the Evidence of a living Miniſtry; and which ſo evidently attended her, in the laſt Teſtimony ſhe bore in a publick Meeting (in great bodily Weakneſs) that moſt or all preſent were reached and deeply affected thereby, and a young Woman was, at that Time, convinced of the Truth; which was as a Seal to the finiſhing of her Service in the Work of the Miniſtry; and, in which, being ſo owned to the laſt, we have no doubt but ſhe now receives the Reward of the faithful Servant, and is entered into the Joy of her Lord.

A Teſtimony

A Testimony from Brighouse *Monthly-meeeting in* Yorkshire, *concerning* John Scott.

HE resided, the greatest part of his Time, in the Town and Neighbourhood of *Leeds*, and did early embrace the Heart-tendering Visitations of God's Love to his Soul, under which he became very solid and religious whilst young; and so effectual was the Power and Prevalency thereof upon him, that before the Expiration of his Apprenticeship, he came forth in a publick Testimony. And as the holy Anointing continued and increased upon him, he grew in the Root, and became well grounded in the Ministry of the Gospel of Peace and Salvation, and seemed ever careful not to go beyond the Line of Truth therein. And as he was not large, so he was not frequent, in his publick Appearances: Towards the Conclusion of his Time, his Ministry appeared still more lively. In our Meetings of Worship, he was singularly steady in his waiting for the Arisings of divine Life and Power, and was ready to join with it, in whomsoever he found it to appear.

He visited, at several times, the greatest Part of this Island; and once, with his dear Friend *John Haslam*, the Kingdom of *Ireland*, and *Holland*: In all which, we have reason to believe his Labours were acceptable to Friends.

He

He was a constant Attender of our Meetings for Discipline, and was of considerable Service therein, having a peculiar Talent for the good Purposes thereof. He was quick of Apprehension, and sound in Judgment, and when concerned to speak to Cases, his Words were few and savoury. He was remarkably tender of having any *disowned*, without first trying, by Gospel Endeavours, affectionately to reclaim them; neither was he less careful, that the Society should not be imposed on by the specious Pretences or superficial Acknowledgments of any. Such was his Regard for Peace and good Order in the Society, that he often employed and exerted his Abilities in that good and laudable Office of a *Peace-maker*, both at home and abroad with Success.

He was a frequent Attender of the Yearly-meeting at *London*, where he was well received, and we hope of Service. His last Journey thither, was with his above-mentioned Friend *John Haslam*, taking Meetings through several of the Inland Counties, which he performed, though very weak in Body; and constantly attended the Meetings in *London*, and appeared very lively and acceptably therein. When these Meetings were over, he, by short Journeys, (visiting some Meetings in his Way) reached our Quarterly-meeting at *York*, which also he attended, notwithstanding the bodily Infirmities which were upon him, and was evidently favoured with the Goodness of Truth.

This

This Meeting being over, and not being able to reach home, he tarried at *York*, and was enabled to sit with Friends there, in their Meeting the First-day after, and appeared to the Satisfaction of Friends, as it was in a degree of the Demonstration of the Spirit and Power. After which, becoming weaker and weaker, on the Fifth-day following he breathed his last, having bore his Ilness with remarkable Resignation and Quietness of Mind, and we doubt not is entered into eternal Rest.

He died at *York* the 3d Day of the Seventh Month 1755, and was buried in Friends Burying Ground in *Leeds* the 6th Day of the same, Aged about Seventy, a Minister Fifty Years.

A Testimony from Marsden *Monthly-meeting in* Lancashire, *concerning* ALICE HALL.

PRECIOUS in the Sight of the Lord is the Death of his Saints; precious the Rememberance of their Lives to his People, and worthy to be recorded, as Examples to present and succeeding Generations; that marking the peaceful End of the Perfect and Upright, many may be induced more steadily to persevere in the Footsteps of the Flock of Christ, and encouraged to enter early into the Vineyard of our Lord, as did this our departed Friend;
who

who having been favoured with the valuable Blessing of a religious Education, under the Care of pious Parents, gave timely Hopes of an Increase in Piety, advancing in Grace as she advanced in Years.

About the Twenty fourth Year of her Age, she was called to the Work of the Ministry, and gave Proofs of her Love to the Almighty, by Obedience to his Requirings, continuing a diligent and faithful Labourer in his Service to the End of her Life.

She was a Person generally beloved, both by Friends and others that were acquainted with her, constantly evidencing, both by Example and Precept, that the Honour of God and the Good of Souls were her chief Concern.

In Meetings she was diligent in attending to the Heavenly Gift, and being influenced by the Holy Spirit, her Doctrine was exceedingly edifying. She hath for several Years been infirm of Body, but strong and fervent in Spirit.

The State of her Mind, towards the Close of her Life, we think can't better be expressed than in her own Words, in a few Lines she sent to the Meeting some time before her Departure, *viz.*

" The Renewings of the same Divine Love,
" which we have often enjoyed together, doth
" at this Time tender my Heart, and maketh
" me humbly thankful to the God of my Life,
" that he hath not only been pleased to call me
" into his Vineyard when young in Years, but
" also

" alſo to be near, from time to time, and favour
" me with his living and powerful Preſence
" now in my old Age, to his Glory and my
" exceeding great Comfort: For which, I am
" very thankful to him, who is worthy of
" all Glory and Honour for evermore." Thus
did ſhe continue fruitful in old Age, and laid
down her Head in perfect Peace, the 3d of
the Ninth Month 1755, in the Seventy fourth
Year of her Age. A Miniſter about Fifty
Years.

A Teſtimony from Newcaſtle *Monthly-meeting, concerning* ARCHIBALD GILLESPY.

HE was convinced of, and embraced, the Principles of Truth in his young Years, and as he gave up in Obedience to the Maniſeſtations thereof, was by the Operation of that Divine Power and Grace, by which he was firſt reached and early called to the Work of the Miniſtry, well fitted and qualified to hold faſt the Heavenly Treaſure, which dwelt largely in him. He was alſo furniſhed with Wiſdom to divide the Word aright, to the Comfort and Edification of many, like the good Scribe, bringing forth, out of his Treaſury, Things new and old. He was powerful and reaching in his Miniſtry, fervent and ſolemn in Prayer, very regular and circumſpect in his Conduct; of a peaceable Difpofition, an humble Life, and godly Converfation; an affectionate kind Hufband, a tender and loving Parent.

He was a due Attender of Meetings for divine Worfhip, as alfo Monthly and Quarterly-meetings for Difcipline, whilft he had Ability of Body, and many times had good Service therein; tho' we don't find that he travelled much abroad in the Work of the Miniftry, except into *Scotland*, and fome of the Northern Counties in *England*, where, we believe, he was well received, and had good Service, not only in ftopping the Mouths of Gainfayers, but his Doctrine, at times, dropt as Dew, and his Speech diftilled as the fmall Rain, greatly refrefhing the tender Plants.

We are fenfible of the great Lofs the Church has fuftained by his Death, though we believe it is his great Gain, who has done a good Day's Work, and as a Shock of Corn full ripe, we doubt not, is entered into the Reft prepared for all thofe that love and ferve the Lord.

He died the 30th of the Tenth Month at *Newcaftle*, and was buried the 2d of the Eleventh Month 1755, in Friends Burying Ground there, Aged near Eighty nine, and a Minifter Sixty two Years.

A Teftimony

A Testimony from Carlisle *Monthly-meeting, concerning* DAVID HODGSON.

HE was born at *Wormanby* near *Carlisle* in *Cumberland*; his Parents were of good Repute and Esteem among Friends and others; and being favoured with a religious Education, as he advanced in Years, came more immediately to experience in himself the Visitations of divine Grace, which teacheth to live soberly, righteously and godly in this present World; and as he gave up in Obedience thereunto, experienced Peace and Justification in his own Soul; and, about the Year 1704, came forth in a publick Testimony to the Universality of the Love of God in Christ Jesus, and to the effectual Operation of his Grace in the Hearts and Souls of Mankind, in order to their Salvation; and his Ministry was attended with a fervent Engagement of Spirit for the Cause of Truth, and the Prosperity thereof.

He attended the Yearly-meeting in *London* several times, in his younger Years, and visited the Meetings of Friends in divers Parts of this Nation; in *Scotland* more generally, and in *Ireland* two different Times: Of which Labours of Love, and Services in the Truth, we have had good Accounts.

He was a diligent Attender of Meetings, and exemplary in timely coming. And though in Meetings for Difcipline he was not forward to fpeak to Affairs; yet was much concerned for Peace and the good Order of the Church, for the reconciling of Differences, and maintaining the Difcipline thereof.

He entertained Friends with great Opennefs and Freedom. He was a loving Hufband, a kind Friend, a peaceable Neighbour, and charitable to the Poor and Afflicted. He bore a faithful Teftimony againft the antichriftian Yoke of Tithes, not only as to paying, but as to receiving them; for being by Law intituled to an *impropriate Tithe*, he refufed to receive the fame in his Life-time; and at his Death, by Will devifed the faid Tithe to the feveral Owners of the Eftates, out of which it was payable.

In the Decline of Life, though he did not enjoy a good State of Health, yet he attended Meetings at home when able, and the Monthly and Quarterly-meetings; though he appeared not much in the Miniftry of late, yet we have Caufe to believe he retained the fame Love and Unity of Spirit, with Truth and Friends, and the Caufe thereof.

As his Diforder grew upon him, which was faid to be of the *Paralytick* kind, his Capacity was in fome degree impaired, tho' he moftly continued fenfible to the End. He departed this Life in great Stilnefs the 14th of the
Eleventh

Eleventh Month 1755, and was buried the 16th of the same, in Friends Burying Ground at *Moorhouse* (a solemn Meeting being first held) attended by many Friends and others.

Aged Seventy nine, a Minister Fifty one Years.

A Testimony from the South Monthly-meeting *in the County of* Warwick, *concerning* John Bevington.

OUR dear and much esteemed Friend *John Bevington*, was one who, by a divine Touch, was prevailed upon in his young Years, to turn his Back upon Folly, and endeavour to walk in the Paths of Virtue and Righteousness; and being naturally of a chearful, active and generous Temper, quick of Apprehension, and of good Judgment, he became more than ordinarily useful in his Generation as a Man, as well as through divine Favour, as a *Christian* and a *Minister*; so that it may be truly said of him, that, as a Neighbour, he was sociable, very serviceable, and lived and died in good Repute; as a Friend, sincere, sympathizing and ready to assist; as a Husband and Parent, tender and affectionate, careful and solicitously concerned, by Precept and Example, to train up his Children in Plainness, Sobriety, and the Principles of true Religion;

Religion; and for many Years, at the Head of a large Family of Children and Servants, demeaned himself as a prudent Oeconomift, with a Heart and Houfe open for the Entertainment of his Friends. A zealous Attender of Meetings, both for Worfhip and Difcipline, and a Promoter of Opportunities of Retirement in his own Family and others: And thus (as alfo in his general Conduct) endeavouring, by a circumfpect and exemplary Life and Deportment, to come up in the Difcharge of his Duty towards God and Man; and having his Eye to the Recompence of Reward, was enabled by Faith to prefs through the Entanglements of an adverfe World, and run with Patience the Race fet before him, though often in the Deeps; largely experiencing, that through many Tribulations the Righteous enter the Kingdom.

As to his publick Teftimony it was found and edifying, which rendered him very near and valuable to many, and well approved amongft us. He travelled not a little, in the Service of the Miniftry, in this Nation. In the Year 1749 he vifited *Scotland*, in Company with *John Lewis*, and had feveral Meetings diftant from the Refidence of any under our Denomination; which Opportunities he particularly mentioned in his laft Ilnefs, as believing the Fields in that part are white unto Harveft: That Journey he vifited Friends in *Ireland*, miffing few if any Meetings in that
Nation;

Nation; and that thefe his Labours of Love tended to real Service, and the mutual Satisfaction of himfelf and thofe amongft whom his Lot was caft, is beyond doubt with us; for we believe he was moved and exercifed therein, under divine Influence.

To thefe his Labours, as a Minifter, we may add, that he, as a Member in our Meetings of Difcipline and Church Affairs, was for many Years remarkably ferviceable. The Lofs of fuch Worthies is really matter of Lamentation, but being fatisfied our Lofs terminates in his eternal Gain, we defire to fubmit to that Providential Arm, who giveth and taketh away as it pleafeth him.

His laft Ilnefs, being a Diforder in his Stomach and Bowels, proved exceeding painful, and having little Appetite, reduced his Strength apace; but that Power that vifited him in his Youth, and had been underneath to fuftain in every needful Time, did not leave him in this his final Conflict, but enabled him to endure it with Patience, and to triumph over Death, the Sting thereof being removed.

Amongft the few Expreffions, through Pain and Difficulty delivered, he fignified, *That though he had laboured abundantly, he had no Merit of his own, but trufted in the Mercies of God, and had Hopes of a bleffed Immortality; and might he but quietly pafs away, the greateft Monarch's Place on Earth, would be difpifed by him, in comparifon of eternal Reft;* and tho' his

Family and Friends were near and dear to him, yet now he could not but beg to be dissolved.

He departed this Life in a very innocent and Lamb-like Frame, at his own Habitation at *Upper Eatington*, the 15th Day of the Twelfth Month 1755, in the Sixty fifth Year of his Age, having been a Minister near Forty Years; and on the 17th of the said Month, his Body was decently interred in Friends Burying Ground at *Upper Eatington* aforesaid, accompanied by many Neighbours, Relations and Friends, which was a very solemn Opportunity.

A Testimony from the Monthly-meeting of Witham *in* Essex, *concerning* ANNA FLACK.

IT having pleased the Lord to remove by Death our worthy Friend *Anna Flack*, the Remembrance of her Zeal and *Christian* Labours engages us to impart, as a Testimony, That having received a Gift in the Ministry of the Gospel of Christ, she appeared in a publick Testimony about the Twenty sixth Year of her Age. Her Integrity and Faithfulness in the Exercise thereof was great, notwithstanding her Afflictions and Trials, of which she had an uncommon Share, which rendered her State *a Life of Sorrows*; but she attained Experience by the Things which she suffered, and being

being faithful, they added to her Enjoyment of the Lord's Goodness, and the Advancement of his Work; so that many in this and the adjacent Counties can from comfortable Experience testify, she was sent of God to water his Heritage.

Her Ministry, accompanied with the holy Anointing, tended greatly to the Encouragement and Edification of the Sincere-hearted, she being frequently and zealously concerned, in the Course of her Service, in true Gospel Love to call unto, invite and warn the Disobedient to forsake the Evil of their Ways, and turn to the Lord with all their Hearts, whilst the Day of his merciful Visitation was extended unto them.

She was sincerely concerned to adorn her Doctrine with a Conversation agreeable thereto, being a good Example in diligent Attendance of religious Meetings, in which she was a true and faithful Labourer in Spirit, for the Resurrection of that divine Life and Power, which is the Crown of all our religious Assemblies. Her grave, weighty and tender sitting therein was affecting to behold.

She was greatly serviceable in the Promotion of our Womens Meetings of Discipline: The Members of which will be no small Sharers in the Loss of so valuable a Friend. She was concerned for the Promotion of Truth in general, also earnestly exercised on Account of her own Family in particular, that they might live

live in the Fear of God; being an affectionate Wife, and a very tender careful Mother to her Children, much beloved by her Neighbours in general, to whom she was serviceable in divers Respects, and the Loss of her is generally lamented by them.

In the latter Part of her Life she had an infirm State of Body, whereby she was rendered unable to travel any considerable Distance; yet she constantly visited and attended Meetings about home when able, and very frequently when under Indisposition of Body. We believe and trust she is at Rest, the Lord calling her from laborious Works to a peaceful Reward.

She departed this Life the 20th of the Twelfth Month 1755, at her House in *Boreham*, Aged about Forty six Years, and was buried at *Witham* the 25th of the same Month, a great many Friends and others accompanying her Body to the Place of Interment.

A Testimony

A Testimony from the Monthly-meeting of Reading *in* Berkshire, *concerning* ISAAC PICKERELL.

OUR said dear Friend removed from *London*, and settled with us the latter End of the Year 1723, where his Company and religious Services have been very acceptable; the Lord having blessed him with a considerable Share of Understanding, both in divine and natural Things, whereby he was well qualified, as well as zealously concerned, for the maintaining that good Order and wholsome Discipline established in the Church, and therein acted with that prudent Care and Circumspection, which evidently denoted that he lived near to the Well-spring of Divine Goodness. He was very assisting, by Advice and otherwise, to Friends in Cases of Difficulty, either of a religious or civil Nature; having a true Sympathy with such as were concerned for the Prosperity of *Zion*, unto whom he was as a nursing Father. Neither did the afflicted Widows, or their Fatherless Children, escape his Regard. And as he truly feared the Lord, and delighted in the Company of his People, so his Heart as well as House was open to such whom the Lord concerned for the spreading of his glorious Gospel.

The

The many good Advices and sweet Opportunities some of us have had with him, renders his Memory dear and precious to us. He was an early and constant Attender of our religious Meetings, whilst Ability of Body permitted, and when there, would wait with that becoming Gravity, which denoted a well composed Mind, waiting in the Gift received for the arising of the Spring of eternal Life, in which his Heart was often enlarged, and his Mouth opened amongst us, to the Reviving of the Spirits of those that were ready to droop, as well as to the Refreshment of the Sincere in Heart; though full in the Discharge of his Duty to the Stubborn and Rebellious.

He was sound in Doctrine, distinct in Delivery, and his Ministry edifying as well as convincing; as many were Witnesses to, not only in these Parts, but likewise in most Parts of *Great Britain*, where his Labour of Love, and Gospel Ministry was very acceptable.

For divers Years past he was afflicted with a Disorder which brought on him great Weakness of Body, but he remained sound in his Memory and Understanding, and in humble Resignation to the Divine Will patiently waited for his Change; declaring, not long before it came upon him, his Satisfaction *in that he found his Day's Work was done, and that he had faithfully served the Lord, his Church and People*; so that we may say, in the Words of the holy Apostle, *He had fought the good Fight*, and kept the Faith, and is gone to receive the immortal Crown which the Lord, the righteous Judge, will give to all those that love his Appearing.

He quietly departed this Life the 23d of the Second Month 1756, and was buried the 1st of the Third Month following, in Friends Burying Ground at *Reading*, his Funeral being attended by many Friends and sober Neighbours; where divers living Testimonies were born to the Excellency of that Power, by which he was raised up and preserved to his Conclusion: Aged near Seventy nine, a Minister about Fifty three Years.

A Testimony from the Mens Meeting at Cork *in* Ireland, *concerning* ANN HART.

BY an Account which she delivered to a Friend before her Ilness, we understand that she was educated amongst the *Baptists*, and, when very young in Years, was often affected with the Ministry of one *Coleman*, a *Baptist* Preacher, who, when Orders came to this City to stop all Dissenters Meetings, dropt the publick Meeting; which occasioned much Thoughtfulness and Exercise in her Mind; and being at some Loss, she went to the publick Worship, but soon grew weary, and dissatisfied with the Deadness and Formality thereof:

thereof: Whereupon, observing that Friends kept up their Meetings at that Time of Persecution, she went to one of them, and was so reached by the Visitation of Truth, through their living Ministry, that she was thereby convinced, took up the Cross and joined with them, (being then about Thirteen Years old) notwithstanding the many Slanders that were raised against them, both by malicious Tongues and abusive Books, as a People denying the *holy Scriptures*, *Prayer*, &c. which she soon found were false. And being concerned to be faithful to the Discoveries of Truth in her own Mind, she witnessed a Growth in it, and received a Gift in the Ministry, in the Exercise of which she was very acceptable to us, being lively and to our Edification.

During her Ilness, she often gave good Counsel and Advice to Friends that visited her, and expressed her religious Experiences in an affecting Manner to them, which were omitted to be taken down; but, in particular, a little before her Decease, she recommended to Friends, *That they should be concerned to invite, and bring into the Mens and Womens Meetings, such Youth as were sober and orderly*; as also, *that they should be weighty in their Meetings, and be careful to keep near to Truth*; *and, as it may open, give Judgment impartially, without Favour or Affection*. And having retained her Integrity to the End, we believe is now entered into those Mansions of eternal Felicity, where

the

the Wicked ceafe from troubling, and the Weary are at Reft.

She departed this Life the 22d of the Third Month 1757, in the Eighty feventh Year of her Age.

A Teftimony from the Quarterly - meeting of Oxfordfhire, *held at* Witney, *concerning* THOMAS GILKES.

WHEN it pleafed Divine Goodnefs to call him into the Miniftry, it was his Care fo to demean himfelf, as to adorn the Doctrine of Truth; and he was a Man much beloved, not only by Friends, but by his Neighbours. We think he might be deemed one of thofe Elders that deferved *double Honour*, being found in Doctrine, diligent in the Lord's Bufinefs, and an excellent Example of Induftry in his Family. And when drawn abroad, in the Love and Service of the Gofpel, (which was frequent while able) he was particularly careful to return home with great Expedition, when he looked upon his Service to be over. So that we think we may fafely fay, God's Glory and the Good of his fellow Creatures were what he efteemed his chiefeft Joy.

His Care over the Church was great; he might be called a fteady Watchman: And it is evident, he ruled his own Houfe well, and brought

brought up his Children in the Nurture and Admonition of the Lord, who hath been a rich Rewarder of his Care; for he was livingly made sensible of his Blessing resting upon him, and even when his outward Man was decaying, and his Race seemed near at an End, the Heart-melting Goodness of the Lord often made his Cup run over, and he felt the Evidence in himself, *that he had fought a good Fight, and kept the Faith,* and we have no Cause to doubt but he now inherits an incorruptible Crown.

May the God and Father of all our Mercies, if it be his Pleasure, raise up many more such worthy Instruments, that his Plantation may be watered, and living Praises more and more ascend to his great and excellent Name, who is worthy for ever and ever.

He was Aged Eighty two; a Minister about Fifty Years.

A Testimony

A Testimony from Ulster *Province-meeting in* Ireland, *concerning* ROBERT RICHARDSON.

HE was convinced in his Youth of the Principles of Truth, and led an orderly exemplary Life according thereto. He was diligent in attending Meetings at home and abroad, and zealous for the maintaining our Discipline; well qualified for visiting Families, and concerned to promote it. He had a few Words in Meetings for near Twenty Years, and though his Expressions were but short, they were frequently attended with Tenderness, being found and suitable to the State of the Meeting.

He had extraordinary Openings of Scripture Passages, which were comfortable and edifying. He was often under Trouble, and sorrowfully expressed his Concern for the declining State of the Church, and the undue Liberties, and the Unconcernedness, which were spreading amongst the Professors of Truth.

In his last Ilness, a few Days before his Departure, among many other weighty and sensible Expressions, he said, *Now I know that my Redeemer liveth; Glory and Honour to his holy Name for evermore.*

He departed this Life the 29th of the Fifth Month 1756, Aged Eighty eight Years.

A Testimony from Norwich *Monthly-meeting, concerning* PETER ANDREWS.

OUR dear Friend *Peter Andrews*, from West *Jersey* in North *America*, being on a religious Visit to Friends in this Nation, deceased in this City; and the lively Sense of his Services, and the Regard we bear to his Memory, engages us to transmit the following Testimony concerning him.

His first Visit to us was in the Eleventh Month 1755, and his Service and exemplary Deportment will remain as a lasting Testimony for him, and to the Truth he preached, in the Minds of many; and we have good reason to believe he was made instrumental, in a very particular manner, to the Help and Furtherance of some amongst us, whom it had pleased the Lord to visit with a fresh Visitation of his Love. And by the Information of other Friends, who well knew him, and particularly our Friend *Edmund Peckover*, who frequently accompanied him, as well as from our own Knowledge, we are enabled to give the following brief Account of his Labours and Travels, from the Time of his Arrival to his Death.

He landed in the South Part of *England*, in or about the Sixth Month 1755, and came directly up to *London*, where he was kindly received

received by Friends, and had very good Service during a short Stay there; but being desirous of being at the Quarterly-meeting to be held at *York*, in Company with several Friends of *London*, he went as directly to the said City as he could well do, being near Two Hundred Miles, and reached there by the 24th of the Sixth Month, at which Time began the Quarterly-meeting; and this our dear Friend had a very memorable and weighty Opportunity in Ministry, in the Meeting of Ministers and Elders at the Opening thereof; but, in the succeeding Meetings for Worship, was mostly silent; yet in those for Discipline, was divinely led to set forth the Nature, good End and Tendency of the same, and very zealously pressed to the keeping them up, in the same Wisdom and Power in which they were first established; evidently setting forth, *that they proceeded from that which gathered our Forefathers to be as a peculiar People unto God*; to the no small Edification and Comfort of many sincere Hearts, who rejoiced greatly in having his Company, which remains fresh in their Remembrance; his Services being as Bread cast upon the Waters, which, according to the wise Man's Observation, *shall be found after many Days*.

After the Quarterly-meeting was ended he went to *Pickering*, where a very large Meeting is kept Annually for Worship, and had seasonable and profitable Service. He travelled

to many other Places in that County, and
Friends were greatly refreshed and edified by
his *Christian* Visit, though not always attended
by publick Declarations in their religious Meetings appointed on his Account, which were
mostly very large, and Expectations high, yet
his Eye was to his great Master's putting forth.
He often was led to famish that too eager
Desire after Words; and in several publick
Meetings he had nothing to say amongst them;
which, tho' a great Disappointment to many
for the present, yet there afterwards appeared
a signal Service in it.

He was at *Yarm*, *Stockton*, *Bainbrig*, and
several other Meetings in and about the Dales;
then came to *Leeds*, *Bradford*, *Wakefield*, *Doncaster*, and so into *Lincolnshire*; which County
he visited pretty generally, also the Isle of *Ely*,
and came into *Norfolk*, and to this Place in
the Eleventh Month 1755, as afore-mention-
ed; was at most, if not all, of Friends Meetings in our County; then went into *Suffolk*
and *Essex*, and returned to *London* the latter
End of the first Month 1756, where he remained a few Weeks, being exceeding ill;
yet was at most of the Meetings in that City,
and was very serviceable, with many other
Friends, in Affairs particularly relating to the
Society in *Pensilvania* at that Time.

He went back again into *Essex*, and so for
Hertfordshire, some Parts of *Buckinghamshire*,
Oxfordshire, *Glocestershire*, and to the Yearly-
meeting

meeting at *Briſtol* in the Fifth Month 1756; and had good Service both in Meetings for Worſhip and Diſcipline, which was well received, and, it is hoped, made laſting Impreſſions on the Minds of many who had the Opportunity of being preſent.

His Indiſpoſition ſtill continued, but did not hinder him from travelling: From *Briſtol* he paſſed through ſome Part of *Gloceſterſhire*, *Wiltſhire*, and *Oxfordſhire*, and got to the Yearly-meeting at *London* in the Sixth Month, and altho' his Ilneſs continued upon him, was enabled to bear ſeveral living Teſtimonies, in the Demonſtration of the Spirit and of Power.

After the ſaid Yearly-meeting was ended, he came down to the Yearly-meetings at *Colcheſter* and *Woodbridge*, where he was eminently ſupported to be ſerviceable in the Churches. At *Woodbridge* he was ſtrengthened to bear a large, powerful and affecting Teſtimony in the laſt Meeting of Worſhip, to the tendering of many Hearts, whoſe States were ſo effectually ſpoken to, as that it may be fitly compared to the Excellency, and glorious Situation which the *Pſalmiſt* deſcribed, when he ſays, *How good, and how pleaſant a Thing it is, for Brethren to dwell together in Unity! It is like the precious Ointment upon the Head, that ran down upon the Beard, even* Aaron's *Beard, that went down to the Skirts of his Garments: As the Dew of* Hermon, *and as the Dew that deſcended upon the Mountains of* Zion; *for there the Lord commanded the Blessing, even Life for evermore*, Psalm cxxxiii. 1, 2, 3. It was indeed a most Heavenly, precious, baptizing Season, (this being the last publick Opportunity our dear Friend had) in which he was wonderfully led to set forth the progressive Steps the Almighty was pleased to make use of, in appearing to *Gideon*, confirming him in the Certainty of his Requirings, condescending to grant his Requests in a very peculiar Manner, and sealing them with his Presence, and giving him Victory over his Enemies, as he was faithful to follow the blessed Author that pointed forth the beginning as well as finishing that great Work, to which that extraordinary Servant of God, *Gideon*, in his Day was called; which memorable Service of our dear Friend, there is great Reason to believe the great Lord, who prepared him for the same, was graciously pleased to fix as a Nail in a sure place; and may it so continue in the Remembrance of those then present, who are left for a small Space yet in Mutability.

He continued very weak in Body all his Stay in *Woodbridge*, being about five Days, and no Perswasions could prevail with him to hinder his setting forward for his Journey, having strong Desires in his Mind to see Friends in this Place again; and to a particular Friend he expressed his Love so great to us, *that he thought he could willingly die with us*. He was favoured to accomplish it in two Days after he left
Woodbridge,

Woodbridge, though with great Difficulty, and lodged at the House of our Friend *John Oxley*, as he had done before, but took to his Bed soon after he got in, to which, the remaining Part of his Time, he was mostly confined.

It being the Time of our Yearly-meeting, many Friends went often to visit him, and he expressed to some, *That he was satisfied he was in his Place, in giving up to follow the Requirings of the Lord, in leaving his outward Habitation, and those near Blessings of a most tender affectionate Wife and dutiful Children.*

The Severity of his Illness kept him mostly *delirious*, yet he was favour'd with some clear Intervals; in one of which, being in a sweet Heavenly Frame of Mind, he broke forth in the following fervent Supplication, viz. *Oh! this poor Soul hath been for many Days on the Brink of the Pit of Distress; but thou, dear Father, dost not afflict thy Children willingly, but for some great and good Cause known only to thyself: Dear Father! suffer not thy Children ever to despair of thy Mercies, but that we may be helpful, as much as may be in our Power, to one another in all such times of Trouble. Dearest Father! thou hast been pleased to open, and to favour with thy Goodness; my Soul is thankful, and can say, thou art worthy of Glory and Praise for evermore.*

He continued to the 13th of the Seventh Month 1756, and then departed this Life, and was interred in Friends Burying Ground

the

the 18th of the same; after an awful Meeting; (his Corps being attended by a very large Number of Friends and others) and no doubt he rests, with the Spirits of the Just made perfect, in those glorious Mansions prepared for all those that hold out in Faithfulness to the End. His Memory is very precious and dear to many who are yet surviving, and we believe it may truly be said, that few Friends who have travelled in this Nation, have been more approved, or had more general Service in so short a Space of time.

A Testimony from Knaresborough *Monthly-meeting in* Yorkshire, *concerning* DAVID HALL.

HE was born at *Skipton* in *Craven* the 22d of the Tenth Month 1683, of honest and religious Parents, from whom he had the Blessing of a religious Education, which he happily improved from his Youth.

In the Eleventh Year of his Age he was seized with the *Small-pox* of a malignant kind, from which he narrowly escaped with his Life, whereby his bodily Strength was much impaired, and his Nerves so affected, that he rarely afterwards could walk steadily; for which reason his Father, thinking him unlikely to bear much bodily Fatigue or Labour,

about

about the Fifteenth Year of his Age put him to the Free-School at *Skipton* (there being at that time no School of Friends that taught the Languages in our Parts) wherein, by his Induftry and Diligence, in a fhort time he attained a competent Knowledge. He was a good Example to his School-fellows, adorning his Profeffion by a grave and exemplary Converfation, and was in great Efteem with his Mafter.

Having gone through the *Claffics*, and left that School, his Father open'd one for Boarders in his own Houfe, which was managed with good Succefs, many Friends, from different Parts of the Nation, fending their Children to be inftructed by him.

About the Year 1711 he came forth in a publick Teftimony, wherein he was very zealous, yet according to Knowledge; and after fome time he had a Concern to go into the Streets at *Skipton* and *Keighley*, on the Market-day, to warn People to Repentance and Amendment of Life. As he grew in the Miniftry, he was concerned to vifit at feveral times moft Parts of this Nation, as alfo *Scotland* and *Ireland*, as by a fhort Journal, he left in Manufcript, does amongft divers other remarkable Paffages of his Life particularly appear. He was very weighty, plain and pertinent in his Teftimony, even to the meaneft Capacities, not affecting to be thought learned, well knowing the Infufficiency of human Literature

Literature and acquired Parts in a Gospel Ministry. He had an excellent Knowledge and Understanding of the holy Scriptures, which he had a peculiar Talent in beautifully allegorizing upon, frequently in his Testimony, to the Information and Edification of the Considerate amongst his Auditors. He had a great Concern for the Youth of our time, frequently advising them, *To make the Religion of their Education, the Religion of their Judgment; and not content themselves with Formality, which is, in religious Matters, no more than a dark, dry and empty Lamp.* Those, more advanced in Years, he called out of *Worldly-mindedness, Indolence, Lukewarmness* and *Indifference;* often reminding us of the Church of *Laodicea,* that *her Case was as vile in the Sight of God, as that of the Wicked and Prophane.*

He diligently attended First-day and Week-day Meetings, at, or before, the Hour appointed, to the Conclusion of his Time; as also Monthly and Quarterly-meetings, till of late Years he was prevented by bodily Infirmities; during which Interval of time, he was concerned to write divers Epistles and Manuscripts to the said Meetings, and Friends in general; Part whereof are published, and Part remain in Manuscript, wherein are contained many good and weighty Advices and Admonitions, suited to most States, Stations and Circumstances of Life.

His

His Life and Conversation was innocent and inoffensive, conducted with Wisdom, Virtue and true Piety; he was a tender nursing Father to the Young in the Ministry, a Strengthener of the Weak, a Comforter of the Feeble-minded, an Encourager of the Faithful in the smallest Gifts. He had it very much upon his Mind, the latter Part of his time, to advise Friends, *Not to be too much discouraged, tho' they might see the Places of such as the Lord had raised up, and truly qualified for the Work of the Ministry, left empty, and but little Appearance in many Places of Succession therein; for the eternal Root remained the same, though the Branches were taken away.*

He was given to Hospitality, a Lover of good Men, a kind Husband, an affectionate Father, a good Neighbour, of a tender and charitable Disposition towards the Poor. May we that are left behind so run, that we may also obtain the Prize, which undoubtedly he hath done, having run well to the End; which, after some previous Ilness, wherein he expressed *his Assurance of Peace with the Lord*, came pretty suddenly upon him the 16th of the Ninth Month 1756, in the Seventy third Year of his Age, having been a Minister about Forty five Years.

N. B. *His Journal and several of his Epistles are since published, and may be had of the* Printer *hereof.*

A Testimony

A Testimony from Mountmelick *Monthly-meeting in* Ireland, *concerning* MARY NEAL, *formerly* MARY PEISLEY.

SHE was, in her younger Years, a Lover of Gaiety and Vanity, till visited by the Lord; she thereupon gave herself up to serve him with full Purpose of Heart.

Being called into the Work of the Ministry, she readily obeyed, yet with religious Fear, being particularly careful not to be too forward; so that her Offerings were like Fruit in its right Season, to the Honour of the Lord, and the Consolation of his Heritage. She was a diligent Labourer in Spirit for the Subjection of Self, and the Prevalence of divine Life; and as she was very careful to rise up in that Life, so was she likewise to sit down in it. Her reverent Solidity, and patient Waiting upon the Lord in Meetings, being very exemplary, and carrying with it a Reach and Awe to those that beheld her.

She was, when out of Meetings, of an uniform Conduct, retired in Spirit, awful and weighty in her Deportment, her Words few and savoury, administering Grace to the Hearers; seeking much to have her Conversation in Heaven, and to draw the Minds of others thitherward. In Friends Families, often drawn forth

forth in the pure Love of God, particularly to the Youth. In the Difcipline of the Church, of great Service ; fo that, though but young as to the time of her Miniftry and Services, fhe ftood in the Authority of Truth as an Elder, and as a Pillar in the Lord's Houfe, bearing the Weight of Oppofition, and Affaults of oppofite Spirits, without giving way, the Divine Power being her Shield, and the Munition of Rocks the Habitation of her Soul.

Under a lively Concern for the Welfare and Honour of every Part of the Society, fhe was at times qualified to impart tender and fuitable Counfel to her Brethren and Sifters engaged in the Miniftry and Difcipline, *That they might have a fingle Eye to the Glory of God, to prefer his Service before their own, and to get their Day's Work well done in the Day time.* She freely gave up herfelf to fpend and be fpent, and to pafs through various Perils, of a very near and exercifing kind, by Sea and by Land ; often under great Weaknefs and Hardfhip of Body, as well as Pain of Mind : Twice fhe vifited the Meetings of Friends through this Nation ; once through *England,* and fince that, through the *American* Continent ; and, by Accounts received, we find her Services abroad correfpond with the Teftimony here given of her.

Since her Return from her *American* Journey, fhe, with fome others, vifited the Families of Friends through this Monthly-meeting, as

fhe

she had done a while before her said Journey. The Weight of that Service lay chiefly upon her, and we believe she discharged herself faithfully therein ; it was finished the 14th of the Third Month 1756, and on the 20th, after an Ilness of about fourteen Hours, she was removed by Death, to the sorrowful Surprise of many, in a Sense both of our own Loss, and that of the Church in general, by the sudden Removal of this worthy Instrument in the Lord's Hand, who we believe was well prepared to live with Christ in his Kingdom, with whom her Life was hid whilst here.

She was indeed a true Burthen-bearer, a valiant Warrior, that turned not her Back in the Day of Battle ; very nearly united, in the celestial Bond, to such as loved Truth above all Things, and has left very few amongst us, equal to her, in respect to a faithful and diligent Application to the great and primary End of our Existence.

On the 24th of the said Month, her Corps was taken into the Meeting-house in *Montrath*, where a solemn Meeting was held on the Occasion, and several Testimonies born, many Friends from adjacent Meetings attending it ; after which, it was decently interred in Friends Burying Ground in the said Town. She died Aged Thirty nine, a Minister about Twelve Years.

Some

Some Account of her last Expressions.

"On the 17th of the Third Month (three Days before she departed this Life) in a retired Opportunity, with several Friends, she was opened to speak of the *Excellency of the Sabbath of Rest*; and, *that when Almighty God had finished his six Days Work in Creation, he appointed a Sabbath, and sanctified it*; and she believed there was there, *who would cease from their Works, and enjoy a Sabbath, in which they would have no Work to do*. She was clear and sweet in the Declaration of it, and the usual Seal of her Ministry attended it.

"On the Day she departed this Life, she lay quiet and still, in a retired awful Frame, and would sometimes raise her Voice with a melodious Sound, through the Efficacy and Virtue of that glorious Grace, which so often animated her to sound forth Praises to the King of Saints: And though she did not then express herself in Words, yet there was *a Language in the Sound*, that richly and fully manifested, that she triumphed over her bodily Pain, and over Death, Hell and the Grave; for she longed to be dissolved, intreating her Lord *to give her a Release, if it was consistent with his holy Will.*

"About Half an Hour before her Departure, her Pain being taken away, she said, *I praise thy Name, O my God! for this Favour.* After which,

"which, she breathed shorter and shorter, and
"quietly departed without Sigh or Groan,
"like one falling into a sweet Sleep; and is
"doubtless gone to enjoy that Sabbath of Rest,
"she so ardently longed for, diligently sought
"after, and so feelingly spoke of in her last
"Testimony; having been a Pattern to the
"Believers in many pious Excellencies, in
"Word, in Conversation, in Charity, in Spirit,
"in Faith, in Purity."

A Testimony from Brighouse *Monthly-meeting in* Yorkshire, *concerning* REBECCA COWEL.

THIS our dear and ancient Friend, was descended of believing Parents in the East Riding of this County, and was one whom the Lord was pleased to visit with the kind and merciful Offers of Life and Salvation in her Youth, which she embraced, and became a chosen Vessel for his Use, and had to tell to others, what he had done for her Soul, before she was Twenty Years of Age. The Testimony she had to bear, to the Sufficiency of the Name and Power of Jesus, was plain, sound and informing. Whilst unmarried, she visited the Meetings of Friends through the greatest Part of this Nation and *Scotland*.

In the Year 1708, she married *John Cowell* of *Leeds*, a Friend of good Repute, and a true Help-mate

Help-mate in the best Things; in whose time, she visited most of the Meetings in *England*, and also those of *Wales*; and since his Decease, in like manner, this and the neighbouring Counties, and once again most of the Meetings in *Wales*; in all which Labours of Love, we have reason to believe she was serviceable to many, as she also was at home, where, in the very Decline of Life, she shone more bright in her Gift than ever.

A few Months before her last Ilness, being appointed, with other Elders, to visit Families, she went through most of our Meetings with much Openness and Enlargement of Heart, to the great Satisfaction of Friends, which the more endeared her to her fellow Members in Christ, and when the Time of her Removal came, made their Loss the more sensibly felt. She was zealous for preserving good Order amongst the Women, and was often engaged in their Meetings of Discipline to good Satisfaction.

Her Care for the Poor, especially those of her own Sex, was very considerable, to whom her Charity, as well as Advice, was often extended. She was frequent in attending of Meetings, even when old Age and Infirmities of Body seemed sufficient to prevent her. In her last Sickness she endured great bodily Afflictions, with very remarkable Patience and Resignation to the Divine Will, and often dropped many comfortable and edifying Expressions,

pressions, to her Relations and Friends who frequently visited her; as also at other times breaking forth in holy Praises and Thansgiving to the Almighty, for his manifold and abundant Blessings; and, not long before her Exit, said, *Though my Weakness of Body is great, and my Pains hard to be born, yet my Holy Helper is near; I am often refreshed, I am often comforted, I have nothing too much, nor nothing too little, and all is well.* In this Heavenly Frame of Mind she continued to the 5th of the Fifth Month 1756, when she departed without a Sigh.

Aged near Seventy nine, a Minister near Sixty Years.

A Testimony from Devonshire-house *Monthly-meeting, concerning* ABRAHAM FARRINGTON.

THIS worthy Minister and Elder having had Drawings in Spirit for several Years, as we are informed, to visit the Churches of Christ in this Nation and *Ireland*, in the Service of the Gospel: When he apprehended the Time approached, wherein he was to enter upon this weighty Engagement, he settled his outward Affairs; and having the Concurrence and Unity of the Brethren, embarked on board a Vessel bound from *Philadelphia* to *Dublin*, in Company with three Friends from *Europe*, who

who had performed a religious Visit to the Churches in *America*.

He landed at *Dublin*, after a safe and prosperous Voyage of about four Weeks. He visited the Meetings of Friends in *Ireland*, and by the Accounts received from thence, had very weighty and acceptable Service there. After he had laboured faithfully in that Nation to strengthen the Brethren, and assist in building up the waste Places in *Sion*, he embarked for *England*; and having visited the Churches in some of the Northern Counties, and attended the Yearly-meeting at *Penrith* (where his Labour of Love, in the Work of the Ministry, was to Edification and Comfort) he came up to this City to the Yearly-meeting, where his Service was truly acceptable.

After the Yearly-meeting was over, he attended the Yearly-meetings of *Colchester*, *Woodbridge*, *Norwich*, and the Quarterly-meeting at *York*, and visited many Meetings in the Northern and Midland Counties; from whence, good Accounts have been received of the weighty and affecting Labours of this our dear deceased Friend.

He returned again to *London* the latter End of the Twelfth Month 1757, and having travelled with great Diligence, and laboured fervently, his Health was impaired; nevertheless, he attended Meetings till his Disorder encreased so as to render him incapable of further Service.

As this our dear worthy and honourable Friend spent but little time in this City, we cannot from Knowledge and Experience give such a Testimony concerning him, as might be thought requisite; yet, as some of us partook of the Benefit of his religious Labours, we find ourselves engaged to give forth this Testimony concerning him.

His Conversation was innocently chearful, yet grave and instructive; he was a Man of a weighty Spirit, a Valiant in *Israel*; a sharp Reprover of libertine and loose Professors, but tender to the Contrite and Humble, and a Lover of good Order in the Church.

He was strong in Judgment, sound in Doctrine, deep in divine Things; often explaining, in a clear lively Manner, the hidden Mysteries wrapt up in the Sayings of Christ, the Prophets and Apostles; and it may truly be said, he was well instructed in the Kingdom, bringing forth, out of his Treasure, Things new and old.

His Ministry was in Plainness of Speech, and attended with divine Authority, reaching the Witness of God in Man, and to the Habitation of the Mourners in *Sion*; frequently pointing out, in a lively Manner, the Paths of the exercised Travellers, and the Steps of Heavenly Pilgrims; by which he was made helpful to such as are seeking the true Rest, which the Lord hath prepared for his People. It may truly be said, he was eminently gifted

for

for the Work of the present Day, remarkably qualified to expose the Mystery of Iniquity, and to point out wherein true Godliness consisted.

His Distemper encreasing, he was confined to his Bed, at the House of our Friend *Thomas Jackson*, in *Devonshire-square*, where all necessary Care was taken of him. During his Illness, he was very sweet and tender in his Spirit, and remarkably patient. He uttered many comfortable and Heavenly Expressions, and several times said, *He apprehended his Time in this World would be but short* ; and seemed fully resigned to quit Mortality, having an Evidence, *that he should be cloathed upon with Immortality, and be united to the Heavenly Host.*

He had frequently been heard to say, in time of Health, *That he thought he should lay down his Body in this Nation, and not see his Friends in* America *more* ; to which he appeared freely given up. He often expressed his Desire, *that he might be favoured with an easy Passage* ; which was graciously granted.

He departed this Life, the 26th of the First Month 1758, like a Lamb, without either Sigh or Groan, as one falling into a sweet Sleep, Aged about Sixty six Years ; and on the 30th of the same, his Body was carried to *Devonshire-house*, where a large and solemn Meeting was held, which was owned by him whose Presence is the Life of our Meetings ; and from thence his Body was carried, by Friends, to their

Burying Ground in *Bunhill-fields*, a large Concourse accompanying it, and was there decently interred amongst the Remains of many of our primitive Worthies, and valiant Soldiers in the Lamb's War, *who loved not their Lives unto Death, for the Word of God and Testimony of Jesus.*

A Testimony from Tottenham *Monthly-meeting, in the County of* Middlesex, *concerning* DANIEL BELL.

OUR eminent and worthy Friend *Daniel Bell,* was the Son of *Jonathan* and *Rebecca Bell,* of *Cockermouth* in *Cumberland,* both descended of reputable Parents, and well esteemed in the Society.

He was born the 12th Day of the Twelfth Month 1685; and being soberly and religiously inclined from his Youth, was often favoured with the tendering and refreshing Influence of Divine Love ; so that when very young, he was frequently drawn to solitary Places for Retirement and Prayer ; *and,* as he has several times occasionally mentioned, *renewed his Resolutions to persevere in Obedience to those early Reaches of Divine Grace and Favour ;* and was often fully persuaded, that by continuing faithful therein, *he should be conducted safely through the various Occurrencies that might attend him in in this Life*; frequently remembering the Importance of that solemn Advice of Christ to his Followers, *Seek ye first the Kingdom of God and his Righteousness, and all these Things shall be added unto you.* And as he continued faithful in Obedience, he found it effectually verified in himself.

Soon after his coming to *London*, which was in the Year 1703, he entered into an Apprenticeship; and his circumspect and religious Deportment drew the Notice, and gained him the Affection, of solid Friends; and joining in an intimate Conversation with some of the most religious young Men, they had many precious Opportunities of Retirement together, to their mutual Edification, and Growth in the Grace of our Lord Jesus Christ; which hindered not, but promoted, their Success in what they engaged in of temporal Concerns.

He came forth in the Ministry about the Year 1705; and his Service, in that Capacity, was well approved by Friends and others. About the Year 1708, he had a Concern to visit his native Country; and having obtained Leave of his Master, and with the Concurrence of the Monthly-meeting he belonged to, he set out from *London* the 25th of the Second Month 1708, accompanied with some Friends from thence to *Uxbridge*, where there was a Burial, which occasioned a large Number of People, who were attentive to the Testimony born, and the Lord's Power was in Dominion, to the tendering of many Souls. And one of the Friends accompanied him into *Cumberland*, visiting Meetings in the several Counties they passed through, where they had many tendering and comfortable Seasons. And being come to his Father's Habitation : — *Please to take his own Account of the Reception he met with there*, viz.

"My dear Parents, said he, received me
" with much Gladness; and that Evening
" many Friends came to see me, and our
" Hearts were cemented together in the En-
" joyment of Divine Love, which was largely
" shed abroad amongst us. Blessed be the
" God of Truth for ever, who remembers his
" breathing Seed. On the Third-day Morn-
" ing I went to *Pardsey-crag* Meeting, and
" called to see our dear Friends *James Dick-*
" *inson* and Wife, who went to Meeting, and
" a glorious Time we had, to the Joy and
" Satisfaction of many. And tarrying some
" Weeks in the County, I visited the Meetings
" in general, where we had many comfortable
" Seasons; and I accompanied several Friends,
" appointed to visit Families, and had good
" Satisfaction in our Visit; the Lord's owning
" Power did attend us in a wonderful Manner;
" he was pleased to open the States of Friends
" Families very particularly, to the Edification
" of his People, in the Places where we
" came."

At

At the Quarterly-meeting for *Cumberland*, he met our Friend *John Bell*, and from thence they continued together till they returned to *London*, vifiting Friends Meetings in the Counties through which they paffed, where they had many fatisfactory Times. In that Journey he had good Service, for the Comfort and Edification of the Faithful, and his Teftimony had a great Reach on many of the Youth.

In 1710, he vifited the Meetings twice in *Kent*, *Suffex*, *Hampfhire* and *Surry*. In 1711, he entered upon a Vifit to Friends Meetings in moft Parts of *England*, *Scotland* and *Ireland*, where feveral were convinced by his Miniftry; and he returned to *London* the 6th of the Fourth Month 1713: Soon after which, he travelled in the adjacent Counties, and alfo in the Weftern, vifiting Meetings.

In the Year 1713, he took a Journey in the Weftern and Northern Counties. In 1715 and 1718, he travelled in the South and Weft Parts: In 1744, in the North and Eaft. In 1745, 1746, and 1747, he travelled in the North and Weft Parts. In 1748, he made a general Vifit to the Northern and Midland Counties; and to the fame in 1750: And his laft and concluding Vifit to thefe Parts, was in the Year 1755. Since which time, he frequently travelled into the adjacent Counties, in the Service of the Gofpel.

He was found and edifying in his Teftimony, often drawn forth in Points of Doctrine with

with great Clearnefs, which tended to the Opening the Underftanding into the Doctrine of the *Chriftian* Faith and Practice. He was very affectionate for the Youth, and often engaged, in his publick Miniftry, for their Good ; his Counfel to them was weighty and of great Importance, delivered in fo tender and affectionate Manner, as made him truly aimable in their View : In fhort, we believe him to have been a fanctified Veffel for the Lord's Ufe. And being often times favoured with the qualifying Influences of the Divine Spirit, his Doctrine dropt as the Dew, to the great Refrefhment of the Heritage of God; and there are many living Witneffes, that can fet Seal to his Miniftry and Labours of endeared Love amongft us.

He was conftant in attending Meetings, both for Worfhip and Difcipline. His Converfation was exemplary, fincere, and courteous ; not tenacious, but condefcending. He was diligent and induftrious in Bufinefs, when at liberty from religious Duties, and the Service of the Church. He was a loving Hufband, a tender and affectionate Parent, a kind and gentle Mafter, well beloved by his Relations and Friends, and efteemed by his Neighbours.

The laft Time he was at Meeting, he was remarkably favoured with Power from on high ; which was fo demonftrated by the Fulnefs and Clearnefs of his Teftimony, as to

be

be taken particular Notice of by divers Friends that were prefent.

In his laſt Ilneſs he was attended with the Over-ſhadowings of Divine Goodneſs; and though the Profpect of lofing fo dear a Relation, and fo worthy a Friend, could not but be Matter of Sorrow and Affliction; yet, in the Midſt thereof, the fweet Frame of Mind in which he was, when confined to his Chamber and his Bed, has caufed great Joy and Comfort to all about him, his Soul being filled with Prayer and Praifes to the God of his Salvation, in whom he had believed; and he who had been his Morning Light, he found to be his Evening Song: Breaking out often in Heavenly Expreſſions, faying, *Grace, Mercy and Peace, abounded to his great Conſolation*; and that *he had done his Day's Work.* On a Friend coming to pay him a Vifit, a few Days before he died, he faid to him, *The Lord has been my Stay and my Staff, and has helped me along, and I find him to be fo now.*

He departed this Life the 24th Day of the Second Month 1758, at his Houfe at *Tottenham* in *Middlefex*, and was honourably buried, the 2d of the Third Month following, in Friends Burial Ground at *Winchmore-hill*, the Meeting being attended by many Friends from *London* and the adjacent Counties, and feveral weighty Teftimonies born, to the Comfort and Edification of thofe prefent; and we have not the leaſt Doubt, but this our worthy Friend is
gone

gone to that State of everlasting Rest and Peace, where the Wicked cease from troubling, and the Weary are at Rest.

Aged Seventy two, a Minister Fifty three Years.

A Testimony from Ratcliff *Monthly-meeting, concerning* JOSEPH OLLIVE.

AS the Memory of the Just is blessed, we have Cause to believe a Blessing will rest upon those, who retain such a living and thankful Remembrance of them and their past Services, as faithfully to follow their Example: And as we have been large Partakers of the religious Labours of this our dear and honourable Friend, we esteem it our Duty to give forth the following Testimony concerning him.

He was the Son of *Benjamin* and *Elizabeth Ollive* of *London*, and was born at *Walthamstow*, in the County of *Essex*, the 19th of the Ninth Month 1692. He was early favoured with a merciful Visitation of Divine Kindness, to which he gave up when young and tender in Years; and as he grew up, by keeping close thereto, he became largely acquainted with the Operations of the Spirit of Truth upon his Soul, and, being preserved in Faithfulness, was made a solid and useful Member of the Society.

About

About the Thirty fifth Year of his Age a Dispensation of the Gospel was committed to him to preach. His first publick Appearances were in the Life and Wisdom of Truth, which nearly united him to the Brethren; and as he grew in his Gift he was not forward, but cautious, preferring his Brethren, and more especially those that were Strangers; and it may be truly said, his Labours were very acceptable, being greatly to the Comfort and Edification of the Church.

And though, by reason of bodily Infirmities, Travelling was more difficult to him than most of his Brethren in the Ministry, yet he frequently visited the Meetings of Friends in divers Parts of this Nation, during a Course of many Years; and his Services therein were well received by the Faithful.

He manifested an affectionate Regard for his Relations, exercising the tender Care both of a Friend and a Father over them; was a just and kind Master, and much beloved by his Servants; generous and exemplary in his Neighbourhood, affording constant Relief to some, and occasional Assistance to many others of the Poor: He often dispensed of his Liberality in private, being far from Ostentation in what he bestowed. His *Christian* Compassion and Benevolence led him to assist such, as either publickly or privately applied to him, by judicious Advice and Information, and
sometimes

sometimes by suitable Application, when it appeared necessary.

His natural Capacity was extensive, being improved by a good Education, but more so by the Influence of that Inspiration of the Almighty, which gives a right Understanding. He was largely concerned in the Management of Affairs relating to the Society. The Assiduity of his Attendance, and the industrious Exertion of his Abilities in the Cause of Truth, and for the Help of the Brethren, rendered him a very useful Member of this Monthly-meeting, of the Meeting for Sufferings, the Morning-meeting, and the several other Meetings established by Divine Wisdom, for particular as well as general Service; wherein he appeared to be extensive in Knowledge, deep in Experience, distinguishing in Judgment, and audible in Expression.

He was a kind Entertainer of Friends in general, and a great Encourager of Women Friends, to come up in their proper Services in the Discipline of the Church.

Towards the Conclusion of his Time, we were deprived of his Company at our Evening-meeting at *Bromley*, bodily Weakness rendering him unable to endure the Evening Air; yet he very frequently attended our Week-day Meeting at *Ratcliff*, where such as were rightly engaged to wrestle for a Blessing, had the Help of his Spirit, in an holy Labour and Exercise, to dig through all Obstructions, that they might get

get to the Spring of divine Refreshment, whereby he was often enabled to bear a living Testimony for God and his Truth ; which tended much to the Comfort of such as were honestly concerned, and to the stirring up the pure Mind in all.

He very nearly sympathized with the Afflicted in Spirit, and was often made instrumental for their Relief ; he had a great Regard for the Honest-hearted, though ever so weak and feeble in the Church ; and was frequently concerned to interceed for them, when favoured in the House of Prayer, that they might be strengthened, and come forward to do their Day's Work in the Day time.

He gave several transient Intimations of late, to some of his Relations and Friends, signifying *an Expectation that his Time here would be but short* ; the last of which he dropped with a remarkable Serenity and Chearfulness of Spirit.

It pleased Divine Providence to take him from the Dangers and Troubles of this probationary World, without passing through the Pains of a tedious and afflicting Sickness. He departed this Life the 25th of the Fourth Month 1758, by the sudden Seizure of an *Apoplexy*. A fresh Instance of the great Necessity of seeking a timely Preparation ; the Consideration whereof we hope may be a Means to excite us to Diligence and Watchfulness, that Fearfulness may not surprize us,

when

when that awful and awakening Time may come, that we ſhall be ſummoned from Works to Rewards.

We have Cauſe to believe it has been the ſteady Concern of this our dear deceaſed Friend, for a long Series of Years, to diſcharge himſelf, and ſo to watch, that he might be ready to meet the Lord at his Coming. And we doubt not but his Removal is to him a happy Tranſlation into the Manſions of eternal Reſt and Glory; yet we cannot but be ſenſibly affected with the Loſs of ſo ſerviceable and valuable a Member in the Church.

His Body was decently interred in Friends Burial Ground at *Ratcliff* on Firſt-day, the 30th of the Fourth Month aforeſaid, after a very large and ſolemn Meeting, which was favoured with a good Degree of the Divine Preſence, and attended by a great Number of Friends and others from the ſeveral Parts of this City.

He died in the Sixty ſixth Year of his Age, a Miniſter about thirty Years.

A Teſtimony

A Testimony from Reading *Monthly-meeting in* Berkshire, *concerning* MICHAEL TURPIN.

OUR dear and worthy Friend, *Michael Turpin*, was born at *Hemel-Hempstead*, in the County of *Hertford*, the 3d of the Sixth Month 1668; and after living at *Albans* in the said County about Sixteen Years, removed to this Town about the Year 1726, where he resided about Thirty one Years; in which Time he was of good Service to this Meeting, being well qualified for the Work of the Ministry, to which he was called about the Twenty third Year of his Age: And by strictly adhering to the divine Gift bestowed on him, grew in the Life of Religion, and had a lively and powerful Testimony frequently to bear in old Age, increasing in his Gift as he grew in Years: And though not a Man of much Literature, yet, when under divine Influence, he discovered a good Understanding, being well instructed in the School of Christ. He was zealous in Testimony against *Pride, Covetousness, all Libertinism,* and *whatever is not subject to Truth*; also, that our *Christian* Discipline might be maintained upon its ancient Foundation. He was a true Mourner in *Sion*, one who sighed for the Abominations of the Times, and truly sympathized with others in the like Condition, to whom he often had a Word of Encouragement, which he suitably administered greatly to their Comfort: But to the lukewarm, indifferent, formal Professors, his Testimony was close and piercing; and by keeping his Place in the Authority of Truth, he was a Check upon some forward and unqualified Spirits, which sometimes appeared amongst us.

He was often (especially toward the Conclusion of his Time) extraordinarily drawn forth, in fervent Supplication to the Almighty, for the young and rising Generation, and that those who were in undue Liberties might be reclaimed, and those who were at Ease in a Profession and outward Conformity, without a real Possession of the blessed Truth, might be, by a fresh Visitation, awakened and stirred up to a Sense of their States and Duty.

His Life and Conversation was exemplary and edifying; his Deportment and Countenance solid, weighty and awful; he loved and sought Retirement, slept little, was temperate and industrious, conscientiously concerned that he might not bring any Reproach on his holy Profession by Insolvency; and therefore, and for the Benefit of his bodily Health, he occupied a considerable Part of his Time in such Business as he was capable of, though the Profits arising therefrom were very small.

In his last Ilness, which continued about three Weeks, he was enabled to bear the
Extremity

Extremity of his Pain with remarkable Patience and Stilness; and, in the Depth of Humility, begged of the Lord, *That he would be pleased to release him from his Affliction*; who in Mercy granted his Request; and he is, we doubt not, safely arrived through a Sea of Troubles to the Port of endless Joy, and is an Inhabitant of that glorious City (of which he had a Vision a little before his Decease) where there is no Need of the Light of the Sun, neither of the Moon, for the Glory of God doth lighten it, and the Lamb is the Light thereof.

He quietly departed this Life, in great Stilness, the 11th of the Ninth Month 1757, and was buried the 15th following, in the Burying Ground belonging to Friends at *Reading*, in a very plain but decent Manner, according to his particular Desire, in the Eightieth Year of his Age: A Minister about Fifty seven Years.

A Testimony from Wigton *Monthly-meeting in* Cumberland, *concerning* HANNAH WILSON.

HANNAH WILSON was born the 7th of the Fourth Month 1681. She was Daughter of *Joseph* and *Mary Steel* of *Moresgate*, who gave her a strict and religious Education; for which, she often expressed great Gratitude to Providence and her virtuous Parents, with strong Desires that she might tread in the same Steps, and follow their godly Example.

In 1715 she married *Richard Wilson* of *Cockermouth*, and in 1736 was called to the Work of the Ministry, in which she was faithful according to the Gift received. In the time of Health, frequent in Heavenly Meditation by her Fire-side, exhorting those about her, and in the Family, *To remember their Latter-end, and seek a City that hath Foundations; that when the Bridegroom came, their Lamps might be trimmed, and ready to enter with him.* And frequently said, *It has been my early Desire from my Infancy, that I may live the Life of the Righteous, that my last End may be happy with them that die in the Lord; and, Oh may this be all our Portion at last!* with much more to the like Effect at different times.

During her last Ilness, which continued about two Weeks, she was very resigned, whether Life or Death; and said, *Thy Will be done, O God! I am ready if thou please now, for I have no Guilt upon me; I prayed for Patience to bear my present Affliction, and thou hast given it me; nay, more than I have asked for: Blessed by thy holy Name. My Cup overflows with thy Goodness, now, in this Time of Need and great bodily Weakness; for which, my Soul, and all that is within me, reverently bows and worships afresh.*

At

At another time she said, *This Death is an awful Solemnity to all that are capable of thinking; and yet, Thanks be to God, I have not the least Fear of it; for the holy Lord that hath been with me at times, all my Life long, will be at my right Hand through the Passage of Death, and conduct me to the Regions of Light.*

At another time, after a solemn Silence, she said, *Gracious and holy Lord, remember our Off-spring, the Youth of this present Generation; Oh! visit them afresh and afresh, till it be effectual; and grant that the Sufferings of many of their worthy Ancestors, in Goals and Dungeons for the Testimony of thy Name, and which many sealed with their Blood, may sink in their Minds; that it may be a Spur on them to Faithfulness, that they may not trample on their Ashes by a contrary Conduct: Oh! let a double Portion of their Spirit rest on them; that from our Seed, Judges as at the first, and Counsellors as at the Beginning, may be raised up among them: And, O holy Lord! bless the Youth of this Meeting, and all Ages and Degrees in it; Oh! do thou, when ever they meet, be in the Midst of them, and surround them with thy living Presence: Be with such as are not able to attend the Assemblies of thy People; let thy Light shine round about such in their solitary Chambers, for their Comfort and Support; and graciously be near all under Affliction, whether of Body or Mind, and help them that are seeking after thee; be thou Strength in all times of their Weakness, that they*

they may have to testify of thy Goodness in the Land of the Living. And, Oh! grant, where Hardness of Heart has entered, that it may be done away; and give such Hearts of Flesh, that nothing but Love may rule in the Church, or in our Families: Thou art sufficient for all these Things; take us, we beseech thee, into thy holy Protection, that we may be safe under the Shadow of thy Wing, where we may magnify thy Name, for thou art worthy of Worship and Praise for ever; with more of the same Import.

After which, desiring some present to mind the Manifestations of the Spirit of God in their own Minds, and be obedient thereto, which would give them Happiness in Life, and Peace in Death, she remained quiet; and departed on the 26th of the Eleventh Month 1758, and was buried in Friends Burying Ground at *Wigton*.

Aged Seventy seven, a Minister Twenty two Years.

A Testimony

A Testimony from Marsdon *Monthly-meeting in* Lancashire, *concerning* CHARLES HARRISON.

OUR Friend, *Charles Harrison,* from his Youth had strong Desires in his Mind after the true Knowledge of God, and our Lord Jesus Christ; and, frequenting the Meetings of particular *Baptists,* was much tossed with divers Winds of Doctrine, and strong Temptations of the Enemy of his Soul. Whilst in this State, he went to a Meeting of the People called *Quakers,* where our honourable Friend, *John Fothergill,* exhorted *to an inward Waiting upon the Lord, in Faith, to receive Power over every evil Thought.* This Doctrine made so deep an Impression upon his Mind, *that* (as we, some of us, have often heard him say, with Tears of Joy) *he was as if he heard the Sound of his Voice for many Days.* Hence forward he attended our religious Meetings, and in a little time it pleased the Lord to deliver him from those strong Temptations and Fears, and to raise him up to preach the Gospel. His Ministry was acceptable and edifying, his Life and Conversation being very eminently correspondent with the Doctrine he preached.

During his last Illness, he was much visited by Friends, and many religious People of other Denominations; to whom, tho' under great Weakness of Body, he was often engaged to declare the Goodness of the Lord, in a very powerful and affecting Manner.

He departed this Life, in perfect Peace, the 14th Day of the Ninth Month 1758, and was buried in Friends Burying Ground at *Sawley* the 16th of the same, in the Eighty ninth Year of his Age, having been a Minister Fifty Years.

A Testimony from Kendal *Monthly-meeting in* Westmorland, *concerning* WILLIAM HARTLEY.

OUR beloved Friend, *William Hartley*, was born near *Broughton* in the County of *Lancashire*, of reputable Parents, and had his Education in the Principles of the Church of *England*. In his youthful Days he was of a very gay and sprightly Disposition, altho' he had frequent Intervals of serious Reflections, wherein he clearly beheld the airy State and Condition he was then in; yet, as he was obedient to the Convictions of Divine Grace, the momentary Pleasures of this frail Life were sullied in his Eye; and becoming more and more religiously inclined, a Dissatisfaction with the Forms of Worship he was brought up in, increased so, that about the Twenty first Year of his Age he was convinced of the Principles of Truth as held forth by us, and joined the Society;

Society; in which he continued an unshaken Example of true Piety, through the various Afflictions and Vicissitudes of Life; having been a diligent Assistant in transacting the weighty Affairs of the Church, and particularly serviceable in that of visiting Friends Families, wherein he was excellently qualified.

In about the Sixty second Year of his Age, his Mouth was opened in a publick Testimony to the blessed Truth, and his Ministry being accompanied with a divine Authority, (though he was mostly short) his Labour of Love generally tended to the Comfort and Edification of the Hearers.

And when the Time of his Dissolution drew near, he seemed to have an undoubted Evidence of an happy Futurity, frequently breaking forth in much tender Advice, Counsel and Encouragement to his Family, and Friends who came to visit him, in no less lively and affecting a Manner than in the time of Health. Thus was he owned in his last Moments by the Divine Presence, wherein his Soul greatly delighted, which considerably alleviated his bodily Pain, and was an inexpressible Consolation to his dear Wife and Children, to whom he had fully discharged himself; having been a loving Husband, an affectionate and exemplary Parent, and, in his Neighbourhood, a most faithful Friend and Adviser. A constant Attender of Meetings so long as Ability of Body would permit.

What

What shall we say more concerning this our deceased Friend, than that *Blessed are the Dead that die in the Lord? yea,* saith the Spirit, *from henceforth they rest from their Labours, and their Works follow them.*

He died the 3d of the Second Month 1759, in the Sixty eighth Year of his Age, and was buried the 6th of the same, in our Burying Ground at *Crook,* in the County of *Westmorland.*

A Testimony from the Six-Weeks Mens-Meeting at Waterford *in* Ireland, *concerning* ELIZABETH BALFOUR.

IT has pleased Infinite Wisdom to remove from us, by Death, our dear and well beloved Friend *Elizabeth Balfour,* whose Services, during the few Years she resided amongst us, were very acceptable: We therefore are concerned to give, in a brief Manner, a Testimony of her.

She was of a pleasant and chearful Disposition in Conversation, yet attended with Gravity and Meekness, which rendered her Company agreeable and instructive: In her Deportment solid, in her Ministry plain, living and powerful; not forward in appearing, but watchful and attentive to observe strictly the Motion of Life; so that when concerned, it was

was both seasonable and suitable; and notwithstanding she was sometimes sharp in Reproof, to such as brought Reproach on our holy Profession, yet she was tender in Sympathy with *Sion*'s Mourners, to whom she had often a Word of Comfort and Encouragement to administer. She was also gifted in Discipline, having good Service in Meetings for it here and elsewhere, being zealous for preserving good Order, and that *Christian* Plainness and Moderation should be observed in all Respects.

She was likewise serviceable in Family Visits; a Work she much approved of, but went upon with Awfulness and Fear, being sensible of the Weight and Exercise which attends the rightly concerned therein, and that nothing short of *Divine Wisdom* can enable or qualify for the faithful Performance; which therefore she not only waited for, but was often favoured with.

More may be said concerning the Services of this our dear deceased Friend, if we were to particularize; but we chuse Brevity, as well as being cautious of expressing any thing which may be thought like Encomiums on her, having nothing in View but to attribute the Praise of all to the Almighty, Great and Gracious Being, whose Works they are, and which alone do praise him; and likewise to animate and encourage present and future Generations to follow her pious Example, that

so

so they may (as we believe she has done) when they finish their Course, by fighting a good Fight, and keeping the Faith, receive the Crown of Righteousness, which is laid up for all them that love the Appearing of our Lord; to whom, through, in, and over all, be the Thanksgiving and Praise, Dominion and Renown ascribed for ever.

She departed this Life the 1st Day of the Eighth Month 1758, in the Forty second Year of her Age; a Minister about Twenty Years; and was interred in Friends Burying Ground at *Waterford*, after a solid Meeting of Friends and others, wherein the Power of that Truth, in which she lived and died, was evidently manifested.

Some further Account of ELIZABETH BALFOUR, *with her dying Expressions.*

ELIZABETH, the Wife of *Archibald Balfour* of *Waterford*, and Daughter to *James* and *Sarah Tomey* of *Limerick*, was by the Fear of the Lord, (which is the Beginning of Wisdom) co-operating with the great Advantage of a religious Education, preserved in her early Years from the Follies incident to Youth; being dutiful to her Parents, to whom she was often a Joy and Comfort in the Lord; and a good Pattern, both by Advice and Example, to her younger Brothers and Sisters.

It

It pleafed the Lord to call her to the Work of the Miniftry about the Twenty fecond Year of her Age, altho' much in a Crofs to the natural Part ; but finding that nothing but Obedience would be acceptable to the Almighty, fhe gave up to his Call, and difcharged herfelf according to the Ability received, to the Satisfaction and Comfort of fenfible Friends, where her Lot was caft. She vifited this Nation generally, and fome Parts thereof feveral Times ; alfo the South Weft Parts of *England,* in the Year 1742, in Company with *Elizabeth Fennell* (then *Peafe.*) As to her farther Service, the Reader is referred to the Teftimony of Friends of *Waterford* concerning her : And in the Station of a Wife, was tender and fympathizing beyond what can be exprefled in Words, or ever underftood, except by fuch as have been favoured with fuch a Blefling.

She was feized with her laft Ilnefs on the 10th of the Seventh Month 1758, and on the 13th apprehending fhe was near her End, in great Agony of Spirit faid, *My Pain and Weaknefs is fo great, that I think I can't hold long ; I am fo diftreffed and poor in Mind, that I fear I am not prepared for it.* Upon which fhe wept bitterly ; yet faid, *She could not accufe herfelf of acting amifs, that occafioned the Lord to withdraw from her, unlefs the laft Time fhe had any Thing given her to fay in Meeting, fhe pleaded Excufe fo long, that the Meeting broke up ; and it then ran through her Mind,* There

is

is that scattereth and yet encreaseth; and there is that with-holdeth more than is meet, and it tendeth to Poverty; adding, *and I have found it so.*

A Friend, whom she dearly loved, coming to see her, and finding her thus, spoke very encouragingly to her, saying, *He had Faith to believe, the Almighty would not take her hence, before he gave her a full Assurance of eternal Happiness*; upon which she seemed easier in her Mind, but in great Fear and Poverty till the 22d; from which time, till her Departure, many comfortable Expressions were dropped by her, the Substance of some of which is as follows.

Being that Morning very weak, she looked as if going off in a very still Manner; and being asked to take something, she desired *not to be disturbed*; and soon after said, *I thought I was going quietly and sweetly, for all is now well*; *I now can say*, Not my Will, but thine, O Lord, be done; *now Death seems near, and I am willing, having got an Evidence of eternal Peace.*

After some time of great Weakness, she said thus; *It is a fine Thing to be preserved alive in the Truth; it is more than all besides, and what I have often desired for; my Heart is filled with divine Love, but am not able to express what I feel.* She desired *her Love to be remembered to several Friends in particular*; adding, *and to all the Friends of Truth; to whom my Mind has often*

often been nearly united in sincere Love : Tell them, that there is a Mansion of eternal Rest prepared for me, where I hope we shall meet again, never more to part. Remember *my dear Love to all my dear Friends in this City ; they have been kind, yea, affectionately kind to me since I came amongst them ; also to Friends of* Cork *and* Dublin, *and every where, where my Lot has been cast.* O Lord *! preserve thy People here, who have been highly favoured, and also those in the Place of my Nativity ;* Oh the Sheep's Clothing *! but not the Life ; may the Lord open every sensible Eye to see it : I have often desired to be favoured with a feeling Sense of this State ; the Lord grant it me unto my End, and unto all the Sincere-hearted.* Lord *! open the blind Eyes, and cause them that are gone astray, to return before it be too late.*

To some Friends, who were by her, she said, *I could not express these Things of myself in my present Condition ; nay, I durst not :* (having signified a Care that rested on her Mind in this Respect, since the time her Mouth was first opened in a publick Testimony) *I thought I should have nothing to say ; but feeling the Renewings of Divine Life amongst us, (for which my Soul praises the Lord) I am made willing to drop what opens, while I have Strength given. My dear Love is to my beloved Sister in the Truth,* Susannah Hatton ; (who was then abroad on Truth's Service) *she will be sorry for my Removal, as we have loved one another dearly ;*

dearly; but I am going to eternal Rest and Peace, where, I trust, we shall meet again, and be separated no more.

She desired a particular Friend, that visited her, to lay her out, and see that every Thing was plain; saying, *I love Plainness in my Heart:* And cautioned a young Woman, who sometimes did that Office for the Dead, to avoid putting so much needless plaiting upon the Sheet that covered her, as she had seen her and others do; saying, *I have been often troubled at it, and I request thou mind it for the future; for Plainness in every respect is most becoming us as a People; any Thing to the contrary being unanswerable to our Profession.* At another time she expressed herself thus; *How little doth the World, and the Comforts I had in it, look now in my View; there is nothing in it worth our Notice, but to press after the better Part; nothing else now has any Beauty in my View: The Lord, if it be his Will, suffer me not to be long here; I hope the Work is pretty well, and nigh accomplished.*

Being in great Pain, she said, *This is hard Work; the Affliction of this Body is very great: And it is an awful Thing thus to look the Almighty in the Face; yet, through Mercy, I am freed from any Guilt that I know of. Oh! if it be so dreadful for those that have led pretty innocent and circumspect Lives; what will become of them that are loaded with the Guilt of Sin? If the Righteous scarcely be saved, where shall*

shall the Wicked and Ungodly appear? A Woman of another Perfwafion being prefent, fhe added, *And there is no Mortal that can give any Help to remove the Guilt of Sin, at fuch a Time as this; fo let none deceive themfelves with fuch Notions; for if they do, they will find it a Deceit.* She warned a young Woman, that came to fee her, againft Pride and High-mindednefs; and fet before her the great Danger many poor Souls were in, if they fhould be fummoned hence in their prefent unprepared State; faying, *How miferable would my prefent Condition be, when attended with fuch Affliction of Body, and ready to launch into Eternity, if that was my Cafe!*

One Morning, after a painful Night of great Weaknefs, both of Body and Mind, infomuch that her Voice was fcarce to be heard; after lying ftill for fome time, fhe prayed very fervently, with an audible Voice and great Power, to the following Import:

" O Lord God Almighty! thou that dwelleft
" in the Heavens,' and the Heaven of Heavens
" cannot contain thee; yet haft thou promifed
" to look down on him that is poor and con-
" trited before thee, and that trembles at thy
" Word: May it ftand good with thy Hea-
" venly Will, to fulfil it this Time to thy poor
" diftreffed Handmaid, who thou knoweft has
" been often contrited, and trembled before
" thee. Thou that haft been with me in
" fix

"six Troubles, forsake me not in the seventh;
"if thou doest, I am undone, for I have no
"Strength but what comes from thee: Thou
"that hast been Strength in Weakness, and a
"present Help in every Time of Trouble, O
"be graciously pleased to look down upon me
"now in Mercy, in this Time of the greatest
"Affliction I ever met with; let thy Presence
"be near, else I perish for ever: Thou that
"hast been with me all my Life long to this
"Day, and only knows my Condition and
"great Weakness of late, forsake me not now.
"— I feel a little of the Revivings of thy an-
"cient Goodness, for which my Soul praises
"thy great and holy Name. — O Lord! be
"pleased to remember my dear Husband, be
"thou his Comfort and Support; also my dear
"Parents, Brother and Sisters, and all my near
"and dear Friends. Lord God Almighty!
"grant that their Eyes may be so kept unto
"thee, that thou mayst be with them when this
"Time of deep Trial comes.—Thou hast been
"near at this Time, beyond what I expected;
"Strength in Weakness, Riches in Poverty
"indeed."

Soon after the above Prayer she spoke thus;
*Now the Beloved of my Soul is come, but not empty-
handed: Oh the Preciousness of his Love! his
Time is the best Time; thy Servant is now ready.*
After which, she lay very still and quiet (tho'
in great Pain of Body) inwardly breathing and
praising

praising the Lord, as was visible to every sensible Beholder; often signifying, *That she had nothing to do but to give up the Ghost, when the Lord's Time was come*; and being earnestly desirous to be endued with Patience to wait his Pleasure therein, which she expressed, *she could not attain to without his Aid, more especially when in such grievous Pain of Body*; the Lord was pleased to grant her Request, and endued her therewith to Admiration.

Some time after, she spoke thus; *Lord! be with me in the pinching Time of separating Soul from Body, and give me an easy Passage; Oh! grant for a Sign, that I may stretch at Ease, if it be but for a few Moments before I go hence; and give me, at that Time, a renewed Assurance of Peace with thee.* Which Petition was also graciously granted her; as, for several Hours before her Departure, she complained of no Pain of Body; saying, *All is well: The Lord is my Righteousness; I have Peace, Peace, sweet Peace; quite easy both in Body and Mind, and humbly thankful for it: Oh the Joy that I feel! What signifies all the Trouble and Pain we can go through here, if we can attain to this State at last:* My Peace I give unto you *(said our Lord.) I have thought of this Saying to Day, and I witness it.* In which contented Condition, accompanied with a remarkable Degree of Heavenly Innocence and Cheasfulness of Spirit, she continued unto the last; and

leaning

leaning her Head backwards, as if falling into a sweet Slumber, in a few Minutes drew her last Breath; and we doubt not, is entered into that full Fruition of eternal Rest and Peace, which she had a sweat Earnest of, never to feel any more Pain.

F I N I S.

www.ingramcontent.com/pod-product-compliance
Lightning Source LLC
Chambersburg PA
CBHW030343230426
43664CB00007BA/512